What Life Should Be About

Elegant Essays on the Things That Matter

John P. Weiss

WHAT LIFE SHOULD BE ABOUT

For my parents, John and Patricia Weiss.
And for my sister, Leslie Elizabeth.

Acknowledgments

Writing can be a solitary existence. Many thanks to my wife Nicole, and son Conner, for tolerating my creative life. And warm thoughts for Skye. Our year together was too short, and you will never be forgotten.

Contents

1. How the Spirit of Small Things Will Sustain You — 1

2. How Comfort and Conformity Are Dream Killers — 5

3. How Would Your Life Improve If You Just Accepted It? — 9

4. The Most Important Question to Ask Yourself in a Relationship — 13

5. Become a Charming Gardener Who Makes Souls Blossom — 18

6. How Many Years Must Pass Before We Set Ourselves Free? — 25

7. The Number One Thing to Avoid in Your Creative Work — 30

8. Why the Convenient Path You're On Might Be Leading You Astray — 34

9. Why the Treasures You Have Matter Less Than the Experiences You Live — 38

10. How Bright Your Candle Burns Is All About Choices — 43

11. Why Coffee Shops Are Teachers, If Only We'd Pay Attention — 47

12. If Your Creative Work Doesn't Please You, What's the Value? — 53

13. What a Little Boy and His Airplane Can Teach Us About Love   57

14. What Matters Most Is How You Walk Through the Fire   61

15. Eliminate One Thing to Improve Productivity and Happiness   66

16. The One Habit I Wished I Discovered in My Twenties   71

17. Three Things I Gave Up That Greatly Improved My Life   76

18. How to Get Revenge for All the Things That Defeated You in Life   82

19. The Precious Thing at the Heart of Your Creative Work   88

20. Guess What Matters Far More Than the Position?   94

21. What Marcel Proust and Robert Frost Can Teach Us About Finding Happiness   100

22. One Powerful Strategy to Defeat Problems and Critics   106

23. How to Stop Feeling Irrelevant and Embrace Life   111

24. We Are All Broken   116

25. How the Culture of Open Options Is Making Us Miserable   121

26. The Most Important Thing We Bring to Another Person   127

27. A Note On the Windshield   132

28. The Unexpected Movie That Made Me Realize What Really Matters   138

29. The Most Important Kind of Freedom   144

30. My Best Answers to 9 Life Questions from a Reader 149

31. The Monsters Will Come in Your Life: Here's How to Vanquish Them 154

32. The Most Important 3 Words to Ask Yourself Before Pursuing a Goal 160

33. How to Turn Apartness Into Your Creative Asset 165

34. Love and Sacrifice: Why the Days Are Long But the Years Are Short 171

35. How One Act of Kindness Can Rekindle a Loved One's Memory 177

36. The Flower of Your Life Will Wither Without Care 182

37. Why Grace Is Found in the Mundane 187

38. What a Little Soul Taught Me About Being Grateful 192

39. This Is How Ghosts Make You Sick 198

40. Do You Know What Kills More Dreams Than Failure? 202

41. This Is What He Did After the Plane Crash 208

42. This Is How to Dance With Loss 213

43. You Can Reinvent Your Life and Be Happy 220

44. Here Is the Antidote for Modern Life 227

45. Do You Make These Mistakes at Work? 231

46. This Is What an Octopus Can Teach You About Life 237

47. What Happened to the Gift of Empathy? 243

48. Are You Aware of the Good Bones in Your Life? 249

49. This Is the Damage of Labels 254

50. What Monks Know About Better Living 259

51. How to Get Your Life Off Autopilot 268

52. The Art of Emotional Wintering 276

53. Why Your Second Mountain Is the Answer   281

54. Guess Who Has the Most Power in a Relationship?   288

55. How to Be Memorable in Social Settings   294

56. This Is What Happens When You Simplify Your Life   302

57. How Trying to Be Happy Makes You Miserable   310

58. How to Escape Your Family to Save Yourself   317

59. Do You Make This Mistake in Conversations?   323

60. How to Age With Elegance   331

61. This Is Why You Need to Say Yes   336

62. What Life Should Be About   342

63. Are You Aware of the Nasty Habit Killing Your Dreams?   348

64. You Need These People in Your Life - But You Ignore Them   354

65. How to Escape a Life of Mediocrity   360

66. How the Power of Simplicity Can Improve Your Life   364

67. Never Get Out of Bed Before Noon   370

68. The Exciting Whisper Moving Through the Aisles of Your Spirit   373

Also by John P. Weiss   377

About the Author   378

Chapter One

How the Spirit of Small Things Will Sustain You

It was the orange Schwinn bicycle that crushed me in the end.

It's funny how the most unexpected things can give release to tightly held emotions. Such was the case for me after the conclusion of my father's memorial service.

I organized every facet of my dad's memorial, from the music and photos presented to the catered reception and clean-up. I was the strong one who comforted my family, thanked all who came and tipped the funeral home manager.

I collected the last boxes of memorial photos and mementos, stuffed them in my car, and got ready to leave. And that's when the small photo fell out of a box and landed softly on my shoe.

It was an old Polaroid of my father sitting on an orange Schwinn bicycle. The bicycle belonged to me when I was ten years old. It was a birthday gift from my parents.

I sat in the front seat of my car, gazing at the photo. My father, who was a robust man standing six feet tall, looked ridiculous straddling my bike.

And then the tears came.

That singular photo brought back everything I loved about my father. His generosity, love, protection, guidance, and steadfast loyalty to me and our family.

It's been over forty-seven years since that photo was taken, and even now it teleports me back to my childhood and feelings of love and reassurance.

On a human level

Dad's decline was a slow and steady unraveling of a man I loved and respected deeply. A retired administrative law judge, former United States Marine, and intellectual polymath, Dad was formidable.

And yet, behind those penetrating eyes and learned intellect was a man who got up early to brush his community of stray cats. Even when the fog of dementia crept into my father's capacious mind, his decency and generosity of spirit remained. Near the end of his life, at the memory care facility, Dad always smiled and thanked the staff for their care and kindness.

"Those with dementia are still people and they still have stories and they still have character and they're all individuals and they're all unique. And they just need to be interacted with on a human level."
—Carey Mulligan

At one point, Dad was carrying around a small stuffed animal. It's strange how, later in life, we sometimes return to our childhood. Perhaps because our souls yearn for the simplicity and reassurance of that magical time in our lives.

The stuffed animal was a small thing. A gift from one of Dad's nurses. Yet it gave him peace and comfort.

In our busy lives, we sometimes forget to slow down and consider the small things that give us peace and comfort.

Memories are roses in our winter

The author and columnist George Will once wrote that memories are roses in our winter.

The elderly often flip through photo albums which help conjure the comforting past when dreams and the bloom of youth held promise for the future.

But we don't need to wait until we're old to take advantage of memories and the objects that invite them. We just need to slow down, take a break from the social media and frenzied pace of modern life, and travel back in time.

"Nothing is ever really lost to us as long as we remember it." — L.M. Montgomery, The Story Girl

Beyond photos, objects and keepsakes from the past are the small things that can sustain us. They're unique because they exist in the present and past, like friendly, tangible ghosts.

If we hold them and close our eyes, we can time travel.

Small things give me hope

The other day I spent some time with a few of my parent's things. Each one of them took me back to my childhood.

"Often, small things give me hope when big things feel so oppressively bleak." — Julien Baker

There was the wooden elephant Dad brought back from Japan after World War II.

The beautifully carved elephant sat throughout my childhood, in the living room of our home. To this day, he's a kind of tranquil sentinel, protecting memories of those early days.

My father had immaculate, copperplate handwriting crafted with elegant fountain pens. As a boy I used to watch, mesmerized, as Dad penned legal decisions on yellow legal tablets.

My mother, who I also loved deeply, passed away in 2021. She left behind magical objects from my past, as well.

Her prized possession was a little figurine dog that she kept from her childhood. It sits today in my art studio, a constant reminder of Mom's spirit that brings me daily peace.

Not everything worth keeping has to be useful

When our lives come to an end, we leave things behind.

Some of these things are sold, given to others, or thrown away. But often, a few are cherished as comforting keepsakes.

"Not everything worth keeping has to be useful." — Cynthia Lord, *Rules*

These keepsakes are the small things that have the power to sustain us.

My mother's little dog statue accompanied her from childhood to her 87th year, providing comfort and fond memories. Dad's wooden elephant was there in the living room throughout all our family celebrations. And now the elephant sits in my home, watching over my family.

I write with my father's fountain pens and try to channel a bit of his calligraphy in my hand. When I hold the pen, I feel like a little piece of Dad is with me.

The spirit of small things soothes our hearts and warms our souls. It can bring us peace if we're willing to slow down and travel to the past.

Cherish the small things your loved ones left behind. Hold them, close your eyes, and take wing to the past.

These keepsakes and lifelong objects will transport you back in time, where the spirits of loved ones are waiting with open arms, and your soul can rest a bit from the trials and tribulations of daily living.

Chapter Two

How Comfort and Conformity Are Dream Killers

It's hard for people to rise above their opinions of themselves.

This curse of self-limiting beliefs can often be traced back to childhood. Either an unsupportive parent or careless teacher did or said something devastating, and we carry the wound forward.

The injured little voice inside our head whispers, "Just do enough to get by. Don't rock the boat. Don't risk it."

What's sad is that our doubts are frequently far from the truth. But doubts are comfortable. Doubts give us an excuse to not try. Doubts are the status quo.

Ask yourself, "What if my doubts are not true?"

What if?

An indefensible self-mutilation of the soul

A few years ago, I was sitting in a restaurant with a good friend, and he asked about my writing.

"I don't know," I told him, "I work hard on my stories and essays, but there doesn't seem to be much return on investment. It's a lot of work. New readers join my newsletter each week, but just as many unsubscribe every time I publish. I'm thinking about quitting and going back to painting."

My friend listened attentively as I bemoaned the capricious nature of social media algorithms and how online readers prefer clickbait titles and cat videos over elegant essays about life lessons.

Basically, I was having myself a little pity party, and indulging in self-doubt about my writing.

"Self-pity is spiritual suicide. It is an indefensible self-mutilation of the soul." — Anthon St. Maarten

My friend suggested that maybe I needed to make changes and break out of my comfort zone. This got me thinking that maybe my self-doubts were not true. Maybe I had simply become too comfortable in my writing, and needed to change?

I analyzed my work closely and realized that I had fallen into a comfortable style and approach. I had been using copywriting skills and emulating a few successful online writers. As a result, my work was derivative and boring.

What I realized is that comfort and conformity are the enemy. They're dream killers because when we stay safe and copy others, we deny our true potential.

So, I changed things up in my writing.

I started to focus on more elegant prose and tried to connect with readers on a deeper level. After that, I had one of my best years of online writing.

Show me your friends, and I'll show you your future

We are all creatures of habit. This is a good thing if the habits are healthy and productive.

Unfortunately, our habits often reflect the path of least resistance.

We do things subconsciously because they're comfortable and familiar. Like mindlessly clicking on the TV every night instead of exercising. Or following the same old formula in our writing or creative work.

Beyond comfort and conformity, our environment plays a huge role in our potential creative and personal success. This is because environment is stronger than our will. It wins over time.

Stock your kitchen with unhealthy food, and that's what you'll be eating. Put a big screen TV in your house and that's what you'll be watching. And what's crazy is that we complain to friends about weight gain and never having the time to read.

Who we spend most of our time with also determines the course of our lives.

Hang out with people who like to drink and party and soon that will become your lifestyle. Alternatively, hanging out with people who like to exercise and feed their minds will rub off on you, too.

"Show me your friends and I'll show you your future." — *Dan Pena*

I'm not suggesting you dump your friends, but you should avoid any bad habits they might have. And perhaps try broadening your circle to new friends whose good habits and success you might want to emulate.

The enemy of growth

If you want to follow your dreams and find success, avoid comfort and conformity. What's easy and familiar seldom gets you where you want to go.

"Conformity is the jailer of freedom and the enemy of growth." — *John F. Kennedy*

Surround yourself with people who inspire you, and whose positive example will help fuel your dreams and success. Create a home and work environment that helps you make good decisions.

Do these things, and you can change the opinion you have of yourself. You can become the person you always dreamed of being.

And when you get there, be sure and take the time to inspire and help others who are still struggling. This is how we not only change ourselves and others for the better but maybe even the world.

Chapter Three

How Would Your Life Improve If You Just Accepted It?

I couldn't help but smile when the sturdy, self-assured woman in the restaurant placed her order.

The stuffy waiter struck me as a Vegan, determined to suggest healthy options, but the delightfully direct woman was having none of it.

"Bring me a hot fudge sundae, with extra whipped cream and cherries," she said cheerfully, as her colorful necklace and matching earrings sparkled against the restaurant lights.

She was glowing and elegantly dressed. Even her small purse slung over the chair matched her necklace and earrings.

I admired the woman's style and self-confidence.

Skeletons dancing in their own closets

We live in a society where physical appearance is worshipped, making it hard for those struggling with weight. Body shaming is a real thing, and it can leave lasting psychological scars.

Some robust people are active and in excellent shape, but their overall body type camouflages their underlying fitness. They often endure judging eyes and whispers from slender but narrow-minded people.

"The self-righteous scream judgments against others to hide the noise of skeletons dancing in their own closets." — John Mark Green
I suspect the woman in the restaurant was no stranger to the cruelty of others. No doubt boys teased her as a little girl. Maybe her skinny college roommates disregarded her?

All the more reason why I admired this self-confident woman.

Adversity can destroy or shape a person. Those who are knocked around by the sharp edges and irritants of life sometimes emerge as brilliant pearls.

Part of reaching that place of deep personal power and self-assuredness involves more than developing a thick skin and steely determination.

It involves the power of acceptance.

Know when to let go and then do it

When I was a teenager, I fantasized about becoming a rock star.

My musical journey began with years of classical piano lessons. I became fluent on the keyboard and discovered that my tenor voice could mimic some of my favorite singers.

I joined a high school rock band, and then another rock band in college. At parties friends would goad me into playing the piano and singing.

I sang at a karaoke bar once and was approached afterward by members of an established local band. They asked if I'd like to be their lead singer.

But alas, deep down, I knew the truth. I was a decent singer, but not remarkable.

I accepted the fact that being a rockstar was not in my future.

Once I accepted that fact, I permitted myself to move on. I found a career that suited my abilities, and I developed my deeper talents for artwork and writing.

"Some people believe holding on and hanging in there are signs of great strength. However, there are times when it takes much more strength to know when to let go and then do it." — Ann Landers

This is the power of acceptance.

It frees you to pursue the things better suited to your skills, talents, and abilities. And it allows you to move on, to the better life that you deserve.

Some struggles aren't worth it. They steal our time and energy, preventing us from pursuing the things we were meant to be doing.

Nothing to do with resignation

It's not always easy to let go of something that feels so very important to you. Whether it's a relationship, career, passion, or pursuit.

The key is to look for recurring clues. Those breadcrumbs of evidence suggest maybe, just maybe, this person or thing or activity isn't right for you.

Maybe you're being held back from becoming the best version of yourself?

That's when you should consider acceptance. Try it on, like a comfortable sweater. How does it fit? How does it feel? What would you do with the freedom it can provide?

"Acceptance of one's life has nothing to do with resignation; it does not mean running away from the struggle. On the contrary, it means accepting it as it comes, with all the handicaps of heredity, of suffering, of psychological complexes and injustices."— Paul Tournier

Imagine how your life could change if you embraced acceptance, let go of what's not working, and started focusing on the areas where your skills and talents shine.

There are many things I've accepted in life. I won't be a rockstar. As much as I work out and eat right, I'm never going to look like Brad Pitt. And that's okay because accepting these things means I can focus on the stuff that matters more.

What matters more to me? Loving my family. Reading great books and writing elegant stories and essays. Drawing cartoons, painting pictures, and shooting classic black and white photographs.

I'll never forget what the self-confident woman in the restaurant showed me.

Namely, that acceptance is a powerful thing. And life is too short to deny yourself a hot fudge sundae with extra whipped cream and cherries.

Chapter Four

The Most Important Question to Ask Yourself in a Relationship

It was the second time in a week my partner and I responded to their apartment.

As a young patrol officer, I had grown accustomed to the rhythms of domestic violence in our community. Angry and emotionally damaged people seem to hurt the ones they love with alarming regularity.

We could hear shouting as we climbed the stairs, stepping over a plastic bag of empty beer bottles. "Police department," my partner shouted as we knocked on the door.

Inside, everything went silent.

Slowly, the door was unlatched and opened. She was crying, with mascara running down her red cheeks.

"Where is he?" my partner said. "Over there, on the couch. He's been drinking again, but he didn't hit me," she said.

Thus began yet another domestic violence investigation. Our job was to determine if a crime occurred, and who the primary aggressor was. And to provide professional resources for the victim.

This time, there had been no crime. Just a loud argument, which prompted the neighbors to call. The boyfriend decided to leave and stay the night at a buddy's house.

We talked to the young woman for a while, went over the domestic violence pamphlets, and offered to phone on-call crisis support professionals. She declined.

Before we left, she said something I never forgot:

"He makes me feel so bad about myself."

Narcissists live in fear of humiliation

There are many attributes to look for in a significant other, but we tend to focus on the superficial ones.

Namely, looks and money.

American culture is enamored with physical appearance, celebrity, and wealth. This is why Hollywood icons are trailed by armies of paparazzi.

Social influencers analyze fashion trends, celebrity relationships, and other amusements. Boring stuff like depth of character gets short shrift.

Of course, the private lives of many Hollywood stars are far from idyllic. Look no further than the feud in the courtroom between actor Johnny Depp and his former wife Amber Heard.

Cellphone videos played for the jury reveal slammed cabinets, verbal jousting, and the unraveling of a dysfunctional relationship. Celebrities may seem like they're above the fray, but they struggle in relationships too.

In Hollywood and society, often the prettiest and most successful people are narcissists.

The late author and psychiatrist Gordon Livingston, in his book *"How to Love,"* wrote the following:

"Unable to tolerate criticism, narcissists live in fear of humiliation. This causes them to be attuned to any hint of disapproval and they are prone to lash out when criticized. They manifest feelings of entitlement: The rules that apply to everyone else do not apply necessarily constrain them because of their sense of their own 'specialness.' In a traffic jam, they are the people in expensive cars passing on the shoulder. They are often preoccupied with fantasies of success, power, or beauty. They are, in a word, arrogant. They are also prepared to take advantage of others when it suits their needs."

What causes the selfishness we see more and more in society today?

We have seen a rise in selfishness

One would think that every high school kid receives education focused on how to form and sustain a close relationship.

Yes, there is sex education, but little in the way of how to select a life partner. Thus, kids learn from their immediate families, friends, and media influences.

If you're lucky enough to have loving, well-adjusted parents, then you might be able to craft something similar in your own life. Unfortunately, many kids have dysfunctional parents or live in broken homes.

With at least half of all marriages ending in divorce, and the media feeding us misplaced priorities for relationships, it's no wonder more and more people are becoming self-absorbed and selfish.

Consider the following line from Suzy Kassem's book, *"Rise Up and Salute the Sun: The Writings of Suzy Kassem"*:

"In the last 10 years, we have seen a rise in selfishness: selfies, self-absorbed people, superficiality, self-degradation, apathy, and self-destruction. So I challenge all of you to take initiative to change this programming. Instead of celebrating the ego, let's flip the script and celebrate the heart. Let's put the ego and celebrity culture to sleep, and awaken the conscience. This is the battle we must all

fight together to win back our humanity. To save our future and our children."

In my twenty-six-year career in law enforcement, I witnessed countless dysfunctional relationships. They spanned all gender, ethnicity, sexual orientation, and socio-economic status.

Often the common denominator was self-centered people.

A lack of interest in the needs of others

In Gordon Livingston's book *"How to Love,"* he shared the following observation:

"Self-centered people frequently seem successful. Their ability to get others to conform to their opinions and satisfy their needs may appear to be a valuable life skill; over time these qualities are revealed as manipulative and a lack of interest in the needs of others becomes a highly unattractive trait."

If we are to find happiness in our relationships, it must begin with discernment. We need to look past superficial qualities like looks and money.

Two extremely important qualities to look for in a partner are **kindness** and **empathy**.

People may be on their best behavior in the early stages of a relationship but be on the lookout for little clues. How does he treat the waiter in a restaurant? Does she cut vehicles off and yell at motorists in traffic? Is he looking at his cellphone or you?

Kind, empathetic people step outside themselves. They envision what it's like to walk in the shoes of another. Money and looks are nice, but kindness and empathy in a partner are probably the best predictors of your future happiness.

The most important question to ask yourself in a relationship is this:

How does this person make me feel about myself?

I never forgot the young woman in her apartment, saying, "He makes me feel so bad about myself."

My partner asked her, "Why do you stay?"

"Honestly, I don't know," she told us.

She deserved better, and so do you.

Yes, sometimes circumstances are complex and it's not easy to free yourself from a dysfunctional relationship. But with planning, time, friends, and even professional support, it's possible.

Look for kindness and empathy in a significant other. Ask yourself if the person you're with makes you feel good about yourself.

Life is too short to remain unhappy.

Chapter Five

Become a Charming Gardener Who Makes Souls Blossom

My wife is a hospice nurse who has the privilege of helping people near the end of life's journey.

She tells me that people near death don't fixate on wealth, fame, sex, possessions, or popularity. They focus on relationships, love for family, and friends.

It's easy to take the important people in our lives for granted. Ambitions and dreams animate our lives, sometimes at the expense of the people we love.

We spend years focused on ourselves and the things we want. But then one day a diagnosis, accident, or old age alights on our shoulders. So, we turn to the ones we love for help.

Will the ones we love be there for us in our time of need?

Perhaps the answer comes in another question:

Have we been there for them?

I wish I had stayed in touch with my friends

Bronnie Ware is the author of the best-selling memoir *"The Top Five Regrets of the Dying: A Life Transformed by the Dearly Departing."*

As a former nurse who spent years working in palliative care helping patients in the last weeks of their lives, Ware learned a great deal about what matters most in life.

She wrote a blog post about the regrets of the dying which gathered tremendous attention from readers. It led Ware to publish her best-selling book *"The Top Five Regrets of the Dying."*

Here are the top five regrets:

I wish I'd had the courage to live a life true to myself, not the life others expected of me.

I wish I hadn't worked so hard.

I wish I'd had the courage to express my feelings.

I wish I had stayed in touch with my friends.

I wish that I had let myself be happier.

Each of the above regrets carries tremendous wisdom if we slow down long enough to appreciate them.

For me, the one about staying in touch with friends resonates deeply.

Fight for them

I had a buddy who took his life years ago. He went through a difficult divorce and became unmoored, but he did a good job of hiding his pain.

One day he showed up at my house, out of the blue.

I remember inviting him in. We sat on the couch and had a beer. He talked about this and that.

In hindsight, his visit was a little out of character, but at the time I thought it was just a random visit. A week later he took his life, and I was devastated.

"I think if I've learned anything about friendship, it's to hang in, stay connected, fight for them, and let them fight for you. Don't walk away, don't be distracted, don't be too busy or tired, don't take them

for granted. Friends are part of the glue that holds life and faith together. Powerful stuff." — Jon Katz

I replayed the day of his visit in my mind over and over. What could I have done differently? How did I miss that his visit was either a cry for help or a final goodbye?

His loss still stings so many years later.

Life and loss have taught me that friends are precious. We must cherish them. Fight for them. Pay attention to their behavior. Hold them close.

The problem, however, is that life gets in the way.

The charming gardeners who make our souls blossom

I am blessed to have wonderful friends. But among them, only a few keep in touch regularly.

Truth be told, I need to be better about staying in touch. I tend to be hermitic, immersed in my reading and creative life.

The reality is that lives diverge. Careers, relationships, and raising kids take precedence. Sometimes we move away. Or we move on.

Other times we sort of outgrow friendships. Shared interests we might have had in college change. Or the person we knew then isn't the same now, and vice versa.

If we're lucky, we might be blessed with one or two lifelong friends.

The kind of friends who never seem to change. Keepers of shared history, secrets, dreams, and unshakable loyalty.

"Let us be grateful to people who make us happy, they are the charming gardeners who make our souls blossom." — Marcel Proust

These rarest of friends are the kinds of people who not only make us happy, and they bring out the best in us. We feel better about ourselves in their company. Somehow, they lift us.

Don't you want to be that kind of friend to others?

When the rest of the world walks out

It's never too late to become the kind of friend your friends deserve.

What follows are five suggestions for how to become a better friend. They're more subtle than the usual advice about remembering birthdays, calling frequently, etc.

Embrace these tips, and there's a good chance your life will improve. Because kindness and helping others channel a kind of divinity, and we need that in this broken world.

"A real friend is one who walks in when the rest of the world walks out." — Walter Winchell

Of course, there are many ways to be a good friend, but hopefully, these five suggestions will help.

Make it about them

It's natural to want to share everything that's going on in your life when you reconnect with a friend. Just make sure you're not monopolizing the conversation.

Whether it's a phone call, zoom session, or in-person get-together, be a good listener. Ask questions. Take an interest in what they have to say. Don't interrupt or steer the conversation to yourself.

"There is a difference between listening and waiting for your turn to speak." — Simon Sinek

Your attention is a wonderful gift. Your friend will appreciate it and hopefully return the same courtesy.

Banish one-upmanship

It's natural for friends to talk about their careers, successes, vacations, and kids' accomplishments, but we must always remember that it's not a competition.

The definition of success and happiness in life varies from person to person. For instance, I view free time as more valuable than financial wealth. Also, I'm more interested in my friend's passions than their bank accounts.

Don't boast about your income, investments, possessions, or fancy vacations with friends. Doing so makes you look small like you're trying to one-up them.

If a friend talks about an amazing vacation, don't try to one-up them with tales of your even better vacation. Just be happy for them.

In short, spend less time talking about yourself, and focus on your friend. Truly listen.

Banish one-upmanship because friendship is not a competition.

Forgive

I have a childhood friend who tearfully confided in me years ago that he had broken the law.

The fact that I was a police officer at the time only made my friend feel more ashamed and embarrassed.

He explained the financial greed behind his crime, and that he faced federal prison time. He apologized and said how much our friendship meant to him. He asked for nothing but my forgiveness.

"Forgiveness is the fragrance that the violet sheds on the heel that has crushed it." — Mark Twain

I told a work colleague about my friend's tearful confession, and my colleague callously said, "Well, he's a crook and I'd dump him as a friend. You don't want to associate with a known felon."

What would you do?

I ended up standing by my friend because I knew deep down, he was a good person who temporarily lost his way. I wrote a letter to the Judge, acknowledging my friend's mistake and suggesting constructive approaches to punishment.

My friend served six months in federal prison, where some of his talents were put to good use. He has since married, fathered two wonderful children, and found success in his profession.

We remain loyal friends.

Solace

Years ago, a friend of mine was going through a divorce. His wife had moved out, taking many of the furnishings and possessions they once shared in the house.

It was my friend's birthday, and we took him to coffee at work. My friend tried to appear upbeat, but it was clear that he was down.

"I know that there will be solace for every sorrow, whatever the circumstances." — Anne Frank, The Diary of a Young Girl

After work, on a whim, I picked up a six-pack of my friend's favorite beer and showed up on his doorstep.

I rang the doorbell, and when my friend opened the door, a broad smile flashed across his face. Stepping into his house, I saw the missing pieces of furniture and felt the emptiness.

To this day, my friend still talks about that impromptu birthday visit, the beer we shared, and the solace the visit brought to his wounded soul.

Be there for your friends when they need you. Bring them solace.

Notice

I have a close friend who notices the little things. He remembers what my favorite dessert is. And the fact that I love writing with fountain pens.

On more than one occasion he has gifted me lovely fountain pens.

Taking the time to notice the little things that your friends love and cherish is a wonderful way to surprise them with gifts and acts of kindness.

"This small act of thoughtfulness hit the heartstrings that quietly ask, who's taking care of you? Who's thinking of you?" — Christina Tosi, Dessert Can Save the World: Stories, Secrets, and Recipes for a Stubbornly Joyful Existence

Perhaps you notice a favorite author in your friend's library, and later, purchase the author's most recent book as a gift for your friend. Or you notice your friend's favorite flower and show up one day with an entire bouquet.

When we notice the little things that friends value, it shows how much we care. Take the time to notice.

The bonds that sustain us

Friendships shelter us from the storms of life and celebrate our successes.

They are the bonds that sustain us when marriages fail, finances falter, disaster strikes, and all is lost. And they are the bons vivants when times are special, and we long to share our good fortune.

Don't neglect your friendships. Use the five suggestions above to nurture your friendships.

Because when you become a better friend, everyone wins, and the luster of life will shine a little brighter.

Chapter Six

How Many Years Must Pass Before We Set Ourselves Free?

During my afternoon walk a few days ago, I encountered some balloons tied to a pole.

They wanted to fly away and explore, much like people with dreams and ambitions. But a string tethered the balloons to a pole, denying their skyward longing.

When I returned days later the balloons were deflated on the ground, still attached to the pole. They seemed sad and defeated, like an exhausted animal ensnared in a trap.

A lot of people are like those balloons. Dreams lift them, but then life often comes with strings attached. And the strings tether and prevent them from taking off.

"I'd be smiling and chatting away, and my mind would be floating around somewhere else, like a balloon with a broken string." -Haruki Murakami, The Wind-Up Bird Chronicle.

We bob about on the breeze of our ambitions, but the strings in life hold tight until our spirits wane and our dreams deflate. For some, the struggle ends quickly, and they give up. For others, it can take years before they wither in defeat.

The question is, how do we cut the strings holding us back? How do we set ourselves free?

You must learn to live on fault lines

Suleika Jaouad's future was exciting and bright.

She attended The Juilliard School's pre-college program for the double bass, earned a BA with honors from Princeton University, and an MFA in writing and literature from Bennington College.

She fell in love and moved to Paris to pursue her dream of becoming a foreign correspondent. But then, like those balloons tethered to a pole, her life became entangled by strings.

Strings that tethered her to a hospital bed.

It began with a persistent itch on her legs, followed by exhaustion and lengthy naps. Doctor visits and misdiagnoses followed, until finally her illness was discovered: Acute myeloid leukemia.

Suleika was only 22 years old.

She was given a 35 percent chance of survival and would spend the next four years in a hospital bed, fighting for her life.

"You must learn to live on fault lines." — Suleika Jaouad

A popular blog Suleika started during her illness caught the attention of the *New York Times,* and this led to an Emmy Award-winning series of published articles called *"Life, Interrupted."*

After endless rounds of chemotherapy, a clinical trial, and a bone marrow transplant, Suleika left the hospital. Her new freedom led to a 100-day, 15,000-mile road trip across the United States.

All these experiences led to her affecting and inspirational book, *"Between Two Kingdoms: A Memoir of a Life Interrupted."*

Suleika didn't allow illness to ground her dreams. She realized that life is precarious. That one must live every moment and cut the strings holding you down.

We all live on fault lines. There will always be uncertainties, inconveniences, obstacles, limitations, fears, and doubts.

If we give in to these things, we become tethered like balloons to a pole.

Unable to chase our dreams.

Grounded.

I don't believe in circumstances

How about you? What are the strings holding you back?

The question to ask is: *Am I to blame for the strings holding me back?*

"People are always blaming their circumstances for what they are. I don't believe in circumstances. The people who get on in this world are the people who get up and look for the circumstances they want, and if they can't find them, make them." — *George Bernard Shaw, Mrs. Warren's Profession*

Yes, we all have limitations. There are obligations, rent, mortgages, expenses, and family members who depend on us.

But even with life's obstacles, we have the latitude to chase our dreams and soar.

Yet often, we don't.

We allow unhealthy habits, excuses, fear, and negative thinking to tether our dreams and ambitions. Before we know it, the years click by, and we end up deflated like those withered balloons.

Don't let this happen to you. It's never too late to change your trajectory and cut those strings.

Here are a few suggestions:

Stop keeping up with the Joneses

Nobody really cares if you have a BMW or not. If you spend your life comparing yourself to others, you'll forever be unhappy. Better to chase the passions and dreams that make you happy.

Accomplishment trumps approval

If your self-esteem hinges on the approval of others, you'll never be happy. Who wants to be tethered to the whims of other people's judgment?

Focus on accomplishment. On developing rare and valuable skills.

The world is full of posers and mimics copying what everyone else is doing. Study, practice, put in the time, and then develop your unique vision.

Opportunity and success often grow out of earned accomplishments.

Lemons out of lemonade

Suleika Jaouad made lemonade out of lemons. From a hospital bed, she wrote her inspiring *"Life, Interrupted"* columns, and has since become a devoted advocate for those living with illness and enduring life's many interruptions.

Whether it's an unexpected illness, job change, or other challenges, explore how you can use the experience to make lemonade out of lemons.

Stop wasting time

Endless social media scrolling, hours of television, unnecessary commitments, and inefficiency all keep us from attaining our dreams and ambitions. Also, there will always be other people happy to spend your time for you.

There are countless books, articles, and videos about time management. None of them will help if you're not honest with yourself.

Take a sober look at how you spend your time. Those YouTube benders add up. While you're partying or sleeping in, someone else is at the gym or up early finishing a novel.

Success rewards discipline and effort.

Stop wasting time, embrace discipline, make some sacrifices, and craft a schedule that supports your dreams and ambitions.

How many years must pass before we set ourselves free? Unlike those deflated balloons, you have the power to free yourself. Cut the string that's holding you back and let yourself soar.

Chapter Seven

The Number One Thing to Avoid in Your Creative Work

The genre-blending music of Jon Batiste is all about feeling good.

Watch his entertaining, high-energy music video *Freedom* to gain an appreciation of Batiste's upbeat sound and artistry. He recently won five Grammy awards, including the coveted *Best Album of the Year* for his LP *We Are.*

Batiste is a Juilliard trained musical dynamo. He's a jazz pianist, singer, songwriter, composer, dancer, bandleader for the Stephen Colbert late show, and more.

An article at Billboard.com noted that Batiste *"performed on and co-produced all of We Are, wrote or co-wrote all but a couple of the album's tracks, and played bass, keyboards, piano, strings, mellotron and even the theremin (!!) over the course of the LP."*

PBS.org wrote the following about Batiste:

"Born into a long lineage of Louisiana musicians, Jon Batiste is a globally celebrated musician, educator, bandleader, and television personality whose musical skill, artistic vision, and exuberant charisma have garnered him the well-deserved title of 'crowned prince of

jazz.' Jon is recognized for his originality, jaw-dropping talent, and dapper sense of style."

Talent, hard work, and exceptional training account for much of Batiste's success. But perhaps the most important quality that helps him stand out is originality.

The importance of being weird

Josh S. Rose is a director, filmmaker, and photographer based in Los Angeles, California.

According to his website, *"Rose spent over two decades as a creative director in advertising before breaking off on his own to pursue his passion for documentary photography and creative filmmaking."*

In an interview on *The Gray Matters* podcast, Rose talked about the importance of being weird in photography. Finding your quirks. Your uniqueness.

Rose noted that we have democratized photography because everyone has a smartphone in their pocket. Everyone is a photographer now.

The problem is a *"homogeneity of imagery out there."* Everyone is taking the same photos, selfies, food shots, and shallow depth-of-field portraits.

Instagram has become a sea of similarities.

Many of the photos are good, thanks to today's technology, but they're all mostly the same. *"In the old days, you had a quirk. Something that made you different,"* Rose says on the podcast.

"I never set out to be weird. It was always other people who called me weird." — Frank Zappa

Rose's advice for creatives is to figure out what's unique about you, to the exclusion of everything else.

The question is, how do you find your original voice?

Follow your vision

It's fine to admire the creative work of others and to use it for inspiration. But then, if you want your work to stand out, you must turn inward.

You must find your vision.

Photographer Cole Thompson echoes Josh Rose's *"find your uniqueness"* advice in a blog post, where he wrote:

"If you could do just one thing to improve your photography, it would be to find and follow your Vision. That is the driving creative force behind all my images. It's not the camera, the software, the location, the rules of composition, following photographic fads, or imitating others.

For me, it's finding my Vision and following it. Knowing what I love and pursuing it. Ignoring what others are doing and creating images that I love, regardless of what anyone else thinks of them."

How do you find your vision? Thompson argues that you should critically analyze your work. He wrote:

"I personally find this recent trend to have one's work critiqued by an expert disturbing. What you are getting is only an opinion and there are many of those out there. And the critiquer's opinions are colored by their Vision and their personal preferences."

No doubt there are experts who can mentor you and help improve your skills. But at some point, you must leverage your vision. Your weirdness. Your unique approach or quality that no one else has.

Once you've identified your unique vision, then you must sharpen it. Refine it. Authenticity is important, but quality has to be there, too.

You're the only version

During an interview with author and CNN host Fareed Zacharia, Jon Batiste said the following:

"There's something about a person that makes them the only version that exists. You're the only version. Why do we try to be like other people? Something that's led into you're existing today is so, so unique. It's so special. You're the only one that will ever exist."

Why do we try to be like other people?

Usually, because we admire them. We want to be like them. Copy their style, look, approach, success, etc.

But alas, there is only one version of each of us.

We can emulate others, and maybe find some degree of success. But we'll never be happy because we betrayed our uniqueness. We silenced our voices.

The number one thing to avoid in your creative work is sameness.

If your creative work looks like everyone else's, dig deeper.

Figure out what excites you. Experiment. Ignore Instagram and keep creating.

Look for clues and themes in your earlier work. Build on that, create every day, and your unique work and vision will emerge.

Jon Batiste grew up in a musical family, in the creative atmosphere of Louisiana. That created a great foundation. Along with his Juilliard education. But he listened to his unique voice. His vision.

That's why Jon Batiste is a Grammy-winning artist, and we're all the richer for it.

How about you? What's your quirk or unique quality that sets you apart? How can you develop it, refine it, and share it with the world?

It's never too late to start sharing the real you with the rest of the world.

Chapter Eight

Why the Convenient Path You're On Might Be Leading You Astray

Lindsey Ross is a conceptual, fine art photographer who likes to do things the hard way.

While most of us are enjoying the convenience, speed, and ease of modern living, Ross is lugging around a 250lb vintage camera and gallons of chemicals in the extended bed of her pickup truck.

Ross shoots gorgeous monochromatic images via a somewhat forgotten process known as wet plate collodion.

Her website notes:

"She became interested in the wet plate collodion process when she viewed a collection of early 20th-century prisoner mug shots. Ross began working with wet plate collodion in 2010. The wet plate collodion process has become the ideal format for Ross, who seeks autonomy and at the same time a sense of connection. Ross finds freedom in taking raw materials and transforming those into pho-

tographs. The slow pace of collodion requires a presence and intimacy that connects her to both the physical and spiritual world."

According to Ross, wet plate was the reigning photographic process from 1850 until about the 1890s. It's how we photographed the civil war and how Yosemite and Yellowstone were first photographed and brought back to Congress, which made them national parks.

Filmmaker Andrew Schoneberger produced a brief, fascinating documentary about Ross and her vintage photography titled *"Lindsey Ross: A Less Convenient Path."*

Most people today are content to take photos with their smartphones since the image quality is getting close to professional cameras. And there are apps to reproduce tintype, wet collodion, and many other effects.

So why would anyone want to lug around unwieldy, inconvenient cameras and gallons of chemicals?

The hard days are what make you stronger

Purpose and meaning in our lives seldom come from convenience. More often they come from hard work, effort, and accomplishment.

A day spent on the couch watching TV or scrolling YouTube videos might be convenient and relaxing, but you won't walk away feeling like you've accomplished something.

"You have to remember that the hard days are what make you stronger. The bad days make you realize what a good day is. If you never had any bad days, you would never have that sense of accomplishment!" — Aly Raisman

Not that downtime is bad, but life today increasingly seems to be about the path of least resistance.

Conveniences like TV remotes, Alexa audio commands, robot vacuum cleaners, and DoorDash deliveries all reinforce our sedentariness.

The convenience of smartphones and texting often replace real, person-to-person conversations. Social media and fear of missing out can prevent us from making things and accomplishing goals.

Passive living has become pervasive, along with obesity and a growing sense of mediocrity. It's like we know all these conveniences must be enjoyed in moderation, but we can't pull ourselves away.

If you've succumbed to today's conveniences at the expense of new accomplishments and personal growth, don't feel bad. It's easy and natural to embrace the path of least resistance, and I've certainly fallen victim at times.

But if you want to achieve your goals and chase your dreams, try to identify the conveniences that are hindering you. For me, it's less zoning out on YouTube videos and more time painting, writing, and photographing.

A less convenient path

It helps if you have a passion that excites and motivates you.

Lindsey Ross fell in love with wet plate collodion photography while completing her Master of Fine Arts degree at the Brooks Institute in Santa Barbara, California.

Ross lives in her cluttered photography studio and trudges all her heavy equipment to inspiring locales like Yosemite National Park. She can only afford to produce one, large image during an outing, and sometimes the image doesn't work out.

Ross accepts these hardships and difficulties as the cost she must pay for her art and passion. She must intuitively know that hardships and difficulties strengthen us, like exercising a muscle. They also move her art forward.

In the documentary, Ross states:

"Convenience is the route that we're all told to choose in life, and it's what society is guiding us towards, and it's what commercialism is trying to sell us. But it all leads to typically the same place. And I don't want to go to the same place. And I don't want to go to the same place in the same way."

Look around the Internet and social media and you'll see a lot of similarities. Everyone is using the same stock photos for their blog posts. People are copying one another, writing about the same themes. All because it's convenient.

Ross notes in the documentary:

"When I think of original experiences and friendships that I've made, they've usually been born out of some type of inconvenience or some type of struggle, so I have typically chosen a less convenient path."

You learn the most through the hard things

How about you? Are you stuck on a convenient path?

There's no shame.

I think a lot of us have become a bit too comfortable with today's conveniences, at the expense of doing the hard things that move us forward.

"It hasn't always been easy. There's a lot of hard moments. Sometimes you learn from the end of the bench. Sometimes you learn from injuries. Sometimes you learn the most through the hard things. If you can keep a good attitude and keep on working, eventually situations change, and you can put those things to use." — *Kyle Korver*

There are plenty of smart people like James Clear, author of the best-selling book *"Atomic Habits: An Easy & Proven Way to Build Good Habits,"* who can help you sidestep conveniences in favor of accomplishment.

But in the end, your desire to change must be stronger than your resistance.

Just remember, if an inspiring person like Lindsey Ross can haul a 250lb vintage camera and gallons of chemicals around in search of classic photos, perhaps the rest of us can get off the couch and chase down our own dreams.

Chapter Nine

Why the Treasures You Have Matter Less Than the Experiences You Live

Imagine traveling with your family out west in the 1800s to mine for precious metals in the great California gold rush.

You work hard, strike it rich, gather all your gold, and book passage on a 280-foot sidewheel steamer ship back to New York. Before departure, you splurge and pay a photographer to capture images of your family.

The ship sets sail with over 10 short tons of gold prospected from California. You celebrate onboard with other successful prospectors.

There is a layover in Cuba, and then you set sail for the East coast. Triumphant, you are anxious to return and show all the naysayers your hard-earned wealth.

Your dreams have come true, life feels glorious, and the future is bright.

But then the weather changes.

Desperation is the raw material of drastic change

On September 9, 1857, your ship (the SS Central America) encounters a Category 2 hurricane off the coast of the Carolinas. Before long, 105 mph winds and heavy seas shred the ship's sails. You're taking on water, and the boiler is beginning to fail.

A leak occurs in one of the seals between the paddle wheel shafts and the side of the ship. The boiler is unable to maintain the fire. Both bilge pumps fail when the steam pressure drops. The paddle wheels fail, and the ship can no longer face the wind. You begin to drift in more turbulent waters.

In desperation, the crew and passengers fly the ship's flag inverted, to signal distress to any passing ships.

No ships came.

There is a lull in the storm and passengers and crew form a bucket brigade, frantically trying to fight the rising water. Others try futilely to get the boiler running again.

And then the second half of the storm began.

The ship was without power, close to foundering, and carried further off-course into the dark, rough seas. By morning, miraculously, two ships in the area are spotted.

Only 153 passengers from the SS Central America, mostly women, and children, made it into lifeboats and were rescued. The remaining passengers and crew met their fate in the cold, briny ocean water.

"Desperation is the raw material of drastic change. Only those who can leave behind everything they have ever believed in can hope to escape." — William S. Burroughs

Some no doubt tried to bundle up their gold and hold onto it as they entered the water. But the gold was too heavy, becoming a death anchor.

The lucky passengers in the lifeboats said goodbye to loved ones and fortunes lost, but at least they had their lives.

What, we may wonder, did the survivors do when they returned to their homes? How did their desperate experience and tragedy change them?

People who face death and survive often view life differently. Gratitude and the simple joys of daily living become more important than chasing fame and fortune.

Experiences matter more than things.

There is no torrent like greed

The SS Central America went down with roughly eight million worth of gold ($765 million by today's standards). An enterprising treasure hunter named Tommy Thompson figured out where the shipwreck lay and convinced investors to fund recovery.

Thompson received millions from investors, and with the use of an underwater robot, he recovered approximately 100–150 million worth of gold.

But then things got complicated.

According to Wikipedia:

"Thirty-nine insurance companies filed suit, claiming that because they paid damages in the 19th century for the lost gold, they had the right to it. The team that found it argued that the gold had been abandoned. After a legal battle, 92% of the gold was awarded to the discovery team in 1996."

Thompson went on to bilk his investors and absconded with his fortune. He went into hiding in 2012, living a life on the lam with his girlfriend and assistant, Alison Antekeier. In 2015 US Marshals caught up with Thompson, and he was extradited to Ohio to face a judge and his investors.

"There is no fire like passion, there is no shark like hatred, there is no snare like folly, there is no torrent like greed." — *Siddhartha Gautama*

Thompson originally agreed to surrender 500 gold coins, but then claimed he couldn't remember where they were. Wikipedia notes:

"On November 28, 2018, a jury awarded Investors $19.4 million in compensatory damages: $3.2 million to the Dispatch Printing Company [which had put up 1 million of 22 million invested] and $16.2 million to the court-appointed receiver of the other investors."

I doubt that Tommy Thompson is a happy man. Running from the law, living in motels, and hiding gold coins from investors must be exhausting. Not to mention, sitting in a prison cell can't be much fun.

In contrast, I'll bet the survivors of the SS Central America found a deeper kind of happiness than Thompson's pursuit of greedy wealth.

Because the survivors, despite losing loved ones, were given a second chance at life. And second chances often breed gratitude and appreciation for people and experiences over money and possessions.

Time's relentless melt

Remember those photographs that the gold rush miners had taken of their loved ones before boarding the SS Central America? Turns out a great number of them, despite years at the bottom of the ocean, survived intact.

Fine art photography blogger Keith Dotson published an interesting podcast transcript about these recovered photos. Dotson notes:

"145 photographs were recovered and 11 were sent to Boston for conservation. How these daguerreotypes managed to survive is quite a wonder-given how delicate they are, and the ambrotypes too-those are imaged onto glass and are understandably quite fragile."

Daguerreotypes are photographs taken by an early photographic process employing an iodine-sensitized silvered plate and mercury vapor. Ambrotypes are an underexposed, underdeveloped, wet-collodion negative on glass that, when viewed with a dark background, appears as a positive image.

"All photographs are memento mori. To take a photograph is to participate in another person's (or thing's) mortality, vulnerability, mutability. Precisely by slicing out this moment and freezing it, all photographs testify to time's relentless melt." — Susan Sontag

Dotson's blog post notes that the best surviving photos *"were the ones that were sealed in the best cases, some made of wood wrapped with leather, and others in an early form of thermoplastic."*

Dotson describes these *"faces from the deep"* as *"haunting."* One affecting photograph shows a beautiful young woman in a dark dress with lace. As Dotson describes: *"Her lustrous, jet-black curls cascading down onto her bare shoulders."*

When I look at the photo, I like to think that this young woman was one of the survivors. That she made it back to New York, found meaningful work, started a family, and lived with grand memories of her exploits and gratitude in her heart.

If she did survive, I'll bet she found happiness in the little things. The scent of her baby's hair and garden flowers. The embrace of close friends, and the company of good books.

Unlike Tommy Thompson, who allowed greed to sully his life, I hope the woman in the photo enjoyed a long life of family, passions, experiences, and the glory of everyday living.

Time will melt for all of us. How do we want to spend it? What's truly important, and what's superficial?

In the end, we need very little to be happy. The best of life is seldom found in treasures and possessions. It's found in our experiences, the people we love, and the passions we enjoy.

There's nothing wrong with financial success, but it won't guarantee happiness. Perhaps this is why so many lottery winners end up unhappy.

The real treasures in life are your health, family, friends, passions, and experiences. Chase these, and you will have a life well-lived.

Chapter Ten

How Bright Your Candle Burns Is All About Choices

Everyone has a light within them.

Deep down, we all want it to burn bright. But keeping the flame alive requires effort.

The strong winds of adversity, loss, hardship, and pain can threaten to blow out our flame. Our job, however difficult, is to keep the flame lit.

For those of us whose flame is strong, we must use our light to help others kindle their flame.

So that they can illuminate the world, too.

"No one is useless in this world who lightens the burdens of another." — Charles Dickens

Paul Reid is a UK photographer whose light is burning bright, even if his work is often in black and white. His monochromatic photography was recently featured on the cover of *Black and White* magazine.

Reid shoots portraits, street images, and weddings. He likes to get involved in his wedding photos, capturing unrehearsed, unposed moments that capture the energy and light of his subjects.

I discovered Reid's work by accident while researching the Leica Q2 Monochrome camera online (Reid uses the same camera in his work).

Reid's beautifully shot and poignant short film *"Dreams"* left me moved and inspired, due to its marriage of words and imagery.

A flame can go out at any moment

Sometimes we are the hero in our story, and other times we are the villain.

Most of the time, we're probably just spectators. Going through the motions of life, watching what happens as if we have no agency over the outcomes.

It's easy to fall into a rut.

Endless routines and habits dull our spirit and the light within us can dim. Youthful dreams are stowed away in the dark cabinet of our minds. We focus on work, the mortgage, relationship challenges, that next promotion.

Occasionally, we peek inside the dark cabinet, to see the dull eyes of our dreams staring back at us.

The eyes are lugubrious and pleading as if they're saying, "Don't forget me. I'm still here. Waiting. Hoping. Praying."

Paul Reid's short video *"Dreams"* explores the importance of chasing our dreams.

In his video narration, Reid says:

"My father would tell me that there is a plan for me. My mother still tells me that all of my dreams will come true someday. Their hair is now as white as flames on candles. Wonder if they got everything that they wanted in life? Theirs is the greatest achievement of all, a love that has lasted a lifetime. My candle is burning too. A flame can go out at any moment. I've still got time."

Where are you at with your dreams?

Have you peeked inside that dark cabinet in your mind lately? What changes could you make in your life to free those dreams?

Get up and do something

It's not easy to climb out of a rut, but if we are to nurture our candle flame, climb we must.

There are people every day who find a way. Sometimes all it takes is bold action, like quitting your job and moving.

For others, positive change is incremental.

Think of the movie *Shawshank Redemption.* The actor Tim Robbins brilliantly plays the protagonist, Andy Dufresne, who was sentenced to two consecutive life terms in prison for the murders of his wife and her lover. Only Andy knows he didn't commit the crimes.

Andy methodically plans his escape from prison. He builds trust, obtains tools, patiently works, bit by bit, toward his goal. It takes years.

Whether it takes years or you're able to make immediate changes to stoke your candle flame and chase your dream, the key is to start.

Don't be that person who never starts. Who just goes through the motions, never changing, always shooting yourself in the foot.

Get up and do something. Every day.

"The best way to not feel hopeless is to get up and do something. Don't wait for good things to happen to you. If you go out and make some good things happen, you will fill the world with hope, you will fill yourself with hope."

— *Barack Obama*

Have something going on somewhere

We've all met clingers. People who are just holding on to where they are. Hoping things will change.

The problem with hope is that without action, it's unreliable. Sometimes the gods smile upon us and improve our circumstances. But mostly it's up to us.

"...it's important to have something going on somewhere, at work or at home, otherwise you're just clinging on." — Nick Hornby

Action is the oxygen that stokes the flames of our candle. But the action must be intelligent.

If you have a dream for a creative passion or better life, start by researching the steps necessary to achieve your dream. The ones you admire who achieved the same dreams usually leave clues.

It might require going back to school, or maybe finding a mentor. Saying no to time wasters (TV, social media, addictions, etc.) to maximize your efforts.

You can be the hero of your own story. If you want your candle to burn bright, and your dreams to come true, then roll up your sleeves and get to work.

And when your candle is burning bright, and your dreams come true, remember to use your light to brighten the lives of others.

In this way, all our candles will burn brightly, and the world just might have fewer shadows of doubt, despair, and hopelessness.

Chapter Eleven

Why Coffee Shops Are Teachers, If Only We'd Pay Attention

Thank God for elegance, and for the people who take the time and energy to embrace it.

There is enough ugliness in the world. Enough foul language, sagging trousers, gossip rags, and nihilistic expression.

The muddy pathway to the low road is well-trodden because it's easy. It requires nothing of us. Mediocrity loves company.

The high road, however, is not easy. It's a steady uphill hike, with the wind in your face. It demands sacrifices and effort, but the reward is more than accomplishment. It's a kind of inner peace.

The gentleman in the coffee shop radiated elegance and inner peace.

This rude world

From the moment he strolled in, I couldn't take my eyes off him. His suit, tie, fedora, and handkerchief were beautifully thought out. This was a man who took care in his appearance, but not for vanity's sake. For self-respect and high standards.

He stood tall, shoulders back. He smiled at the barista and said in a silky baritone, "Good morning, ma'am. May I have a dark roast coffee?"

The barista stared back at him in silence, and then caught herself and said, "Of course, sir."

"If you ask what the ten things that improve the quality of this rude world are, I would say one right away: Elegance!" -Mehmet Murat ildan

The dapper gentleman sat down, sipped his coffee, and began reading a book he had carried in under his right arm.

His elegance and refinement were comforting. Like when my father used to arrive home at night after a long work commute, in his three-piece suit, carrying a briefcase.

Dad was an adult. An attorney who took the high road. Someone to be depended on. A professional who dressed like it. Not in a foppish or elitist way, but simply because he respected himself, his family, his profession, and the people he worked for.

Had I not ambled into the coffee shop to read and write, I never would have seen this dignified, elegantly attired man. Nor would I have ruminated about my father's dignity, elegant manner, and the importance of high standards.

My time in the coffee shop was well spent. Through quiet observation, I learned a lesson easily forgotten in today's dressed-down, casual atmosphere.

The lesson was that elegance still matters.

To be impatient means never really living

A week later the siren song of a hot latte and blueberry muffin landed me back in the same coffee shop. I slung my satchel strap over the back of the chair, pulled out a notebook, and waited for my order.

A line formed after my arrival, and an entertaining theater of drama unfolded. The man in front forgot his credit card and asked if he could pay with a check. Tense expressions on the woman behind him betrayed her impatience.

The coffee shop doesn't take checks and so the man trotted out to his car to look for change. "Oh my God, some people," the woman said to the cashier after the man was gone. The cashier meekly smiled at the woman's impatience and took her order.

"To be impatient means never really living, being always in the future, in what will happen, but which is after all not yet here. Do not impatient people resemble spirits who are never here in this place, and now, in this very moment, but rather sticking their heads out of life like those wanderers who supposedly, when they found themselves at the end of the world, just looked onward, beyond the horizon? What did they see there? What is it that an impatient person hopes to glimpse?" -Olga Tokarczuk, The Books of Jacob

An older businessman behind the impatient woman was completely indifferent. He seemed to be quietly humming to himself. When his turn came, he smiled broadly at the cashier and placed his order.

The cashier gave the businessman some change and said, "Your coffee will be right up, sir." The businessman grinned and said, "Ah, coffee, my dear, coffee. Nectar of the Gods!"

This caused the cashier to giggle a little, and I chuckled as well. And then I realized that the coffee shop and its people taught me another life lesson.

Inconveniences and annoying people will come into our lives. We can greet these things with a furrowed brow and sarcastic words, or we can smile and sing the praises of "Nectar of the Gods."

Clearly, the latter enticed a giggle from the young cashier, instead of a meek reply.

People don't listen when you lecture

It wasn't long before another life lesson presented itself in the coffee shop. This time it was compliments of a bickering, elderly couple.

The old fellow ordered a large cafe mocha, which launched his wife into a lecture about the evils of chocolate and high cholesterol. The old chap held his tongue for a bit while his wife chattered about his last doctor appointment and lab results. She couldn't see that she was embarrassing her husband.

Eventually, the fellow shot back and told his wife that he just wanted "to live a little."

"People don't listen when you lecture. No one wants to be talked down to or scolded."-Scott Thompson

I'm sure the fellow's wife meant well. Perhaps he's terrible at managing his health, and his wife must be the bad guy and remind him about his diet.

But here's the thing. It's all about the way you tell somebody something, and when.

It probably would have been more effective for the woman to let her husband enjoy the mocha, and then, later, tell him, "I love you honey, and I want you around. I know you love those mochas, but I worry about your diet and staying healthy."

Such a statement might prove more effective. Either way, watching their exchange reminded me that all couples quarrel. The key is to figure out how to do it elegantly, and to pick the best time and place to bring up sensitive subjects.

Caffeine does not cure existential exhaustion

A few weeks passed and I found myself in a different coffee shop across town. I was running errands and needed a coffee break.

I heard the bells on the shop's door jingle as a jittery-looking man carrying a satchel wandered in. He was skinny and seemed to walk with an electric rhythm.

In his right hand was an empty coffee cup, which he presented to the barista. He said something about being in a hurry, and that he needed to wake up. "This is empty, and I need it filled up, stat!" he said with a nervous kind of smile.

"I can't remember the last time I've slept and while caffeine does sound like Heaven, I wonder if it'll really be able to help me in this state. After all, caffeine does not cure existential exhaustion."
-Kayla Krantz, The Moon Warriors

The barista chap took the cup and as he filled it asked, "Maybe I should throw in an espresso? That'll wake you up." The comment was said in jest, but the jittery fellow agreed.

"That's actually a great idea!" he said.

I watched the harried fellow, armed with enough caffeine to kill a horse, as he scrambled out of the coffee shop and into his car.

Another coffee shop lesson, I thought. Plan your schedule well and go easy on the caffeine.

Love them anyway

My last coffee shop lesson happened a few years back when I was still living in Northern California. I was enjoying a latte and reading in the coffee shop when I noticed a homeless gentleman outside.

The guy had a shopping cart with him and looked like he'd had a rough night. He slumped down on a bench and went through his pockets, presumably looking for some coffee money.

The manager of the coffee house, a kind woman named Anna, spotted the fellow. I watched as she filled a large cup of coffee and headed outside. I got up and followed her, as I was ready to leave.

Outside, Anna approached the man and said, "This one is on the house, George." He stood up, beaming, and said, "I always knew you were an angel, Anna."

"People are illogical, unreasonable, and self-centered. Love them anyway."-Kent M. Keith, The Silent Revolution: Dynamic Leadership in the Student Council

What struck me more than Anna's kind gesture was the fact that they knew one another's names. Clearly, they have interacted before.

The lesson: Take the time to learn people's names.

When we take the time to meet people and learn their names, we see their humanity more deeply. Instead of viewing them as an abstraction ("the coffee barista" or "the homeless guy,"), we get to know them a little more intimately.

Coffee shops can be teachers. But we must get our noses out of our smartphones and laptops. We need to sit quietly, listen, and observe.

I've unwittingly overheard the most amazing conversations in coffee shops. People sharing advice, heartfelt regrets, and plans for the future.

Such conversations remind me how alike we all are. How we all want pretty much the same things. To be loved. To find some success. To matter in this life. To enjoy a good cup of coffee.

Next time you find yourself in a coffee shop, relax. Sit back. Listen. Watch. Let the world and all its rich life lessons unfold before you.

Chapter Twelve

If Your Creative Work Doesn't Please You, What's the Value?

Linnie figured she'd be dead by Christmas, which is why she reached out to Cole Thompson.

Cole Thompson is a professional photographer who specializes in creating classic images in black and white. One of Cole's most iconic images is the photo he took of *"The Angel Gabriel."*

The Angel Gabriel was eating French Fries out of a trash can on the Newport Beach pier when Cole first met him. Gabriel was homeless and hungry. Cole asked if Gabriel would help him with a photograph, and in return, he'd buy lunch for Gabriel.

Cole describes on his website what happened next:

"The pier was very crowded, and I wanted to take a 30-second exposure so that everyone would disappear except Gabriel. We tried a few shots and then Gabriel wanted to hold his Bible. The image worked and the only people you can see besides Gabriel are those 'ghosts' who lingered long enough for the camera.

Gabriel and I then went into a restaurant to share a meal; he ordered steak with mushrooms and onions. When it came, he ate it with his hands. I discovered he was Romanian and so am I, so we talked about Romania. He was simple, kind and a pleasure to talk with. I asked Gabriel how I might contact him in case I sold some of the photographs and wanted to share the money with him. He said I should give the money to someone who could really use it; that he had everything that he needed."

If it's true that the Lord works in mysterious ways, then perhaps it was divine fate that Cole photographed The Angel Gabriel that day on the pier. Because the photograph went on to play a huge part in Linnie's life.

Wrapped in a crown of thorns

Linnie bought a print of *"The Angel Gabriel,"* and then a year later contacted Cole. She had breast cancer and wanted Cole to photograph her. She felt the photos would be of value to other women facing the same diagnosis.

"Some of the most beautiful things worth having in your life come wrapped in a crown of thorns."-Shannon L. Alder

Cole gently tried to tell Linnie that he was not a portrait photographer and recommended someone else. But Linnie was emphatic that Cole take the pictures.

Eventually, Cole relented and agreed.

The photoshoot wasn't easy since Cole was not skilled with portrait photography and the requisite lighting. But finally, Cole was able to take some intimate, poignant photographs.

Then Cole got the courage to ask Linnie, "What's your prognosis?"

"I'll be dead by Christmas," Linnie said.

I grew up in a black and white world

Cole Thompson knew at the age of 14 that he was destined to be a photographer. He read everything he could find about photography and spent hours processing film in the darkroom.

Thompson is often asked why he focuses on black and white photography, and this is what he wrote on his website:

"I think it's because I grew up in a black-and-white world. Television, movies, and the news were all in black and white. My heroes were in black and white and even the nation was segregated into black and white. My images are an extension of the world in which I grew up."

Cole explains further,

"For me color records the image, but black and white captures the feelings that lie beneath the surface."

Clearly Cole's photograph *"The Angel Gabriel"* seems to capture feelings that lie beneath the surface. After all, it moved Linnie to buy a print, and later reach out to Cole to take her photograph.

Who knows how many women facing breast cancer will see Linnie's dignified photograph and find strength and encouragement from it.

The best success is achieved internally

In a world of garish color, noise, and egos scrambling for attention, Cole Thompson marches to his own beat. His art has appeared in many exhibitions, publications and has received numerous awards. But you won't read about these accolades on his website. Why?

Cole explains on his website:

"In the past I've considered those accolades as the evidence of my success, but I now think differently. My success is no longer measured by the length of my resume, but rather by how I feel about the art that I create. While I do enjoy exhibiting, seeing my work published and meeting people who appreciate my art, this is an extra benefit of creating, but not success itself. I believe that the best success is achieved internally, not externally."

There's a lesson here for all artists longing to create authentic, personal work. You can game the algorithms, emulate work that's popular, and sell your creative soul. But it's a devil's bargain.

In the end, you won't be happy with what you create. Sure, you might make some money following the herd. But the best of what you have to offer may never be revealed.

Thankfully, Cole Thompson followed his heart and realized that "the best success is achieved internally, not externally."

A happy ending cannot come in the middle of the story

If your creative work doesn't please you, what's the value? At this stage in my life, I think about this often.

I want to wake up each day excited about the artwork, photography, and writing that I produce.

Yes, I'd love for it to meet favor with the algorithm gods and rank high on Google. But as Cole Thompson notes, the best success is achieved internally, not externally.

How about you? Are you producing work for the sake of attention and popularity, or because the work sings in your soul?

"Heroes know that things must happen when it is time for them to happen. A quest may not simply be abandoned; unicorns may go un-rescued for a long time, but not forever; a happy ending cannot come in the middle of the story."-Peter S. Beagle, The Last Unicorn

Cole Thompson's photographic art clearly touches others, but that's a byproduct of his fidelity to artistic authenticity.

Whatever became of Linnie?

She was able to get into an experimental program. Years later, with a full head of hair, she reached out again to Cole to take her picture.

And just like before, she wouldn't take no for an answer.

Chapter Thirteen

What a Little Boy and His Airplane Can Teach Us About Love

Timothy loved that toy airplane from the day his grandfather knelt and handed it to him.

"This is for you, my boy. So you can take wing and adventure in lands near and far," his grandfather said.

Timothy and his airplane were inseparable. They loved the backyard, where a makeshift runway scratched into the dirt served as the starting point for imaginary trips.

Timothy had a fertile imagination about people, places, and things. He viewed his toy airplane as a kind of portal to discovery. Oh, the places they could go together.

Timothy's imagination was no doubt stoked by the stories and books his grandfather read to him. "Books, my dear boy, free us. They open worlds beyond our grasp. They teach us about life, and what's important," his grandfather once said before making a strange face.

"The worst moments in life are heralded by small observations."
-Andy Weir, The Martian

"What's wrong?" Timothy asked him.

His grandfather sat back, exhaled a few times, and said, "Old age, Timothy. That's what's wrong." But then his grandfather smiled, and his eyes glistened with a loving sparkle.

Fear is for the winter

The day it happened Timothy knew it must be winter. After all, his grandfather read to him once about fear coming in the winter.

"Oh, my sweet summer child," Old Nan said quietly, "what do you know of fear?

Fear is for the winter, my little lord, when the snows fall a hundred feet

deep and the ice wind comes howling out of the north. Fear is for the long

night, when the sun hides its face for years at a time, and little children

are born and live and die all in darkness while the direwolves grow gaunt and

hungry, and the white walkers move through the woods"

-George R.R. Martin, A Game of Thrones

Timothy didn't always understand the books his grandfather read to him but was told, "Not everything has to make perfect sense. Just listen to the words, and the way they make you feel."

"Come on, Timothy, it's time to go." The words that came from his mother made him feel anxious.

Even little boys can sense endings and final goodbyes. She strolled over to him and knelt in her black dress. "Dad is waiting in the car, honey. We need to leave."

Learn to dance with the limp

The drive into town was not far but the somber mood pierced the boy's spirit.

He ran his fingers over the toy airplane as he gazed out the car window. Little boys may not understand many adult things, but the tenderness of youth is not immune to the pain of loss.

"You will lose someone you can't live without, and your heart will be badly broken, and the bad news is that you never completely get over the loss of your beloved. But this is also the good news. They live forever in your broken heart that doesn't seal back up. And you come through. It's like having a broken leg that never heals perfectly -that still hurts when the weather gets cold, but you learn to dance with the limp."-Anne Lamott

There were many in attendance at the memorial service, but that was not a surprise. His grandfather was beloved in the community.

When the boy asked to see the open casket, his mother was unsure, but his father smiled and said, "It's okay, let Timothy say his goodbyes."

His father dragged a chair over to the open casket and held Timothy's elbow as he stepped up. Timothy was a little afraid, but he steadied himself and then peered down.

Death ends a life, not a relationship

His grandfather's face looked weird. Sort of ashen and completely devoid of life.

Timothy knew, in his young mind, that Poppy (his grandfather's nickname) was gone forever. But he also felt, in a strange way, like Poppy was still with him forever. Still in his heart and mind.

"Death ends a life, not a relationship."-Mitch Albom, Tuesdays with Morrie

After a few minutes, Timothy's mother said, "Are you all set, sweetie? Can I lift you down?" Timothy faced his mother, nodded yes, and outstretched his arms. But as she stepped in to lift him, he said, "Oh, wait."

Timothy turned back and looked down at his beloved Poppy. His wise grandfather, who took the time to read to him, and teach him about life and meaning and adventures.

Timothy surprised his parents when he leaned forward, pressing his left hand against the shiny edge of the casket. With his right hand, Timothy reached into his pocket and withdrew the toy airplane.

He leaned over further, and gently rested the toy airplane on his grandfather's chest. Timothy's mother began to sob quietly.

"I love you, Poppy," Timothy said. "Maybe this will help you get where you're going."

Chapter Fourteen

What Matters Most Is How You Walk Through the Fire

Last year our beloved cat Skye enjoyed a spoonful of cream, sauntered into my son's room, and dropped dead.

He was only a year-old Maine Coon, but apparently, the breed is prone to underlying heart conditions. My wife and I scooped up his limp body and sped to the veterinarian's office, but there was nothing they could do.

We tearfully held his paws on the exam table, said our good-byes, and drove home in stunned silence.

The next morning, I accompanied my wife to a doctor's appointment to get the results of some tests. Her doctor sat down in front of us and said, "You have breast cancer."

Those four words launched my wife and me into the fire. The fire of fear, uncertainty, tests, surgeries, and stress.

On the day of my wife's double mastectomy, I took a cell phone picture of her just before surgery. We wanted to share a photo with family.

My wife held up her right hand and gave a thumbs up.

She was moments away from the fire. The fire of surgery, uncertainty, pain, and fear. Yet she gave a thumbs up for the photo, to tell her family that it will all be okay.

That's how you walk through the fire.

With dignity and grace.

Things get bad for all of us

The late author and poet Charles Bukowski lived a difficult life.

In the 2003 film *Bukowski: Born Into This*, Bukowski says that his father beat him with a razor strop three times a week from age six to eleven years old. He claimed that the beatings informed his writing, helping him understand undeserved pain.

Bukowski suffered from terrible acne as a youth, thus isolating him from others his age. The suffering in the Depression deepened his rage, all of which fueled his writing and worldview.

Bukowski's writing can be blunt and depressing, often transcending our preciousness and treacly optimism. Yet it also finds beauty lurking behind the ugliness of life.

Charles Bukowski may have been a hedonistic alcoholic, but he discovered and wrote about the hard truths of life as he experienced them growing up, on the streets, and in the bars.

Consider the following quote from Bukowski's book *What Matters Most Is How Well You Walk Through the Fire*:

"Things get bad for all of us, almost continually, and what we do under the constant stress reveals who/what we are."

This wisdom echoes the views of the late psychiatrist and Holocaust survivor Viktor Frankl, whose famous memoir *Man's Search for Meaning*, reminds us that we cannot control what happens to us, but we do control how we will respond.

"Everything can be taken from a man but one thing: the last of the human freedoms — to choose one's attitude in any given set of circumstances, to choose one's own way." — Viktor E. Frankl, Man's Search for Meaning

Stress, tragedy, and hardship are inescapable realities in life. Shakespeare called them *"the slings and arrows of outrageous fortune."* They can destroy good people.

They should have destroyed the late singer, Roy Orbison.

Only the lonely know the way I feel tonight

Roy Orbison was famous for his signature dark glasses, jet black hair, and operatic vocal ability.

Less known are the multiple tragedies that happened to Orbison in his life.

In the 1960s Orbison and his young wife were riding motorcycles when she crashed into an open truck door. She died in Orbison's arms.

Two years later, while Orbison was on tour in England, his house burned down, killing two of his three young sons. Then, in 1973, Orbison's brother Grady died in a car accident while enroute to visit Orbison.

"Only the lonely know the way I feel tonight." — Roy Orbison

How does one navigate the tragic loss of a spouse, children, and brother? How does one walk through those fires?

With hope in your heart.

Just months after his young sons perished in the house fire, Orbison recorded an album about the tragedy. It was thought to have been lost forever until his other sons discovered it.

One of the songs on the album is titled *"You'll never walk alone,"* which is a cover of the original by Oscar Hammerstein II and composer Richard Rodgers for their musical Carousel.

Here are the lyrics:

When you walk through a storm hold your head up high
And don't be afraid of the dark
At the end of a storm is a golden sky
And the sweet silver song of a lark
Walk on through the wind
Walk on through the rain
Though your dreams be tossed and blown

Walk on, walk on with hope in your heart
And you'll never walk alone
You'll never, ever walk alone
Walk on, walk on with hope in your heart
And you'll never walk alone
You'll never, ever walk alone

Despite the tragedy of losing two children in a house fire, Orbison found a song of encouragement and hope.

The lyrics *"When you walk through a storm hold your head up high"* reflect Orbison's answer to how we should walk through the fire.

The lyrics echo Bukowski and Frankl. We may not be able to control what happens to us, but we can control how we respond.

One of Orbison's sons said that his father always kept a positive attitude. Orbison was a sensitive man who remained cheerful despite the losses in his life.

If Roy Orbison can do it, how about the rest of us?

You can beat death in life

Those who have read the French Enlightenment writer Voltaire are likely familiar with his most famous work *Candide*.

Candide touches on several subjects, but it mostly wrestles with reality versus blind optimism. It holds the view that we are already living in the best of all possible worlds (of course, people of faith would differ on this view).

The late Professor Peter Gay, in his introduction to a bilingual edition of Voltaire's *Candide*, wrote:

"If this life is a desert, it is our duty to make an oasis in it; if this life is a shipwreck, we must rescue as many as we can, and not forget to sing in the lifeboats."

The world and all its tragedies may be all we get, but that doesn't mean we can't "sing in the lifeboats." We get to decide how we want to respond to life's catastrophes.

Charles Bukowski's poem *"The Laughing Heart,"* tells us we can beat death in life. We can choose to turn darkness into light, as the following lines suggest:

"you can't beat death but
you can beat death in life, sometimes.
and the more often you learn to do it,
the more light there will be.
your life is your life.
know it while you have it.
you are marvelous
the gods wait to delight
in you."

When the fires came for my wife, she bravely gave a thumbs up and held her head high.

When tragedy took Roy Orbison's little boys, he found a way to beat death in life. By inspiring others with his songs of hope.

Sooner or later, you'll have to walk through the fire.

Hold your head high. Do it with grace and dignity. Show the world that you're greater than what it can throw at you. Replace the darkness with your light.

This is how we walk through the fire.

Chapter Fifteen

Eliminate One Thing to Improve Productivity and Happiness

It all started with my paintbox collection.

My wife and I were headed down the coast for a weekend get-away in Carmel, California.

Since I am a landscape painter, I love to paint along the coastline and windswept cliffs of Carmel. I also love the endless art galleries in Carmel.

The night before we left, I found myself crippled with indecision. I had numerous paint boxes (also known as pochade boxes) of varying sizes laid out on my studio floor.

Pochade boxes are smaller than traditional French easels. They fold open, revealing a palette and panel holder. Most pochade boxes include an adapter on the bottom for a tripod.

I loved all my pochade boxes for different reasons but having so many choices paralyzed me. I would pick one up and stuff it in my travel backpack with assorted brushes, panels, solvent container, and a dry box to slide in the wet panels after painting.

But then I'd change my mind and unpack everything, only to repack it again with a different pochade box. This madness went on for over an hour until my wife walked into the room and said, "Just pick one and be done with it."

So, I swallowed hard, picked one, and placed all the remaining pochade boxes back in my overflowing closet.

Of course, this wasn't the only time I agonized about painting equipment. I took a workshop in Idaho once and brought along two different paint boxes (a small and mid-size one).

You should have seen me at the airport, lugging around all that equipment. Just before I got on a connecting flight, one of my backpack seams split open, spilling out my brushes and gear. I had to pay top dollar in an airport luggage store for a replacement bag.

"Everything you own must be able to fit inside one suitcase; then your mind might be free." — *Charles Bukowski*

I knew nothing of minimalism back then, but I sensed that there had to be a better way.

Comfort just doesn't make very good art

Ben Staley is a remarkable director, cinematographer, and photographer. Equally remarkable is how he grew up.

According to his website, Staley was born in Alaska and raised without electricity or running water. There was no TV, and he didn't have a flushing toilet until he went to college.

He read a lot of books.

He spent time in the backcountry on horseback and sleeping in a tepee. His website notes:

"There were a lot of campfires and cold nights and stories told by lantern light. Stories.

Images found in the imagination before a flickering firelight. Narrative architecture flowing forth from multiple voices. Untrained. Unrefined. Instinctual oral tradition. Bits of books and movies and experiences and memories and second-hand hearsay. Stories. Stories got into the blood and became the only path forward."

Love of stories led to Staley's work as a director, cinematographer, and photographer. Such work depends upon a lot of sophisticated equipment. So, it's surprising that one day, Staley sold all his cameras and a backpack full of lenses.

In a compelling video on Staley's *"Adventure & Art"* YouTube channel, Staley explains why he sold all his camera gear:

"I just reached a point where I felt comfortable, and comfort, in my mind, just doesn't make very good art. It's not the ingredient you need."

Staley decided to use only one camera, a Leica Q2. He wanted to "disrupt" his old process and challenge himself.

His photography friends thought he was nuts because the Leica Q2 is a 28mm fixed lens. Not having interchangeable lenses severely limits one's shooting options, especially with portraiture (Staley's specialty).

Staley committed to using just the Leica Q2 for one year, and he found his photography grew in new, innovative ways.

Eliminate complexity

In his YouTube video, Staley asks, "What is the most important component in a portrait?" Is it the camera, the lens, the subject, the light, or perhaps the location?

According to Staley, the most important component in a portrait is **you.**

It's your connection to the subject. And sometimes, the more we surround ourselves with technology and equipment, the more removed we become from the art we're trying to create.

Like when I was paralyzed with indecision over which pochade box to take to Carmel. And when I was traveling to Idaho, lugging far more painting equipment than I needed.

"If you want to achieve greater productivity and happiness, eliminate complexity. "— John P. Weiss

Staley got rid of all his old camera equipment and lenses and forced himself to work with just one camera and a fixed lens.

Granted, the Leica Q2 camera is an exquisite camera. The fixed 28mm lens creates some limitations, but there is freedom in limitations.

By eliminating endless options, you spend less time deciding and more time creating.

Remember my pochade box dilemma? After my Carmel and Idaho painting trips, I sold all but two small pochade boxes (one set up in my studio and the other in my backpack, always ready to go).

I realized that I didn't need all that equipment and weight.

This led to simplifying and removing complexity in other areas of my life, like my wardrobe, subscriptions, unnecessary commitments, etc.

There is eminent freedom in removing complexity in your life. When the tyranny of endless decisions is trimmed away, you can then focus on what's important.

We are our choices

Have you ever been in a nice restaurant after a long day at work, only to be confronted with a large menu of choices? And then the server recites all the specials that evening, further complicating your decision.

Endless options and choices sound nice, but they're exhausting. We become stressed out due to the tyranny of decisions.

"We are our choices." — Jean-Paul Sartre

Speaking of the tyranny of decisions, I visited a camera shop recently to purchase a new system for street photography. The salesman was helpful, but I quickly became overwhelmed by all the options and dense, bloated menus in the Sony and Fujifilm cameras.

Afterward, I spent weeks online, watching comparison videos and evaluating endless camera options, lenses, pros, cons, etc. Talk about complexity!

I bought one camera online, only to grow frustrated with its dense menus and litany of buttons, bells, and whistles. So, I returned it and bought another camera, but it wasn't right either.

I was longing for simplicity.

And then I remembered Ben Staley and his simple Leica Q2 camera. Yes, the camera costs a boatload, but it has a simple menu and gets out of your way so you can shoot amazing photos.

I'm ordering the Leica and will soon be broke. But I'll also be outdoors shooting street scenes, portraits, and the world outside. Because there are stories there, waiting to be told.

No more YouTube comparison videos. No more endless options and indecision. Just the joy of unfettered photography and creative freedom.

How about you? What unnecessary complexity is holding you back in life?

Simplify as much as you can, say goodbye to the tyranny of endless decisions, remove the complexity, and start living the life you deserve.

Chapter Sixteen

The One Habit I Wished I Discovered in My Twenties

Henry sits quietly in his wheelchair, a marooned shell of a man.

He is old, inert, depressed, hardly responsive, and barely alive. Can anything pull him out of the lonely, dark world he inhabits?

Fortunately for Henry, he has Yvonne Russell.

Yvonne is a recreation therapist, and she uses an iPod and earphones to play some of Henry's favorite music from the past.

The whole scene played out on a YouTube video I discovered.

What happens next is nothing short of a miracle. Henry comes alive. Oliver Sacks, the late physician, best-selling author, and professor of neurology says in the video:

"The philosopher Kant once called music the 'quickening art' and Henry is being quickened, he is being brought to life."

We watch in the video as Henry starts to dance with his arms and sing to the music. Afterward, the earphones are removed, and Henry is asked questions.

Normally mute and unresponsive, Henry becomes quite voluble and expressive.

Dr. Sacks goes on to note in the video:

"So, in some sense, Henry is restored to himself. He has remembered who he is and has reacquired his identity for a while through the power of music."

When asked what music does to him, Henry answers: *"It gives me the feeling of love."*

As much as this video demonstrates the power of music, it also shows Henry doing something that is deeply important for happiness.

It's something we can all do but often neglect in this age of rapid distractions, side hustles, and 24/7 busyness.

We read to know we're not alone

I used to read to my mother.

In her final years, the tremors of Parkinson's disease destroyed her fine motor skills. Holding a book was impossible.

A life-long reader, Mom missed the joy of immersing herself in a good book. We tried audiobooks, but she was unable to control electronic devices.

I hired a woman named Suzanne to read to my mother twice weekly when I could not be there, but Mom preferred to socialize with Suzanne. So, I became Mom's reader, enabling her to experience worlds outside her contorted body.

"We read to know we're not alone." — William Nicholson, Shadowlands

Over time I noticed something profound. Because my mother was unable to walk or even hold a book, the world she lived in slowed down.

Conversations became immensely important and pleasurable for Mom. When I read to her, she became quiet and completely transfixed. Meals and desserts were almost holy occasions for Mom.

She was doing something that the rest of us, in our busy lives of commitments and ambitions, often fail to do.

She was savoring the moments.

Opportunities to linger in a positive moment

There are so many things we can savor if we just learn to slow down. We can savor a meal, a relationship, a conversation, a book, a movie, a piece of music, memories, and more.

According to a psychologytoday.com article:

"Savoring just means that we attempt to fully feel, enjoy, and extend our positive experiences. Savoring is a great way to develop a long-lasting stream of positive thoughts and emotions, because positive events cannot always be relied on to make you happier."

Taking the time to savor the things you enjoy can lead to greater happiness in life. It can also lead to greater creativity.

Consider the following excerpt from an article on the benefits of savoring in positivepsychlopedia.com:

"In 'Savoring: A New Model of Positive Experience,' authors Fred B. Bryant and Joseph Veroff posit that savoring may be part of creativity. Although savoring isn't the same as flow — the state of intense absorption that heightens performance — it does share the features of clear focus and attention to the present. When we savor, we pay more attention to details and complexity, which may come in handy later when our brains seek out the raw materials of creative ideas. Experiences that were once savored can become the fodder for written masterpieces, scientific experiments, and great business ideas."

The great outdoors, kind people, amazing meals, books, and deep conversations are more than just nice things to experience.

They are opportunities to linger in a positive moment.

Opportunities to savor.

Another way to exercise being present

My father used to enjoy summer days sitting outside on his patio. He would sip iced tea, relax, listen to the birds, and daydream. In essence, he was savoring the moment.

What's the difference between savoring and mindfulness?

According to an article in OutsideOnline.com:

"Like mindfulness, savoring is another way to exercise being present, but it takes things a step further. 'Mindfulness asks you to observe the present moment without judging it and then let go of it,' explains Fred Bryant, a psychology professor at Loyola University who pioneered the field of research. 'Whereas with savoring, you observe a specific type of moment, a positive one, and then you try to cling onto it and not let it go.'"

Think about the last time you truly savored something? Maybe it was an amazing dinner with a loved one. Or a relaxing walk with your dog.

Remember how good you felt?

Taking the time to savor pleasant moments is good for your health. As noted in the OutsideOnline.com article:

"The benefits of savoring are similar to those of mindfulness: studies have found that it can improve mood, lead to greater life satisfaction, and increase feelings of gratitude and appreciation. But it can also help you remember things more vividly, something mindfulness doesn't do."

If we know savoring is good for us, how come we don't do it more?

They are the only things we'll have

Sometimes we must train ourselves to savor the positive things in our lives. Schedule time to enjoy positive experiences and special moments.

"I've always believed in savoring the moments. In the end, they are the only things we'll have." — Anna Godbersen, The Luxe

Here are three tips to help you savor the good things in your life more.

Identify stressful, negative feelings

It's hard to settle into special moments and savor the experience if you are feeling sad, anxious, afraid, angry, etc. Negative feelings must be dealt with.

Ask yourself **why** you are feeling negative feelings. Identifying the cause of your stress is the first step in dealing with it.

From there, you might seek the advice of someone you trust and respect. Or you can write down the stressor and various solutions. Putting it down on paper makes it less scary and easier to manage. Also, it helps you set it aside, so you can move on to savoring pleasant things.

Beware of cognitive distortions

Cognitive distortions are basically unhelpful thoughts. They can emerge from our insecurities or be caused by a bad experience.

For example, maybe someone on the freeway cut you off on your way to a special event. Don't let red lights, rude servers, traffic headaches, and all the other little frustrations of life overshadow the good stuff. The stuff you want to savor.

Slow down

This is often the hardest one for me. My mind is always thinking about things I've done, and things I want to do. It's hard to slow down and savor the present moment.

If this happens to you, try slowing down your breathing. Inhale slowly, exhale slowly.

Focus on the pleasant things you're enjoying at that moment. Silently say encouragements to yourself, like: "I enjoy this soothing music," or "I love the warmth of this amazing campfire."

Savoring is the one habit I wish I discovered in my twenties. Back then I was young and full of ambition. Who has time to savor when there are dreams to conquer?

But then we age and after the battles are won what is left? Memories.

And if we have learned how to savor, then our memories will be sweeter. They will comfort us through our remaining years and beyond the landscape of eternity.

Chapter Seventeen

Three Things I Gave Up That Greatly Improved My Life

I like to walk my dogs in the early evening when the air is crisp and there are few people to run into.

It's not that I'm anti-social. I simply enjoy solitude, exercise, and deep thinking. Also, there's something magical about a cool winter night. How the stars blink back at you, the breeze licks your neck, and the surrounding stillness expands your sense of being.

The dogs are a good lesson in living in the moment. Their superior olfactory senses and exquisite hearing tell them volumes about the environment. They always know where the rabbits are long before I do, and they can tell the difference between coyote scat and what the neighbor's pug left on the grass.

After making our way through the park and around the waterfall, we cut through the neighborhood on our way home. The many living room windows we pass reveal large, flat-screen televisions glowing on the walls.

And almost without fail, most of those televisions are tuned to cable news programs.

No wonder we're so divided in the United States.

Journalism or sycophancy

I used to be a news junkie. Beyond my online newspaper subscriptions, I loved to flip through cable news shows and opinion programs.

But over the years the tone of these shows began to change. Civil discourse gave way to partisan shouting. Networks lost their journalistic integrity and became unabashedly biased.

People pick news networks that align with their politics, failing to see they are in echo chambers of agreement. Even if you flip back and forth to watch competing networks, the hyperventilating anchors and shouting opinion show guests become intolerable.

At least they did for my wife and me.

At the end of 2019, we had enough and quit watching cable news shows. Sometimes, when friends talked about various news and opinion programs, I felt like I was missing out.

But soon I realized that all I was missing was endless partisan bickering.

I kept a few online newspaper subscriptions, which were all I needed to stay current. Unlike the endless hype, commercials, and repetitive looping of cable news, my online newspapers take less than an hour to read each morning.

"A good reader or viewer is a person who is alert about her newspaper or news channel. A good reader or viewer will never waste her hard-earned money in watching or reading just anything. She is serious. She will have to think if the news she is consuming is journalism or sycophancy." — Ravish Kumar

Yes, sometimes there are breaking news events, which the networks cover with great fanfare and urgency. I used to get sucked into these developments and tune in to watch the endless coverage and speculation.

But after quitting cable news, I realized what a waste of time this was. Often "breaking news" merits little more than a few paragraphs in the next morning's newspapers.

Cable news and opinion shows are designed to suck you in, much like social media. You put up with the banal, relentless commercials because you can't wait to watch the next breaking segment.

What could you do with the time spent watching cable news programs? What books could be read, exercise routines completed, or creative passions enjoyed?

When I quit watching cable news and opinion shows, I suddenly had much more time for books, writing, artwork, and photography.

My wife and I still enjoy quality movies and television series, but quitting cable news programs improved our lives significantly.

The most horrible thing in the world

When I was at university, beer was my alcoholic beverage of choice. It was affordable and always paired nicely with pizza.

About midway through my law enforcement career, I discovered the joys of fine wine. Nothing beats a glass of Silver Oak Cabernet Sauvignon with a steak dinner or a glass of chilled Sauvignon Blanc at a summer pool party.

Later in my law enforcement career, my wife and I moved from wine to craft cocktails. After work, it was fun to relax with a few Manhattans.

Sometimes my cop buddies would come over, and we'd play music and have a little party. It was a lot of fun, except for those times when we got carried away and nursed hangovers the next morning.

"After the first glass, you see things as you wish they were. After the second, you see things as they are not. Finally, you see things as they really are, and that is the most horrible thing in the world." — Oscar Wilde

My father wasn't a drinker. Despite his German heritage, he disliked beer. He never touched wine. He'd allow himself a Bourbon and water when visiting friends for Christmas, but that was it.

My mother came from Irish heritage, where drinking is prevalent. While my mother's parents, surprisingly, were teetotalers, Mom struggled her whole life with the bottle.

I have my mother's blood, and the propensity to like alcoholic beverages a little too much.

When you quit drinking you stop waiting

My law enforcement career showed me firsthand the destruction and ruined lives caused by alcohol, so I worked hard to limit my consumption.

But then I retired and moved to Las Vegas.

My wife and I love the thousands of great restaurants, entertainment, favorable tax climate, and nearly year-round sunny weather in Las Vegas. But Sin City is a strange place to live for someone who doesn't gamble and wants to keep a lid on his drinking.

I have friends here who live two blocks away. There are countless amazing bars. We have backyard pools, and it would be easy to fall into a lifestyle of partying with reckless abandon.

And initially, I did partake in some boozy get-togethers with friends. They were fun, but I knew I was on a slippery slope. After a few wild parties and hangovers, I decided to quit drinking.

Fortunately, it wasn't very hard to quit. I didn't suffer from cravings as some people do. My friends were supportive, but no doubt missed my participation.

The upshot was that I lost weight, slept better, gained focus, exercised more, and became insanely productive with my creative pursuits. I stopped waiting to accomplish goals and simply dove in and got them done.

"When you quit drinking you stop waiting." — Caroline Knapp, *Drinking: A Love Story*

Drinking is a personal choice, and when done responsibly, it can be a wonderful escape and way to relax. But choosing not to drink brings amazing benefits, and for me, it has been life-changing in a positive way.

The power of envy to destroy

When I was a young boy in the late 1970s my best friend got a new bicycle for his birthday. It was an amazing Schwinn bicycle with a stick shift affixed to the crossbar of the bike.

Back then, I thought it was the coolest bike ever, and I was supremely jealous of my friend. Even though I had a very nice Schwinn BMX, my bicycle didn't have the cool stick shift.

"Never underestimate the power of jealousy and the power of envy to destroy. Never underestimate that."— Oliver Stone

I remember being a little teary-eyed and riding my "boring" bicycle back home, where I avoided my friend for several days.

Eventually, I came to realize that we don't always get the things we want in life, and with my mother's urging, I started hanging out with my friend again.

A year or so later, my friend's father passed away after a short battle with cancer. During that difficult time, neither one of us was interested in our bicycles anymore. And I realized how lucky I was to still have my father.

There is debate as to who coined the phrase *"Comparison is the thief of joy."* Whether it was Teddy Roosevelt, Mark Twain, or someone else, I think there's wisdom in the saying.

"When we start comparing ourselves and our possessions to others, we tend to focus on the things we don't have rather than the things we do have." — John P. Weiss

With life experience and maturity, I learned to let go of unhealthy comparisons.

Unhealthy comparisons are couched in jealousy, whereas healthy comparisons find inspiration in the fine qualities and things that others possess. Healthy comparisons fuel self-improvement and personal accomplishment.

I have reached a point in life where I don't care about the possessions of others. But I do take note of people's character and creative talents.

When I read an author who moves me deeply, I compare her writing style and techniques with my own, to learn where I can improve.

When I meet someone who impresses me, I try to identify the qualities that stand out, so that I may work on those qualities in myself.

We all live in a house on fire

I gave up cable news programs, alcoholic beverages, and unhealthy comparisons. As a result, I am healthier, happier, and accomplish more in my personal and creative life.

How about you? What could you give up that would greatly improve your life? Letting go of unhealthy habits can lead to new dreams. And new dreams can lead to a happier, healthier life.

"We all live in a house on fire, no fire department to call; no way out, just the upstairs window to look out of while the fire burns the house down with us trapped, locked in it." — Tennessee Williams, *The Milk Train Doesn't Stop Here Anymore*

Most of the time, deep down, we know the things that are bad for us. The things that are holding us back. And the longer we refuse to make changes, the more we feel trapped.

Don't live your life in a house on fire. Jump out of that upstairs window if you have to. You might get hurt, but then most worthwhile things in life seem to involve some pain.

Give up the things that are holding you back. Your dreams are waiting.

Chapter Eighteen

How to Get Revenge for All the Things That Defeated You in Life

The past often shapes our future, but in the end, we get to decide the outcome.

Music legend Madonna was only five years old when she lost her mother to breast cancer. It was a confusing time. Just two years later, Madonna's father married the family housekeeper.

Madonna had been a straight-A student and was awarded a dance scholarship to the University of Michigan. She continued to earn straight A's at the University of Michigan, but after two years she left school to pursue her dreams in New York.

Unfortunately, New York did not welcome Madonna with open arms.

I had to dare myself every day to keep going

In an interview with Harper's Bazaar, Madonna said:

"The first year, I was held up at gunpoint. Raped on the roof of a building I was dragged up to with a knife in my back and had my apartment broken into three times."

To pay rent, Madonna modeled nude for art classes. Despite many challenges, she remained determined to survive and make something of her life.

In the interview with Harper's Bazaar, Madonna shared two subtle lessons about how to conquer your past and claim a bright future. Here's the first clue she shared:

"But it was hard and it was lonely, and I had to dare myself every day to keep going. Sometimes I would play the victim and cry in my shoebox of a bedroom with a window that faced a wall, watching the pigeons shit on my windowsill."

We have a choice in life when difficult things happen. We can let them break us, or we can learn from them and grow. In the comment above, Madonna said she *"had to dare myself every day to keep going."*

Daring ourselves is a powerful motivational tool. It challenges us to become more than we think we are. When we dare ourselves to achieve more, we change our thinking from defeatist to optimistic.

The sight of her mustache consoled me

In the Harper's Bazaar interview, Madonna went on to share a second way to conquer our past and claim a bright future. She found inspiration and hope in the life of another artist who similarly faced hardship and struggles.

As Madonna explains in the interview:

"And I wondered if it was all worth it, but then I would pull myself together and look at a postcard of Frida Kahlo taped to my wall, and the sight of her mustache consoled me. Because she was an artist who didn't care what people thought. I admired her. She was daring. People gave her a hard time. Life gave her a hard time. If she could do it, then so could I."

Most successful people in life face hardships and struggles. We can find inspiration in the lives of successful people we admire. Learning how they overcame their struggles can help us reorient our thinking.

By identifying powerful qualities in successful people, like Frida Kahlo's daring spirit, we can emulate them and achieve our own success.

Just get lost and get saved

The late motivational speaker Jim Rohn is often attributed to the statement, *"We are the average of the five people we spend the most time with."* In reality, we are influenced by a much wider circle of people.

Beyond our family and closest friends, we are also influenced by our work colleagues, neighbors, acquaintances, and the surrounding culture of where we live.

Sometimes people and the environment you live in can hold you back. If you want to conquer your past and claim a bright future, relocating is a powerful option.

"Negative people can only infest you with discouragements when they find you around... Just get lost and get saved!" — Israelmore Ayivor, The Great Handbook of Quotes

We tend to absorb the values and practices of the people around us. By moving to a peaceful, healthy environment and interacting with quality individuals, we can develop well-adjusted minds and escape an unhealthy past.

Moving can free us from negative influences, places that contain bad memories, and commitments that are holding us back.

Of course, there's a difference between seeking a healthy new start and simply running away from problems. If the problems stem from you (for example, bad personal decisions) and not your environment, then moving away may not help.

Make sure you're moving for the right reasons.

The only crime is pride

Sooner or later in life, you're going to disappoint or hurt someone. It might be a spouse that you let down or your kids that you disappoint. How you deal with it will determine how you move forward in life.

If you want to conquer your past mistakes and claim a bright future, you must learn how to make amends and then forgive yourself.

"All men make mistakes, but a good man yields when he knows his course is wrong and repairs the evil. The only crime is pride." — Sophocles, Antigone

A lot of people believe that refusing to forgive themselves proves that they're more sorry. Mental health expert John Delony, Ph.D., quoted in an article for RealSimple.com, notes:

"We may feel like approaching the world through the worst thing we've done buys us some extra grace, but it doesn't. It actually causes us to enter into relationships in a down position. Perhaps more importantly, choosing not to forgive yourself is really choosing to live life less joyfully."

It's important to disconnect your mistake from your identity because we are many things beyond our shortcomings and blunders.

Self-care is never a selfish act

A big part of conquering our past and claiming a bright future involves self-care. A healthy diet, exercise, sleep, and reduced stress go a long way in keeping us healthy. As a result, our minds are clearer, and we make better decisions.

Learning to set boundaries, saying no to unnecessary commitments, pursuing passions that bring joy and comfort, and listening to our own needs improve our mental health. We are less likely to become susceptible to negative thinking and fixating on the past.

"Self-care is never a selfish act — it is simply good stewardship of the only gift I have, the gift I was put on earth to offer others. Anytime

we can listen to true self and give the care it requires, we do it not only for ourselves but for the many others whose lives we touch." — Parker Palmer, *Let Your Life Speak: Listening for the Voice of Vocation*

Author Philip Roth's painful novella *The Dying Animal*, tells the tale of David Kepesh, an aging literature professor, who has a self-defeating affair with a beautiful young student.

The novel was made into the movie *Elegy*, starring Ben Kingsley as David Kepesh and Penelope Cruz as his young student, Consuela Castillo.

In the movie, Kepesh states, *"When you make love to a woman, you get revenge for all the things that defeated you in life."*

But of course, this isn't true.

Some aging men feel like they're reclaiming their youth if they can be with a much younger woman. Or maybe they think they'll have another chance at life. But really, they're just chasing their fear of aging or hiding from deep insecurities.

The way you get revenge for all the things that defeated you in life is by striving to become a better person, forgiving yourself for past mistakes, leveraging your talents, and helping others.

Our pasts have forgotten us

Our pasts have forgotten us, and our destinies await. To conquer your past and embrace a bright future, use the five approaches listed in this article:

1. **Dare** yourself every day, like Madonna did, to keep going. Doing so will change your mindset from defeatist to optimistic.

2. **Admire** and learn from people who overcame adversity, like Frida Kahlo.

3. **Relocate** to escape an unhealthy past of bad memories and toxic people. But remember, there's a difference between running away from your problems and seeking a new start.

4. **Forgive yourself** by making amends where you can and realizing that your mistakes are not your identity.

5.   ***Practice self-care***, which is not a selfish act but simply good stewardship of yourself.

The above five suggestions can help you get revenge for all the things that defeated you in life. They'll help you conquer your past and claim a bright future.

After all, your dreams are impatiently waiting, and life is too short to wallow in the past.

Chapter Nineteen

The Precious Thing at the Heart of Your Creative Work

My little dog, in his deepest slumber, tends to twitch and growl. He lives a quiet life of leisurely walks, back rubs, and tasty dog biscuits. So, I don't know what possibly frightens him in his dreams.

The other night he was snoozing on my lap, unperturbed by the iPad I set against him. But then his dreams came, and my iPad was bouncing and shaking. With each woof and twitch, I found it harder to read.

Reading and comprehension require a calm landscape devoid of distractions and interruptions. Similarly, to achieve our best creative work in life, we need freedom. Freedom from disruptions, unwanted influences, and imperfect conditions.

I've been thinking a lot lately about art and creativity. Specifically, about how we can arrive at our best work. The kind of work that reflects our deepest, most soulful expression.

The answer lays partly in our past. Namely, our childhood.

Live as only you can

When I was a little boy, I loved to draw birds. I often rendered them with layers of sketchy lines, cross-hatched in a way that created a scratchy depth and density. Many of the lines protruded beyond the outline of my bird sketch, which appealed to me in an abstract way.

My well-meaning elementary school teacher, Mrs. Kossin, often suggested I "clean up" the scratchy lines so that they lay within the drawing. "Try to keep your shading within the form," she'd say. As I erased the excess lines, I also seemed to erase the joy I had for the drawing. It no longer reflected how I saw the bird.

"The one thing that you have that nobody else has is you. Your voice, your mind, your story, your vision. So write and draw and build and play and dance and live as only you can." — Neil Gaiman

Mrs. Kossin meant well, but she unwittingly laid the first brick in the foundation of a creative prison. It's a prison we all confront, sooner or later. And the cement that holds the prison bricks together is *conformity*.

Imagination surrenders to intellect

There is often a right and wrong way to do things, and rules certainly help maintain order in life. But when it comes to art and creativity, rules mustn't overshadow our creative freedom. Unfortunately, well-meaning teachers and even parents sometimes instill order in children's lives at the expense of their creative freedom.

The late art critic Carleton Noyes, in his book *The Gate of Appreciation: Studies in the Relation of Art to Life,* wrote about the innate artfulness that we all have in childhood:

"The child is the first artist. Out of the material around him he creates a world of his own. The prototypes of the forms which he devises exist in life, but it is the thing which he himself makes that interests him, not its original in nature. His play is his expression."

Unfortunately, we tend to lose our childhood artistic instincts as we age. As Carleton Noyes notes:

"Imagination surrenders to the intellect; emotion gives place to knowledge. Gradually the material world shuts in about us until it becomes for us a hard, inert thing, and no longer a living, changing presence, instinct with infinite possibilities of experience and feeling." And so, our childhood instincts succumb to conventionality and conformity. We stop coloring outside the lines. No more red skies and blue trees.

We fall in line with societal expectations. We copy others who are deemed successful or popular. This is why there's so much derivative artwork and writing out there. People emulate their heroes instead of tapping into their childhood creative hearts.

And then there's the world of commerce and social media, which mucks up the artistic waters even more.

When I first began blogging and writing online, I expressed myself freely. I had nothing to sell, nor was I thinking much about gaining followers. I wrote for the joy of it.

Even when I was invited to write a weekly column for a fine art blog, I crafted stories and essays that appealed to my writerly orientation. I knew nothing of copywriting, keywords, and SEO tricks. I wrote from the heart.

Readers of the fine art blog responded positively, and I collected those early pieces into my first book, *"An Artful Life: Inspirational Stories and Essays for the Artist in Everyone."*

But then along came social media and with it my fragile artist's desire to "grow a following." I started to pay attention to all those gurus telling us how to gain more followers.

I hired an expert to teach me copywriting. I took a blogging workshop. I started writing for "content farms" to try and get paid for my articles and stories. And I did make some decent money.

But there's always a cost.

I become a liar

Increasingly, I'm discovering artists and writers who gave up on the capricious algorithms and analytics game. Creators who realized their pursuit of popularity and likes had come at the expense of their creative freedom and artistic happiness.

Yes, income matters, but not at the expense of our artistic and creative authenticity. Who wants to look back on one's body of creative work and realize it was all a lie? Created for a few bucks and the popular mood of the moment, but not for the test of time.

"When money enters in, -then, for a price, I become a liar, -and a good one I can be whether with pencil or subtle lighting or viewpoint. I hate it all, but (with it) so do I support not only my family, but my own work." — Edward Weston

There is one thing that should always stand at the heart of our creative work, and that's vision. Not money, popularity, social media likes, and all the other lies that blur our artistic authenticity and vision.

As children, we have vision. We create what our heads and hearts see, not for the market or what others will approve of. The best artists, writers, musicians, and creatives know this. The rest are busy chasing likes and conformity.

One creative who has stayed true to his childhood creative heart is the black and white fine art photographer Cole Thompson. At the early age of 14, Thompson fell in love with the black and white photography of photographers like Edward Weston, Wynn Bullock, and Ansel Adams.

"When I create an image, I am not trying to document what I'm seeing with my eyes, but rather show you what I'm seeing in my head. Creating a great image has little to do with your eyes and everything to do with your Vision." — Cole Thompson

In one of his newsletters, Thompson wrote about the dangers of conformity and creating for others:

"We got the message: conform and be accepted, conform to earn praise, conform and you will be happy! We were quick learners and so we began to conform, and the more we conformed, the more our Vision receded. The more we sought to please others, the less we

sought to please ourselves...until one day our Vision disappeared. And not only did we lose our Vision, we forgot that we had ever once had one."

If we are to be happy with our creative efforts, we need to embrace our vision and learn to let go. According to Thompson:

Let go of caring what others thought.

Let go of conforming.

Let go of following the rules.

Let go of worry if others would like my work.

Let go of trying to win competitions.

Let go of getting likes.

Let go of photographing 'the right way.'

Let go of trying to please others.

Let go of others' expectations.

Let go of my fear of criticism.

Let go of everything.

I've been trying to do this more in my creative work. It has been exciting and liberating, but also difficult.

Difficult because the algorithms and social media masses seem to favor clickbait, garish color, and cat videos more than soulful writing and monochromatic artwork and photography. It's hard to see one's reach online decline, but the joy of creating authentic work keeps me from becoming a creative liar.

The burden of authenticity

How about your creative vision? How is it holding up? Are you listening to your unique, creative instincts, or have you fallen victim to the approval and opinion of others?

There's no judgment here. Income and approval are strong incentives. In the past, I created work to gain the attention and favor of others. I fell under the spell of social media analytics and the false conclusion that "likes" equate to quality and value (sometimes they do, sometimes they don't).

The more we conform, the more our vision evaporates.

Perhaps this is the burden of authenticity. We accept that our income and popularity might wane in pursuit of our deepest expression.

But sometimes the best art takes time to find its audience. The English poet John Keats and the Dutch painter Vincent van Gogh never knew the fame and accolades that their creative work eventually brought. Thank goodness they stayed true to their creative vision.

"Vision is what's left when you remove all of your fears and insecurities, when you stop complying and conforming, when you ignore what others are doing and you pursue what you love." — Cole Thompson

The precious thing at the heart of your creative work is your personal vision. Betray it for short-term gain or ephemeral social media likes, and you'll never find true joy in your art.

Stay true to the child artist within you. The one who always made you smile, laugh, and express the beautiful vision that only you can share with the world.

Chapter Twenty

Guess What Matters Far More Than the Position?

By the time Nic came into my life, I was a divorced father struggling to parent an unanchored little boy.

My son was intelligent and creative, but he needed structure in his life. He was with me during the week, and then nearly an hour away with his mother every weekend. In the summer, the arrangement switched.

Different households and a ping-pong life led to mixed messages, inconsistency, and unfamiliar waters for a boy adrift.

"Everyone needs a house to live in, but a supportive family is what builds a home." — Anthony Liccione

I was a busy police lieutenant on the cusp of becoming the next police chief. Long work hours and irregular events competed with father and son time, not to mention sleep. My mother often babysat when work pulled me away.

And then I met Nic.

Being a mother is an attitude

A friend invited me to dinner one night, to meet his sister-in-law. "You'll like her, John, she's a nurse. You're a cop. You both love books," my future brother-in-law said.

Nic (short for Nicole) was beautiful, independent, and intelligent. I was smitten, and soon we were dating. Before long, Nic and I bought a home together. Our marriage followed shortly thereafter.

Nic recognized that my son needed more structure in his life. Not wanting to overstep boundaries, she sought my permission to help. I gave it without hesitation.

Many positive changes followed. The TV disappeared from my son's room, and it was replaced with shelves of classic books. On nights when police emergencies called me away, Nic took my son bowling.

"Being a mother is an attitude, not a biological relation." — Robert A. Heinlein, Have Space Suit — Will Travel

To avoid confusion about rules or the lack of them in different households, Nic affixed a poster listing the rules in my son's bedroom. Things like *"Put away toys, don't make us ask twice,"* and *"Finish homework."*

Absent work-related interruptions, we ate dinner together every night and talked about our day. The new structure in my son's life worked wonders. He became an avid reader, a black belt in Tae Kwon Do, and an excellent student.

There were many other positive changes that Nic brought to my son's life, and he has blossomed into a remarkable young man. Now 23-years-old, he is a top student completing his computer science degree and ROTC studies at university. He is also an Air Force reservist.

My son is just starting in life, but thanks to Nic, he has been given a wonderful foundation. A foundation built on structure, discipline, ethics, respect, and love.

I have no doubt there will be many achievements in my son's life, and behind those achievements will be the echoes of Nic's parenting.

Speaking of echoes, there is another woman whose be-hind-the-scenes efforts helped shape a remarkable man.

Unvisited tombs

Sarah Bush Johnston lost her first husband in the 1816 cholera epidemic and was left with her late husband's debts and their three children. Then along came Thomas Lincoln, a widower who had known Sarah and her husband in the past.

Thomas proposed marriage to Sarah and agreed to pay off her late husband's debts. Thomas had two children of his own (a son and daughter) and so their marriage created a bustling household in their small Indiana cabin.

Sarah immediately improved the living conditions in the cabin, insisting Thomas cover up the dirt with wood floors, as well as fix the roof and whitewash the cabin. In short, Sarah humanized their home.

Sarah immediately took to Thomas's young son, who was a bit feral and in need of structure. The boy's mother died of accidental poisoning when he was only 9 years old.

Although she was most likely illiterate, Sarah knew the young boy (who could read) needed a strong education. She helped nurture the boy's intellect and reading comprehension by pro-viding many books. She recognized something special in the boy and helped nurture him.

"...for the growing good of the world is partly dependent on unhis-toric acts; and that things are not so ill with you and me as they might have been, is half owing to the number who lived faithfully a hidden life, and rest in unvisited tombs." — George Eliot, Middlemarch

We all know the rest of the story. Sarah's stepson, Abraham Lincoln, went on to become the 16th President of the United States and author of the Emancipation Proclamation.

Lincoln adored his stepmother, as the following quote from an article in history.com notes:

Stepmother and stepson quickly forged a loving bond. "His mind and mine, what little I had, seemed to run together, move in the same direction," Sarah said. She treated Lincoln as if he was her flesh-and-blood by offering love, kindness, and encouragement. He returned the affection, calling her "Mother." In 1861, Lincoln confided to a relative that his stepmother "had been his best friend in this world and that no son could love a mother more than he loved her."

One could argue that Sarah Lincoln was more powerful than an American president, because without her parental love, nurturing, and guidance, it's unlikely young Abe would ever have succeeded in life.

It's not the position that matters in life, it's the person.

Society today likes to celebrate the rich, famous, and powerful (even though the lives of such people are often plagued with divorces, substance abuse, and unhappiness). Young entrepreneurs aspire to be like Elon Musk, and starry-eyed youths fantasize about becoming influencers and celebrities.

Yet behind the rich and famous, cloaked in anonymity and modesty, are the real heroes. The ones whose selflessness and depth of character we'd be far better off emulating.

It's the loving parents and stepparents who sacrifice much to provide a strong foundation and better life for their children. It's the quiet teachers and coaches who shun lucrative jobs to shape young minds and hearts.

Sadly, society seems to celebrate the glitzy and shallow and ignores the sacrifices and depth of real heroes. The ones without fancy titles who toil in the shadows to make future generations, and the world, a better place.

Do your little bit of good

Many people are familiar with the movie *Pretty Woman*, which is about a prostitute and wealthy businessman who end up falling in love. Julia Roberts plays the prostitute, Vivian, and Richard Gere plays the successful businessman, Edward.

The movie is a Cinderella-type story, and audiences naturally cheer for Vivian and Edward to fall in love, despite the many challenges they face. Yet behind the scenes, there is a seemingly bit player whose professionalism, kindness, and depth play a huge part in Vivian's fairy tale life.

"Do your little bit of good where you are; it's those little bits of good put together that overwhelm the world." — Desmond Tutu

Barney Thompson (played perfectly by actor Hector Elizondo) is the hotel manager in the movie, who runs the hotel like a fine-tuned engine. He is professional, articulate, empathetic, and helps Vivian to fit in with Edward's world of fine dining, operas, and high society.

Barney helps Vivian acquire an evening gown, teaches her how to use appropriate fine dining silverware, and even gives respectful advice to Edward.

Beautiful people like Barney exist in the world, but we take them for granted and often overlook how valuable their contributions are.

Find a purpose to serve, not a lifestyle to live

I eventually became police chief and served in that position for ten years. I am proud of my law enforcement career, my contributions, and the people I helped.

Yet I believe my wife Nic, working quietly and humbly behind the scenes, made a more profound contribution.

Despite the demands of a nursing career (including the challenging years serving as a hospice nurse), Nic invested her free time and energy into molding a feral little boy into a mature, kind, ethical young man.

It's one of the many reasons why I love and respect my amazing wife. She had no interest in joining the elite social circles in our city, keeping up with the Joneses, or impressing people with material things. Her happiness and peace come from loving her family and helping others.

"Find a purpose to serve, not a lifestyle to live." — Criss Jami, *Venus in Arms*

It doesn't matter what your position is in life. The depth of your character and how you treat others matter far more than your job title.

And when you look back on the landscape of your life, what do we want to see? Fancy job titles, money, and fame? Or depth of character and a charitable heart that made the lives of others better?

I prefer the latter.

Chapter Twenty-One

What Marcel Proust and Robert Frost Can Teach Us About Finding Happiness

It is autumn here, where the leaves are turning color and the heat of summer has given way to cooler, more forgiving weather.

It occurs to me this cool morning, as I walk my dogs along familiar pathways and rabbit warrens, that I am in the autumn of my life. A welcome time when the rhythms of living are less urgent, and I can linger without guilt over books, artwork, and the slower cadence of each day.

Twenty minutes into our walk, we crest a grassy hill and the dogs become distracted by the rustle of quail in nearby brush. The dogs resist my gentle tug on their leashes.

The sun's warmth outlasts the chilly morning breeze, and I smile as the dogs roll on the grass and sniff scents near and far. I could meander here indefinitely, but an unfinished essay I began earlier today beckons my return.

"Come on boys," I say, "I have promises to keep and miles to go before I sleep."

Trying to resist the present

The dogs are unimpressed by poetry. They live in the present, unencumbered by regrets of the past and worries for the future.

If humans could do the same, we'd probably be happier, but then what would poets like Robert Frost write about?

"Hurrying and delaying are alike ways of trying to resist the present." — Alan W. Watts

As we continued our walk, I pulled up Frost's famous poem "Stopping by Woods on a Snowy Evening" on my iPhone. I slowly read the four beautiful stanzas aloud to my indifferent dogs:

Whose woods these are I think I know.
His house is in the village though;
He will not see me stopping here
To watch his woods fill up with snow.
My little horse must think it queer
To stop without a farmhouse near
Between the woods and frozen lake
The darkest evening of the year.
He gives his harness bells a shake
To ask if there is some mistake.
The only other sound's the sweep
Of easy wind and downy flake.
The woods are lovely, dark and deep.
But I have promises to keep,
And miles to go before I sleep,
And miles to go before I sleep.

Academics will tell us that Frost's poem is written in perfect iambic tetrameter with a tight-knit chain rhyme typical of a form known as Rubaiyat stanza.

What laypersons like myself will tell you is that the poem captures our yearning for nature, quiet moments, and freedom from the burdens of life.

Robert Frost's poetry reflects his philosophy that life should not be rejected but accepted with all its limitations. According to an article in englishliterature.info:

Frost is a Classicist: He believes in the Aristotelian mean, moderation between extreme views, hope and despair, belief and doubt, self-love, and social commitment. Ethically, he speaks for personal integrity and self-reliance. He is aware that "there is no fixed line between wrong and right" but there are "roughly zones whose laws must be obeyed."

Interestingly, the more you learn about Robert Frost's life, the more you understand how loss and melancholy informed his writing. Yet he found room for beauty and hope in his words, too.

We must hunger for them

We all feel the pull of obligations and the distance between where we are and where we want to go. It seems like we never get to finally arrive. Never get to settle into a time and space that brings eternal peace.

"It seems to me we can never give up longing and wishing while we are still alive. There are certain things we feel to be beautiful and good, and we must hunger for them." — George Eliot

Frost's poem "Stopping by Woods on a Snowy Evening" always resonated with me, but even more so now that I am inching towards the winter of my life.

Having closed the door on one career and arriving late to this life of writing and art, I want the joys of creativity to be my lovely woods. A refuge from accumulated weariness, where there are no more promises to keep or miles to go before I sleep.

Perhaps you feel this too? A longing for arrival, peace, and well-being. The question is, absent death, do we ever get there?

Is it even possible?

Plenty of time and seclusion

Robert Frost was born in 1874 in San Francisco, California, and spent most of his adult life in rural New England. He published

"Stopping by Woods on a Snowy Evening" and other poems in his 1923 poetry collection "New Hampshire."

Frost's poems often drew on his rural surroundings to teach deeper principles on life. By the time Frost died in 1963, he had been awarded four Pulitzer Prizes for poetry, received the Congressional Gold Medal, and been nominated thirty-one times for the Nobel Prize in Literature.

An article about Robert Frost at Gradesaver.com notes:

"Frost was not a happy man; he suffered from serious bouts of depression and anxiety throughout his life and was never convinced that his poetry was truly worthwhile (as evidenced by his obsessive desire to receive a Nobel Prize). He suffered through the untimely deaths of his father, mother, and sister, as well as four of his six children and his beloved wife, all of which contributed to the melancholic mentality that appears in much of Frost's work."

Melancholy is a funny thing. It can invite misery and yet inspire great reflection and artistic expression.

Where and how you chose to live can greatly affect both your melancholy and creative success. For Robert Frost, the bucolic life he lived on 30 acres in Derry, New Hampshire, proved vital to his later literary success.

An article at RobertFrostFarm.org shares the following reflection from Frost's selected letters:

"I might say the core of all my writing was probably the five free years I had on the farm down the road a mile or two from Derry Village toward Lawrence. The only thing we had was plenty of time and seclusion. I couldn't have figured on it in advance. I hadn't that kind of foresight. But it turned out as right as a doctor's prescription."

Time and seclusion. Two obvious yet elusive solutions to finding peace and well-being amidst the noise and relentless hardships of modern life. Despite the melancholic undertones of his poetry, Robert Frost's happiest years were the ones spent in Derry, New Hampshire.

Most people understand the importance of time and seclusion, which is why they book vacations and retreats to rest and recharge. But is there more we can do to feel like we've finally arrived at a place of peace and well-being?

See the world as it really is

Marcel Proust's elephantine, seven-volume "In Search of Lost Time (Remembrance of Things Past)," is the longest novel in history (according to the Guinness Book of World Records).

Proust was a French novelist, critic, and essayist. Considered by critics and writers to be one of the most influential authors of the 20th century, his famous novel explores themes of love, art, time, and memory.

The novel's narrator is searching for his own identity and the meaning of life. William C. Carter, a professor of French and Proust biographer, wrote in a lithub.com article:

"In Proust's case, I think he helps us to see the world as it really is, not only its extraordinary beauty and diversity, but his observations make us aware of how we perceive and how we interact with others, showing us how often we are mistaken in our own assumptions and how easy it is to have a biased view of another person."

Writer Claudia Merrill argues that Proust's main concept was gratitude. In a blog post she writes:

"Although his most famous connotation is the recovery of memory through stimulation of the unconscious — referred to as a Proustian moment, his contribution to a somewhat Eastern outlook on life goes mostly unnoticed. Proust gave us more than just a madeleine moment, he showed us what life could be if only we were grateful."

Proust determined that social climbing and endlessly keeping up appearances will not bring us happiness. As Merrill writes: *"Proust knew that happiness was not found somewhere else, it is found within ourselves, through gratitude for our initial circumstances."*

Merrill goes on to write:

"The final important observation about life Proust makes is that life can be enjoyed to the fullest if we are grateful for each moment as it is. Proust saw those around him in high society becoming depressed and consumed by their melancholy, simply because they were always searching for more. The aristocrats would never be satisfied with what they had, or the circumstances in which they were in, because of their detachment from the present moment."

Proust knew that children are inherently happy with what they have in their daily lives. And they see everything as new and interesting. He recommended "seeing with new eyes" as a way for adults to mimic the perspective of children.

The richest of all people

When do we arrive at that magical place of peace and well-being, where there are no more promises to keep or miles to go before we sleep?

The answer will vary from person to person, for we are all unique and in different seasons of our lives. The key is understanding that the "arrival" we experience, the place of well-being and peace, is not so much a destination or place, it's a state of being within ourselves.

"Your true home is in the here and the now." — *Thich Nhat Hanh*

Robert Frost showed us the benefits of nature, time, and seclusion to restore our spirits. Marcel Proust taught us to see the world as it really is, have gratitude for each moment, and see the world "with new eyes."

"The richest of all people is a little child who is so happy with few simple toys!" — *Mehmet Murat ildan*

We all have miles to go before we sleep, and promises to keep. But that doesn't mean we have to reach the end of our journey to find happiness.

If children can find happiness within themselves, perhaps we can rediscover it too?

Chapter Twenty-Two

One Powerful Strategy to Defeat Problems and Critics

Sometimes naive optimism overcomes experience and cynical wisdom. Even when others disagree.

"If I were you, I'd definitely not go." That was the advice from several law enforcement colleagues I phoned in allied agencies.

I was a recently promoted police lieutenant who received an invitation from a community group to attend an evening forum on "race relations and law enforcement."

The community group was a liberal, progressive, activist organization with an ax to grind for law enforcement. There had been some recent enforcement actions by the Sheriff's Office, and tensions were high.

"If I don't attend the forum, they'll accuse us of ambivalence. Shouldn't we try to listen, share our perspectives, and build some bridges?" I asked a police Captain in a neighboring police department.

"We've attended forums like this before," the Captain said, "It's a bait and switch. They line up detractors to speak, film them lecturing us, and post it to their social media pages. They use us as dupes for their political agenda."

"Well, I think I'm going to attend the forum anyway, and give it my best shot," I told the Captain.

"Good luck," he said with a chuckle.

We forget to be understanding

When I arrived at the community center that evening, I was the only one wearing a suit and tie. I felt like a fish out of water. Everyone else was casual, wearing jeans, shorts, t-shirts, beanie caps, etc.

An organizer for the forum came over and introduced herself. She thanked me for coming.

"We have to stop fearing difficult discussions and start seeing them as opportunities for growth." — Sarah Stewart Holland & Beth Silvers

As people started to sit down, I spotted Jim, a Lieutenant from the Sheriff's Office. He strolled over and sat down next to me. "Looks like we're the only law enforcement reps," I whispered to Jim.

The organizer began the forum, outlining many of the recent issues and concerns regarding law enforcement arrests, race relations, and more. A few others spoke, and then the audience was invited to line up to the microphone with questions and comments.

One of the organizers was filming and recording the speakers. Just like I was warned, the speakers railed against law enforcement. Some called us racist. One woman said, "You don't know what it's like to be treated differently. To be singled out."

After the last speaker, the organizer asked Jim and me if we'd like to respond. I was nervous but agreed to say a few words. I stood before the microphone, and this is what I said:

"Thanks for the invitation to be here tonight. One of you said that 'You don't know what it's like to be treated differently. To be singled out.' I may not know your personal experiences, but I can assure you that I know what it's like to be treated differently. To be singled out."

The room was quiet, and everyone was listening intently. I continued:

"Once I was with my wife and son in a restaurant when a man I arrested in the past walked up and threatened me and my family. At social functions, people often treat me differently because I'm a cop. They complain about traffic citations or a family member who was 'unlawfully arrested.' They make assumptions about who I am, and my career based on biases, stereotypes, television myths, or negative stories from others."

Someone in the audience said, "Yeah, but a lot of cops aren't cool. They harass us for no reason." I replied with:

"I'm not going to tell you that every cop out there is a saint. We're human, and sometimes we stumble. But the reason I'm here tonight is to listen. To hear your stories. And to maybe convince you that our community is stronger when we work together. When we focus more on what we have in common instead of where we disagree."

After the organizers ended the forum, several community members thanked me and Jim for attending. One woman said, "I don't think I realized how hard your job can be."

"We are all so desperate to be understood, we forget to be understanding."— Beau Taplin

At the time I didn't realize it, but that evening I used a strategy that helped disarm the critics. Years later, when I was a young police chief, I used the strategy again.

My heart sank

The anonymous letter had been typed, sealed in an envelope, addressed to "Chief Weiss", and slid under my office door. When I read it, my heart sank.

The letter alleged that one of my Commanders had violated a few of our department policies. The letter threatened to notify the City Manager, Mayor, and local media if I failed to take corrective action.

I knew that some members of my police department didn't like the Commander, but I was saddened that they failed to come to me directly. I had an open-door policy, attended early morning roll calls to be available to colleagues, and strived to treat everyone fairly and respectfully.

I called a mandatory, department-wide meeting (for which everyone received overtime pay). Once everyone was assembled in the squad room, I took out the anonymous letter and read it word for word. And then I said the following:

"I have already shared this letter with the City Manager, City Attorney, and Mayor. Internal affairs will investigate the allegations, and if true, appropriate action will be taken. But I must tell you, I am deeply disappointed that whoever wrote this letter chose not to come to me directly. Anonymous, threatening letters don't reflect who we are. I have always said that when concerns or disagreements arise, we must have the courage and courtesy to talk directly to one another. No gossip. No anonymous threats. And if I have in any way caused you to feel differently about this, we must fix that."

You could have heard a pin drop in the squad room. Everyone was dead silent. I paused for a long moment and ended with:

"We must learn to assume the best in one another, not the worst. I'm going to do that going forward, while we address the content of this letter. And I ask that you do the same."

I had my suspicions as to the author of the letter, but I never treated that person any different. I made my point, the matter was appropriately handled, and there was never another anonymous letter.

So, what's the strategy I use to defeat problems and critics? Do the unexpected.

When we do the unexpected, we surprise our detractors. We open a door that can disarm them. We get to define ourselves instead of our detractors defining us. And sometimes, doing the unexpected can hasten a new understanding, nascent trust, and even an improved outcome.

Doing the unexpected won't always lead to success, but it stands less of a chance if you do it without sincerity and graciousness.

Our world needs a lot of solidarity

Shortly before my retirement as police chief, the County Sheriff and I were invited to a community forum. The topic revolved around law enforcement, the LGBTQ community, and pathways to greater understanding and solidarity.

"To shine, we must push others forward and stand together when needed. The failure of others will never mean your success. Our world needs a lot of solidarity, and this is the time to push the big ideas."
— *Mohammed Zaid*

A few law enforcement voices cautioned me. "I'd be careful, John," one colleague said. "Sometimes protestors highjack these meetings. They want to make you look bad. Score a few political points."

But I didn't listen. I'd learned that doing the unexpected with sincerity and graciousness, often led to better understanding and outcomes.

The flier for the community forum included the words: "A Conversation with Allies."

The organizers did the unexpected. They defined their law enforcement guests as "allies," which made us feel welcome.

If you want to disarm your critics and tackle problems, learn to do the unexpected.

Do it with sincerity and graciousness. In this way, you'll build bridges, foster trust, and maybe even change some hearts and minds.

Chapter Twenty-Three

How to Stop Feeling Irrelevant and Embrace Life

I used to wonder if my dad's old truck had a soul.

It certainly had character, with its dents, scuffs, and temperamental stick shift. Who knows what stories and exploits lay behind the truck's dilapidated exterior.

Dad was no longer a spring chicken when he bought the old truck. He used to struggle at times with the stick shift, and repairs were frequent.

But then, Dad was drawn to old things like fountain pens, hardcover books, and the nostalgic design and feel of early model vehicles. Perhaps the truck's high mileage and gently worn exterior reminded Dad of himself? Older, showing some wear, but still full of dreams.

"A man is not old until regrets take the place of dreams." — *John Barrymore*

When Dad passed away, we sold the old truck to a handyman who used to work on our house. "I love these old trucks," the handyman said before driving off to probably the last chapters in that truck's life story.

If trucks and cars are like people, I'll bet they're happiest when they're useful. But what happens when they retire?

Do trucks and cars still matter then?

The importance of having fun

There's an old mining town along Hwy 95 in Nevada known as Goldfield. In this town with a population of only a few hundred sits a surreal junkyard/art installation named *"The International Car Forest of the Last Church."*

The installation contains a spread-out collection of old cars, limos, delivery trucks, and even a school bus. Many of these vehicles are buried nose first, with their back ends protruding upwards, out of the dirt like ostriches.

"Never, ever underestimate the importance of having fun." — *Randy Pausch*

The entire installation is strange, colorful, memorable, and fun. There was even a music video filmed on the site.

The installation was the brainchild of Goldfield local Mark Rippie, who wanted to out-do similar type installations like Texas' Cadillac Ranch and Nebraska's Carhenge. Rippie got help from artists Chad Sorg and Zak Sargent. The project was 9-years in the making.

It's safe to say that all the vehicles resting at *The International Car Forest of the Last Church* are retired. They no longer matter, at least the way they used to.

But weirdly, they look like they're having fun. As if they're no longer taking themselves too seriously.

If cars and trucks that no longer matter can still have fun, what about us?

We need to master irrelevancy

Growing up, you tend to focus on yourself and your goals. You often have parents, family members, and friends cheering you on.

You pursue a career, promotions, relationships, and the many milestones of life (e.g., marriage, first house, children, career success, etc.). Others depend on you, there's purpose in your life, and you know you matter.

But sooner or later, just like old cars in a junkyard, you will matter less. Maybe your kids will grow up and move away, or you'll lose your job and suddenly be unemployed.

You'll retire and notice fewer email and phone messages. Work colleagues carry on without you since you're out of the game now.

Where once you felt engaged and important, sooner or later you end up feeling forgotten and irrelevant.

The question is: Will you be Ok with mattering less?

In an article for Harvard Business Review, writer Peter Bregman wrote:

"As we get older, we need to master the exact opposite of what we've spent a lifetime pursuing. We need to master irrelevancy.

This is not only a retirement issue. Many of us are unhealthily — and ultimately unhappily — tied to mattering. It's leaving us overwhelmed and over-busy, responding to every request, ring, and ping with the urgency of a fireman responding to a six-alarm fire. Are we really that necessary?"

This notion of mattering less doesn't just apply to older adults and retirees. Think about all the people desperately trying to be liked on social media.

The reality is that everyone has an ego, whether young or old. We all want to matter and be recognized by our peers. The problem is that our self-worth becomes dependent on the opinions of others.

So how do we stop feeling irrelevant and learn to embrace life? How do we learn to matter less and smile more? Focus on the present and celebrate your freedom.

Our egos are always worrying about the past or the future at the expense of the present. Also, worrying about what others think hijacks our freedom. We're more hesitant to do what we want to.

You can do what you want

Irrelevancy brings a kind of freedom.

Consider the old limo in *The International Car Forest of the Last Church*. It's covered with graffiti now, resting atop an aging delivery truck.

It looks ridiculous, but do you think it cares? Heck no. It's having fun. It's retired and has the freedom to look however it wants to.

When we stop worrying about how much we matter, we have the freedom to do what we want.

As Peter Bregman notes:

"When your purpose shifts like this, you can do what you want. You can take risks. You can be courageous. You can share ideas that may be unpopular. You can live in a way that feels true and authentic. In other words, when you stop worrying about the impact of what you do, you can be a fuller version of who you are.

Enjoying the freedom that comes with being irrelevant can help us avoid depression and enjoy life after retirement, even for people who have spent their careers being defined by their jobs."

Whether you're feeling irrelevant from a recent retirement, job loss, relationship change, or another big life event, don't despair. Stop worrying about how much you matter and take advantage of your new freedom.

Here are a few suggestions to overcome feeling irrelevant:

Take pleasure in the activity versus the outcome. Don't worry about how good your artwork is, or how many likes you might get on social media. Learn to enjoy the present moment and the joy of what you are doing.

Listen to others more and talk less about yourself. People love to talk about themselves. Even when they appear to be listening to you, they're often formulating their next thought.

Train yourself to listen more. Ask questions. Resist the temptation to make it about you. This will teach you to let go of your ego and how much you matter. Also, others will think you're the best conversationalist when it's just that you listen well.

Talk to a stranger for the pleasure of it. Random conversations with people we don't know can be very fulfilling. We learn new perspectives, and reports indicate random conversations are good for our health and well-being.

Practice mindfulness or meditation. Carthusian monks spend most of their day alone, praying and thinking in individual cells. Their food is delivered through a small locking window.

Carthusian monks live the most austere and cloistered lives of all Christian monks. They shun the Internet and are unknown to the rest of the world, yet they are some of the most peaceful and contented men you'll ever meet.

Carthusians don't spend their days worrying about how much they matter. Through prayer, mindfulness, and deep solitude, they are free in ways that many of us can only dream of.

The good news is that you don't have to become a monk to practice mindfulness and meditation and doing so can free you from feelings of irrelevancy.

Forever is composed of nows

The International Car Forest of the Last Church shows us that old vehicles may not be useful or matter the way they once did, but they can have a lot of fun in retirement. Instead of driving people around, now they're entertaining people as an art installation.

How about you? Are you ready to stop feeling irrelevant and embrace the freedom that comes from living in the moment? Stop worrying about mattering and spend more time living.

"Forever is composed of nows." — Emily Dickinson

I don't know where my dad's old truck is today. Maybe it's still in service, or maybe it has flowers growing out of its engine block.

The latter doesn't sound so bad. There's peace in the garden, where the sun and rain bring growth, and the flowers quiver in the breeze, indifferent to what the world thinks of them.

Chapter Twenty-Four

We Are All Broken

We surrounded the man's mobile home, evacuated the neighbors, and were waiting for the tactical team to get into position.

Our hostage negotiation detectives managed to get a "throw phone" into the rear of the man's home, in the hopes he would pick it up and talk to us.

Sadly, he never did.

I was a young rookie cop back then. It was my first "suicidal, barricaded gunman" call. I was positioned on the perimeter of the man's modest property, with instructions to keep onlookers away.

The man was elderly and, according to neighbors, suffered from chronic back pain and depression. He had several surgeries that failed to fix his back. As one neighbor put it later, "I think he just had enough. He was broken and unfixable."

"But in the end, one needs more courage to live than to kill himself."
— *Albert Camus*

Hours went by. Efforts to talk to the man failed. And then we heard a gunshot, followed by smoke coming from within the mobile home.

SWAT team members forced entry into the home, where they found the man dead of a self-inflicted gunshot. He had started a fire in his room, but fire fighters were able to quickly extinguish the flames.

Afterward, I overheard several residents in the neighborhood. There were tears, hugging, and questions.

One woman said, "I knew he was struggling. I should have stopped by more." An elderly gentleman chimed in, "Don't blame yourself, sometimes people end up in a dark place. They can't get out."

It's true. Sometimes people end up in a dark place and can't get out.

Unless someone can shine a light for them.

Denial is the ultimate comfort zone

David Goggins knows what it's like to be in a dark place. His father was a physically abusive alcoholic who beat Goggins and his mother.

As a child, Goggins was forced to work late into the evening at his father's skate rink. Goggins would try to sleep on the skate rink's office couch, only to get up early for school.

Goggins and his mother finally escaped his abusive father, but they were poor and Goggins bounced between schools. Being the only black kid in school he was often bullied and threatened.

There wasn't a lot of light being shined in Goggins's world until he met Sister Katherine.

"Denial is the ultimate comfort zone." — David Goggins

Goggins and his mother moved in with his grandparents for six months, and they sent him to Annunciation, a small Catholic school. He was only 8 years old in the 2nd grade, and unable to read.

Sister Katherine was a small woman in her sixties, with a gold front tooth. She took no prisoners. She was gruff, no-nonsense, yet dedicated to her students.

In Goggins's inspirational book *"Can't Hurt Me"* he explains why Sister Katherine made a difference in his life:

"She didn't know my backstory and didn't have to. All that mattered to her was that I turned up at her door with a kindergarten education, and it was her job to shape my mind. She had every excuse in the world to farm me out to some specialist or label me a problem, but that wasn't her style. She started teaching before labeling kids was a normal thing to do, and she embodied the no-excuses mentality that I needed if I was going to catch up."

And catch up he did. Despite poverty, prejudice, physical abuse, obesity, and even a heart defect, Goggins went on to become a Navy SEAL and the world's top endurance athlete.

A lot of Goggins's philosophy is about helping yourself.

"No one is going to come help you. No one's coming to save you."
— *David Goggins*

In essence, what Goggins is saying is that if you're in a dark place, you must find the light within. There may be an occasional Sister Katherine to help light the way, but when she's gone, then what?

The art of assisting discovery

Kind and caring people may come into our lives, and sometimes they can correct a wayward path. Many of us have been blessed by the love and kindness of others.

For me it was my high school journalism teacher, Helen Oreb. I was a shy, introverted high school freshman. My entire elementary school education had been in private schools, so I knew no one when I attended my local public high school.

I was an average student in high school, but Helen Oreb was quick to notice my greatest talent, which was drawing and cartooning. With Oreb's urging, I became the high school newspaper's editorial cartoonist.

"The art of teaching is the art of assisting discovery." — *Mark Van Doren*

The campus newspaper was a place where I could fit in, and my self-esteem grew as fellow students complimented my cartoons.

Just like David Goggins's 2nd grade Sister Katherine, Helen Oreb believed in me. She shined a little light to lead the way.

There's a lesson here for all of us. Every day, we interact with loved ones, friends, co-workers, and strangers. Every interaction is a chance to shine a light of encouragement and hope.

After all, there are wounded, broken people everywhere. We may not see their wounds, but we can usually tell when people are sad, struggling, or just not themselves.

The slightest light of encouragement and understanding tells people that they matter, that someone cares.

Most people never listen

Dan Milnor is a former photojournalist with a YouTube channel where he muses about photography, travel, exercise, the outdoors, van life, making photo books, culture, and more.

In a recent video post, Milnor returned from a road trip all over the United States. He admonished viewers to stop talking about "red states and blue states," arguing that such terms are just media and political creations to further divide Americans.

Milnor said that every state is a mix of political persuasions. Sure, some states in the aggregate may swing red or blue, but such divisive and simplistic labeling misses the point. And the point is that people are far more interesting and complex than just their political orientation.

Milnor points out that people are different regionally. Don't think that where you're from is better. Milnor says that our mission statement should be to "listen to other people."

"I like to listen. I have learned a great deal from listening carefully. Most people never listen." — Ernest Hemingway

After all, we are all broken. Everyone has their stories, battles, and wounds. When we listen, we give another the gift of attention. We show that we care and that they matter.

Listening is an act of kindness. To those who are wounded and maybe in a dark place, you're shining a little light for them. Helping them find their way.

The place where the light enters you

Like everyone else, I've had experiences in life that wounded me. That made me feel broken.

People like my family, friends, and Helen Oreb (among others) shined a little light, leading me out of the darkness. So, I've tried to pass it forward.

I do this by paying attention to others. I follow Dan Milnor's advice and listen to other people. I try to shine a light.

The suicides I responded to as a young police officer taught me that darkness can win if we're not careful. We constantly must pay attention to our physical and mental health. And sometimes, that may require the help of professionals.

Time and maturity taught me that I could shine a light on my own darkness. Each trying time, personal loss, and medical challenge taught me that wounds are not only survivable but instructive.

"The wound is the place where the Light enters you." — *Rumi*

The light that Rumi is talking about has to do with knowledge, experience, deeper understanding, acceptance, hope, and God.

It's the hard knocks of life that shape us. They helped shape who David Goggins became. They shaped me, and they'll shape you.

Try to remember this when the darkness intrudes in your life.

Chapter Twenty-Five

How the Culture of Open Options Is Making Us Miserable

Raise your hand if this sounds familiar. You and your honey decide to spend the evening watching a Netflix movie. But then you spend forever browsing through selections and trailers, and now it's time for bed.

According to the author Pete Davis, you fell victim to "Infinite Browsing." We are so attached to the idea of keeping our options open that we never commit to anything.

Davis's book, *"Dedicated: The Case for Commitment In An Age Of Infinite Browsing,"* invites readers to join the "counter-culture of commitment" rather than forever keeping their options open.

The problem with options is that they delay commitment. Despite the apparent "connectedness" of the Internet, we are a society increasingly disconnected and commitment averse. We have a "sharing" economy where no commitment is required.

Instead of getting to know your local restaurant owner and servers, you can have your meals delivered to your house. And now there are "ghost" restaurants designed solely for delivery.

Sure, some ghost restaurants popped up in response to the COVID pandemic, but they're likely going to stay.

We develop low-key online "relationships" from behind our computer screens instead of committing to real, in-person relationships that require effort, accountability, and commitment.

We can't keep up with it

What about those "laptop warriors" traveling around the world, blogging about their freedom and lack of commitments. I'm sure they mean well, but what are they building? What is their legacy? What roots have they planted?

We are a society addicted to novelty, but novelty gives way to diminishing returns. How many of the latest video games can you play before the novelty wanes, and you ask yourself where you're headed in life?

We chase novelty at the expense of depth. And depth most often comes from commitment, and a sustained effort to build something of true value.

"The novelty business is astounding. We can't keep up with it." — *William Hanna*

Things of true value don't usually happen overnight. They take commitment and years of hard work to bear fruit. But the rewards can be tremendous.

People remember the big moments in Martin Luther King Jr.'s life. For example, his letter from a Birmingham Jail, and his famous 1963 "I Have a Dream" speech on the steps of the Lincoln Memorial.

What people don't remember is Martin Luther King Jr.'s less exciting backstory. As Pete Davis describes in his book:

"We remember Martin Luther King Jr. for his cinematic dragon-slaying-his iconic speeches and confrontations-but what's lost is all the long-haul work that queued up those moments. King makes

clear in Stride Toward Freedom, his memoir of the Montgomery bus boycott, just how much time he spent in the mundane work of winning the community's trust, joining local organizations, weaving together coalitions through multiple meetings, and planning efficient public gatherings."

It seems harder than ever for people today to commit to a place, cause, community, or even another person, for the long haul. We want to keep our options open, and in so doing, we deny ourselves something of vast importance.

In fact, this may be one of the most important things missing in our lives today. What is it? *Meaning.*

Increasingly today, private lives have grown, and public lives have shrunk. We talk to our neighbors less, resist joining clubs or organizations, and focus on keeping our options open instead of committing to something.

The question is, where is the meaning in keeping our options open? What will we eventually build? What purpose will we attach our lives to?

Go throw your TV set away

Years ago, I read Robert D. Putnam's book *"Bowling Alone: The Collapse and Revival of American Community."* His book chronicled the decline in church attendance, PTA membership, bowling leagues, and memberships in numerous other clubs.

Putnam pointed to many factors, such as generational change, urban sprawl (longer commutes), larger classrooms, and especially television.

"So please, oh please, we beg, we pray,
Go throw your TV set away,
And in its place you can install
A lovely bookshelf on the wall.
Then fill the shelves with lots of books."
— Roald Dahl, Charlie and the Chocolate Factory

TV encouraged lethargy and passivity. People began watching more sports than playing sports. TV meant fewer kids playing outside after school, and fewer neighbors visiting on their porches.

It's not that TV and social media are evil. Sometimes it's healthy to relax and escape into a great movie or video. But increasingly, TV and social media have become the default forms of entertainment at the expense of real social interaction.

"Americans no longer talk to each other, they entertain each other. They do not exchange ideas, they exchange images. They do not argue with propositions; they argue with good looks, celebrities, and commercials." — Neil Postman, Amusing Ourselves to Death: Public Discourse in the Age of Show Business

Everyone today seems to be glued to their screens, absorbed by addictive social media algorithms. Is this where we expect to find meaning and purpose?

Could this be why we're seeing higher levels of teen and adult suicides? Could this be why so many people are miserable and adrift in their lives?

The fear of closing doors

It makes sense early in life to keep your options open. Especially when you're growing up, discovering your talents, interests, etc. But sooner or later you must make some decisions. Like what kind of career you want to pursue.

Much of education today is about preparation for advancement. Yes, universities offer students plenty of clubs, activities, and subcultures to attach themselves to. But the overarching theme seems to be more about careerism and advancement than professionalism and craftsmanship.

As Pete Davis notes in his book:

"Clubs pitch themselves as resume lines and career offices guide you toward whatever will make you the most marketable. Students who take them up on the offer are often accused of chasing prestige and feeding their ego. But in my experience, what ladder climbers are doing has less to do with prestige and ego (money) and more

to do with fear — *the fear of closing doors. Attaining prestige, they think, is the best way to avoid losing options."*

What if universities spent more time fostering professionalism instead of careerism? Pete Davis notes: *"To be a professional is not some individual designation. It means something to join a profession. Once we are initiated into a profession, we 'profess' — declare publicly — that we intend to perform our craft to the highest standard."*

Professions serve society. They have codes of conduct, traditions, initiations, etc. Pete Davis writes: *"At their best, professions do not just exist to serve their practitioners — they ask their practitioners to commit to serving the profession's public mission. In exchange, they orient and give meaning to their practitioner's lives. They place you in a larger story."*

What do I owe to my times?

What do we owe to the dead, the living, and those yet to be born? It's easy to forget the millions who came before us. The ones who struggled, fought, sacrificed, and created the order and systems of today's society.

It's also easy to lose sight of our neighbors as we focus exclusively on our own needs, advancements, careers, and open options.

"What do I owe to my times, to my country, to my neighbors, to my friends? Such are the questions which a virtuous man ought often to ask himself." — Johann Kaspar Lavater

And what about our obligations to the unborn? Those who will inherit whatever we contribute or fail to contribute.

Whether we realize it or not, we are all linked together on this earth. Individual actions have ripples seen and unseen. If we get sucked into "infinite browsing mode" and forever keep our options open, we'll miss out on committing to something greater than ourselves.

Humanity is our ultimate community

I often think of the police chief who hired me as a rookie police officer back in 1989. That police chief spent his entire, long career in the same police department. He was totally committed to his city.

Even after he retired, he remains active in his community. He volunteers at his church and community events, mentors others, and has created a legacy of commitment, service, and professionalism.

Through his dedication and commitments, he has nurtured and sustained the local values and morals of his community. In this way, he honors those who contributed before him, those in his midst, and those who will follow him.

"A true community is not just about being geographically close to someone or part of the same social web network. It's about feeling connected and responsible for what happens. Humanity is our ultimate community, and everyone plays a crucial role." — Yehuda Berg

You can do the same. Steer clear of infinite browsing in your life. Seek a good education or training that can lead to becoming a professional of some kind. And then, commit to a place, cause, community, or person for the long haul.

Do this, and you will find meaning and purpose in your life.

Chapter Twenty-Six

The Most Important Thing We Bring to Another Person

The pathway began at the edge of our backyard, leading into the shadows and solitude of the deep woods.

It was nothing more than a well-trodden deer trail, yet it became an escape route from the frustrations and uncertainties of life.

The path opened to a cluster of tall trees. I was ten years old when I first ventured down the trail and discovered them. They swayed in the breeze, trunks creaking and groaning like old men steadying against the wind.

Twisting limbs jutting skyward blurred into the broad canopy of foliage high above. Was it my imagination, or were the limbs inviting me to scale their intertwined arms? What secret or prize awaited at the top of their lofty reach?

Balancing on the tips of my Keds high-top sneakers, I strained to reach the lowest branch. Finding purchase, I lifted myself up, thus beginning a journey I would repeat for years to come.

Ascending higher and higher, I clung tightly to the safety of the branches. Curiosity about what I would find at the top was stronger than my fear of falling.

At last, I climbed past a tangle of limbs and rose above the canopy of leaves and branches. The sunshine and blue sky above were bright, and my eyes took a moment to adjust.

Nestled and seated securely amongst the top branches, I closed my eyes. There was a breeze, and I could feel the entire tree below me gently swaying back and forth. It seemed like the tree was breathing.

"Trees are as close to immortality as the rest of us ever come."—Karen Joy Fowler

I felt completely safe and at peace. Whatever troubles or worries that drove me into the woods that day seemed to melt away.

The secret of the treetops was that sanctuary and peace could be found there. In the years that followed, I often returned to my arboreal refuge. It became a haven from the vicissitudes of life. A place to recharge my spirit and cleanse my soul from the stains of life's hardships and sorrows.

Not that my childhood and teen years were bad, but there were occasional family struggles, friendship turbulence, and other growing pains. I needed a place of tranquility and silence, and the trees gave me that. And more.

A series of losses, from beginning to end

So many of the things I have loved and took comfort in are gone now. My parents have passed on, along with a supporting cast of family and friends who loved and nurtured me along the way.

"Life seems sometimes like nothing more than a series of losses, from beginning to end. That's the given. How you respond to those losses, what you make of what's left, that's the part you have to make up as you go." — Katharine Weber, The Music Lesson

Our family home in the hills of Los Gatos, California, was sold many years ago, and I live in a different state now. I can no longer trace that old pathway to my cluster of welcoming trees. Even if I could, ascending their branches now would probably be unwise.

When I close my eyes and even in dreams, I can walk through every room of our family home and its surrounding grounds. I see the faces and hear the voices of loved ones long gone. I miss them all, but time and maturity have taught me to make peace with loss.

What helps is that sense of serenity I found high in the treetops. Nestled in the canopy and swaying in the soft rhythms of the mountain breeze, a divine silence crept into my soul.

This notion of peace found in silence remains with me today. When I was younger, I thought the lesson of the trees was to seek sanctuary in your life. Places to recharge and renew your spirit.

But the trees had a deeper lesson for me to learn.

Something beyond the moment

So much of our lives are assaulted by clamor, commitments, expectations, interruptions, and the hurly-burly of daily living. No wonder we flee to the stillness of lakes and the serenity of mountains. We instinctually know that nature and silence are good for our souls.

Healthy and restorative as these outdoor sanctuaries are, the good news is that we can replicate them at home. A simple backyard garden or quiet room for reading, prayer, or reflection can effectively calm our hearts and minds.

Even better, we can train ourselves in the practice of restorative breathing and meditation to create a kind of sanctuary within ourselves. An inner peace.

People who set aside regular time for meditation, prayer, and/or quiet reflection tend to be calm and peaceful. Ever notice such people are often a pleasure to be around? It's as if their stillness and centered calmness are infectious.

Just as trees communicate and take care of one another via an interconnected root system, people are connected as well via our shared humanity. And those who have learned how to quiet their own souls can help others to do the same.

How? Through the power of silence.

"Perhaps the most important thing we bring to another person is the silence in us, not the sort of silence that is filled with unspoken criticism or hard withdrawal. The sort of silence that is a place of refuge, of rest, of acceptance of someone as they are. We are all hungry for this other silence. It is hard to find. In its presence we can remember something beyond the moment, a strength on which to build a life. Silence is a place of great power and healing." — Rachel Naomi Remen

People love good listeners. We want so badly to be heard and to have someone listen quietly and validate what we are feeling.

As Rachel Naomi Remen notes in the above quote, the most important thing we bring to another person is the silence in us. The space for another person to take refuge.

Lighten the burdens of another

When we listen and offer silence, we give another person the space they need to talk. To be heard. To know someone cares.

We become a sanctuary for others.

The trees taught me a lot about being a sanctuary. Sitting atop their limbs and branches, above the canopy, the trees offered a silent place of refuge. No judgment, no advice, just silent sanctuary.

The deeper lesson was that we need to take care of one another, just as trees take care of each other.

The trees, in their silent embrace, took care of me. I was only a ten-year-old boy, and they were like wise old men, cradling me through my insecurities and fears.

"No one is useless in this world who lightens the burdens of another." — Charles Dickens

A lot of people wonder about the meaning of life. They consume self-help books and chase money, fame, and possessions to find happiness.

Hopefully, time and wisdom will teach us that love is the meaning of life. Just like those wise old trees, we are meant to take care of one another.

Learn how to become a sanctuary within yourself, and then use the power of silence to become a sanctuary for others. I can't think of a better way to honor the wisdom of those old trees.

Chapter Twenty-Seven

A Note On the Windshield

I blame it all on the evening breeze.

If not for that late afternoon gust of wind, the note beneath my driver's side windshield wiper would never have flicked up, catching my attention.

I would have driven home, and the rainstorm that arrived later that evening would surely have disintegrated the note's flimsy paper. I don't believe in fate, and I hope things don't happen for a reason because the note altered my view of life.

Had I not worked late that day, maybe the note would never have found its way to my car's windshield. But what's the point in speculation, we can never really know why life unfolds the way it does.

When the breeze lifted the edge of the note into view, I was annoyed. No doubt another windshield advertisement. I stepped out of the car, lifted the wiper, and grabbed the small piece of paper.

The handwritten note was clearly not an advertisement. The letters were printed in lower case, and this is what they said:

"I hate you! I never want to see you again! You said you were work-ing late but here you are, parked outside her apartment. Cheater! Don't call me, and don't show up at the Blue Dish. We're through! -C"

What are the odds that some guy who's cheating on his lady would have the same car as me? I chuckled at the thought and stuffed the note in my pocket.

...

My wife Carole and I have been married for 25-years. Our son and daughter are grown up now, living and working in the city. We've had our ups and downs, like any couple, but remain devoted to one another.

I suppose I have my father to thank for the longevity and joy of my marriage. He once told me, "Find someone who's kind. Looks are great, but they're a terrible predictor of compatibility and happiness. A kind person may have flaws, but kindness reveals character. And strong character can sustain a marriage."

When I got home that evening, I told Carole about the note and read it to her.

"Oh dear," she said. "Can you imagine her boyfriend's shock? He must have gone to see her, only to be accused of cheating. All because your car, apparently, looks like his."

"Yeah, poor guy," I said, adding, "Lousy luck. Although there must be a backstory. He must know a woman who lives in the apartments next to where I parked. Maybe he cheated in the past?"

"Too bad you don't know who she is," Carole said. "Then you could tell her what happened. Maybe her boyfriend is a good guy?"

...

The next day at work, I pulled the crumpled note out of my pocket. I almost threw it away that morning, but something told me to hang onto it. I read it again. The part about not showing up at the "Blue Dish."

I did a Google search for "Blue Dish," figuring it must be a diner or restaurant. Sure enough, there was a Blue Dish diner on 5th Street. On my lunch hour, I decided to swing by there and see what I could find out.

The diner had a 1950's theme to it, with cozy booths in front and big round-cushioned bar seats in the back. I sat down on one of the bar seats and a heavy-set woman behind the bar welcomed me.

"What can I get you," she said.

"How about your club sandwich and a water," I said. I noticed her name tag, which said Madge.

"Hey, can I ask you a question?" I asked Madge.

"Sure thing, sweetheart," she said.

"Do you have a woman who works here with a first initial of "C" in her name?"

Madge looked at me warily. "What's this about? Are you a cop or something?" she said.

"No, no, I'm not a cop. It's just that I found this note on my windshield yesterday, and I think it was meant for someone else."

I told Madge the whole story and handed her the note.

"Yep, that's Cindy's handwriting alright. I'll be damned. I guess you and Steve, her boyfriend, have the exact same car. Cindy is off today, but she'll be in tomorrow. Why don't you stop by then?"

I thanked Madge, ate my lunch, and headed back to work.

...

I told one of my co-workers, Joe, about the windshield note and all that transpired. Joe was a good deal older than me, and I always respected his advice and wisdom.

"Good for you for trying to fix the misunderstanding," Joe told me. "That's all we can really do in life, try to make things better. Sometimes things work out, sometimes they don't. But at least we know we tried. It's the effort more than outcome, I think, that spreads a little grace in the world."

I wasn't sure if I was spreading any grace in the world, but the next day I found myself back at the Blue Dish, nervously seated in a booth. It wasn't long before a pretty, young woman entered the diner and disappeared in the back. A moment later she emerged, wearing a "Blue Dish" apron and a name tag that said, "Cindy."

"What can I get for you?" Cindy said with a cheerful smile.

"Just a coffee, and perhaps a few minutes of your time?" I said.

"For what?" she asked.

I handed her the note she left on my windshield. She stared at it and then back at me.

"Did Steve put you up to this? I don't want to see him!"

"No, no, I don't even know Steve. You put this note on my windshield. Look outside across the street. Do you see the white Infinity? That's my car."

Cindy stared at my car, then the note, and then back at me.

"Oh my God!" she said.

...

Cindy asked the manager if she could take her break early. She slid into the booth, and I told her the whole story. She shook her head, teared up a little, and confirmed that Steve also had a white Infinity. The exact same make and model.

"I'm so stupid," Cindy told me. "I guess I was just being insecure."

Cindy explained that Steve's ex-girlfriend lives in the apartments next to where I had parked my car. She assumed he parked there and was having an affair with his ex-girlfriend.

"I don't mean to get personal, but has Steve been unfaithful in the past?" I asked Cindy.

"No, he's always been great. Really sweet and kind. But his ex-girlfriend used to be a model. She's really pretty. When I saw his car, um your car, well, I thought the worst."

"Well, Cindy, you're a beautiful young woman. I wouldn't worry about his ex-girlfriend," I said.

"Thanks, that's sweet. And thank you for taking the time to find me. I really need to call Steve and clear this whole thing up."

We slid out of the booth. Madge called to Cindy and pointed to her wristwatch.

"Mind your own business, Madge! Can't you see I'm busy!" Cindy said. It surprised me, but then I knew all of this must have been stressful for her.

Cindy surprised me with a hug and thanked me again.

...

That evening Carole and I sat on the back porch after dinner and enjoyed some coffee. I told her all about Cindy and Steve and the outcome of my visit to the diner. I also told her about my co-worker Joe's advice about "spreading a little grace in the world."

"There's been times when I did the right thing to help people and things didn't work out. And there's been other times when they did," Carole said. "The times it didn't work out used to discourage me, but not anymore."

"Why is that?" I asked Carole.

"I'm not sure. I doubt there's a cosmic scorecard that keeps track, but acts of grace just make me feel better, regardless of what happens."

"That sounds like a good philosophy to me," I told Carole.

...

The following week, just for fun, I invited my co-worker Joe to join me for lunch at the Blue Dish diner. I had grown fond of their club sandwich and was curious to see how Cindy was doing.

When we arrived, we spotted Cindy in the parking lot outside the diner. She was passionately kissing and embracing a handsome young man.

"Well look at that," Joe said. "Looks like she patched things up with her fellow. We watched as the young man walked over to a motorcycle, slipped on a helmet, and rode off.

"I thought you said her boyfriend had a car like yours?" Joe asked.

"I guess he has a motorcycle too," I said.

Joe and I entered the diner and Madge seated us in a booth. I introduced Madge to Joe and then we ordered our lunch.

"I'm so happy you did what you did for Cindy," Madge said. "She and Steve got back together. In fact, you should say hello, he's in the diner right now." Madge pointed to Steve, who was seated across the diner from us.

I noticed a small bouquet of flowers on Steve's table.

"Isn't that sweet?" Madge said. "He brought some flowers to surprise Cindy with.

Just then, Cindy strolled into the diner, with a smile on her face. Madge smiled back at Cindy and pointed to the corner of the diner. Cindy turned around and spotted Steve, waving to her with one hand, and holding the flowers in the other.

Cindy cheerfully walked over to Steve, giving him a kiss and a hug.

"Ah, young love. Isn't it beautiful?" Madge said.

Chapter Twenty-Eight

The Unexpected Movie That Made Me Realize What Really Matters

Just when I was about to retreat to my library and swear off any more uninspired Hollywood films, along comes a movie that restores my faith in originality and creativity.

So many of today's movies are formulaic, rely on CGI at the expense of great storytelling, or want to tutor me with a political agenda.

Sometimes I just want to escape into a gorgeously filmed movie with an original story, fascinating characters, and philosophical offerings to rock my world.

What's the movie that did all that for me? *Pig.*

Don't let the minimalist movie title or the seemingly absurd storyline dissuade you. Sometimes thoughtful movies with tremendous life lessons come unexpectedly packaged.

Part of this movie's packaging involves a small pig that lives in the Oregon wilderness with her companion, Robin "Rob" Feld (played by Nicholas Cage).

Feld is a famous Portland chef turned recluse who lives in a dilapidated forest shack. He and his beloved pig forage for rare truffles, which Feld sells to a young restaurant dealer.

But then the truffle hunting pig is abducted, and Feld returns to Portland on a quest to rescue and reunite with his pig.

I know, this sounds like a terrible plot. In fact, my wife and I almost didn't rent the movie, but the artful cinematography (compliments of Patrick Scola) in the trailer won us over.

Does it give you wings?

So much of life involves mundane routine. Our dreams and passions often take a backseat to the needs of today. Years can click by and sometimes we start to feel dead inside.

Some people are shaken out of their life stupor by a tragic event, like the loss of a spouse, or getting fired from a job. Others reach a kind of bottom and decide on their own that it's time to make changes.

You'll have to watch the movie *Pig* to learn why Robin Feld is the way he is, but I suspect many will nod in agreement with Feld's wise observations about life.

Namely, about what's real and what's not.

"How do you know if something is real? That's easy. Does it change you? Does it form you? Does it give you wings? Does it give you roots? Does it make you look back at a month ago and say, 'I am a whole different person right now'? If yes, then it's real. The evidence of truth and reality, lies in how much something can touch you, can change you, even if it's from very far away. Distance is only the evidence of what can be surpassed." — C. JoyBell C.

In one amazing scene in *Pig*, Feld (recently bloodied from an underground fight) seeks information about his stolen pig in a fancy restaurant. Feld asks to see the chef (played brilliantly by David Knell), who once worked for Feld.

Arguably the best scene in the movie, Feld is unimpressed with the pompous chef, who we learn has abandoned a personal dream and sold his soul for something he doesn't even believe in.

How about you? What dreams have you set aside because people, conventionality, or expectations buried your passion?

Journey towards the sacred mountain

Watching the movie *Pig*, and that exquisite scene with the chef, made me realize that what really matters is what's inside of me.

The people I love. The dreams I have. My passion for writing, creating art, and black and white photography.

We waste far too much of our precious time on stuff that's not real. Chasing likes on social media. Worrying about our status. Emulating others instead of teasing out from within our unique gifts and talents.

We fasten on to the surface of things, the facades, instead of going deeper where truth and meaning reside.

"The reflection on the surface of the water is often mistaken for the mysteries that lie beneath. Likewise, the reflection of the moon is mistaken for its own light. In the quest for wisdom, each person must emerge from the illusions of the world and begin the journey towards the sacred mountain."

— Thomas Lloyd Qualls, Painted Oxen

So much of life involves superficial stuff. Probably because we need a bit of surface-level chit-chat to navigate our days more easily.

We ask people "How are you?" to be polite. We don't expect a long answer about the person's marriage, mortgage woes, lost dreams, etc.

The surface level is where a great deal of life plays out, much like Shakespeare's "All the world's a stage, and all the men and women merely players."

Except life is much more than merely playing our parts. Beneath each of Shakespeare's *"Seven Ages of Man"* are the dreams and passions that accompany our various stations through life.

Dreams and passions don't care if we're children, middle-aged, or elderly. They keep whispering in our ears because they want desperately to wake us. They want to prevent us from just living on the surface of things.

What's inside of you

A friend of mine recently introduced me to the world of Dan Milnor.

According to Milnor's website:

"Daniel Milnor once worked as both a fragrance model and a hot tub installer but is better known as a reformed-journalist, photographer and writer who is now, once again, performing these duties in his role as 'Creative Evangelist,' for Blurb Inc., the world's premiere indie publishing platform."

Beyond his photography and writing, Milnor is an outdoorsman who enjoys bicycling, fishing, canoeing, and overall adventuring. He's also an avid reader with a sharp mind.

In one of the many Dan Milnor videos I watched, he told an interviewer something profound:

"In essence, the only thing that matters is what's inside of you, and what you're trying to say in the way that you want to say it."

Milnor's observation rings true for me. The creative work I'm most proud of has always been my personal work. Because it's the most honest. The most real.

We don't get a lot of things to really care about

In the movie *Pig*, the pompous chef goes to great lengths to defend his food and restaurant, but it's all a lie.

Robin Feld tells the chef:

"They're not real. You get that, right? None of it is real. The critics aren't real. The customers aren't real, because...this isn't real. You aren't real."

How can our lives be real if we're not being who we really are? Who we know we can be or become?

Feld warns the chef:

"Why do you care about these people? They don't care about you. None of them. They don't even know you because you haven't shown them. Every day you'll wake up, and there will be less of you. You live your life for them, and they don't even see you. You don't even see yourself. We don't get a lot of things to really care about."

Why do we worry so much about superficial things, like social media likes? I understand that growing a big audience can lead to lucrative financial deals, but will this be the work you're proud of? The real you?

Popularity often has nothing to do with depth and authenticity. Clickbait and pornography attract more eyeballs online than poetry and poignant short stories, but which would you rather produce?

"We don't get a lot of things to really care about." — Robin Feld, *Pig*

Think about the truth of the above statement. Our lives are filled with many responsibilities. Work demands. Errands. Commitments.

If we're not careful, other people will define our lives for us. They'll set the agenda and expectations. If we deny who we really are or want to become, then we're not living an authentic life. Nothing is real. We're just actors on a stage.

We don't get a lot of things to really care about. For Robin Feld, it was his beloved pig and simple life in the woods.

For us, it might be our families, friends, meaningful work, and unique passions. As Dan Milnor points out, the only thing that matters is what's inside of you.

Work on being you. Hone your skills and gifts. Share your authentic self with the world, so people can celebrate who you really are.

Do this, and you'll have fewer regrets and an authentic legacy to be proud of.

Chapter Twenty-Nine

The Most Important Kind of Freedom

The quickest way to spot dead people is to look at their eyes.

There's a vacancy. When they blink back at you, there's no luster. No hope.

If our eyes are windows to the soul, why have so many of us permanently drawn the shades? Maybe because we're trapped in a kind of default setting.

I was a cop for over 26-years, and I met a lot of dead people. Some of them were my colleagues.

I'm not talking about bodies with toe tags in the morgue. I'm referring to the living dead. People who are going through the motions, but not really living.

In Richard Paul Evans's book, *"The Walk"*, a kind woman who works in a diner shares this nugget of wisdom:

"I meet dead people at the diner every day. People who have given up. That's all death requires of us, to give up living. The thing is, the only real sign of life is growth. And growth requires pain. So to choose life is to accept pain. Some people go to such lengths to avoid

pain that they give up on life. They bury their hearts or they drink themselves numb until they don't feel anything anymore. The irony is, in the end, their escape becomes more painful than what they are avoiding. Ultimately we decide whether our lives are good or bad, ugly or beautiful. Some people in this world have stopped looking for beauty, then wonder why their lives are so ugly. Everyone carries divinity in them. Only through helping others can we save ourselves."

I read *"The Walk"* during a challenging year in my law enforcement career. It wasn't the suicides, highway fatalities, or domestic violence incidents that rattled my faith in humanity.

It was the sense of purposelessness I saw in so many people.

To choose life is to accept pain

Books have always been a refuge for me. Great authors, through their stories and essays, help us see things more clearly. For example, reading *"The Walk"* underscored an important life lesson for me: *To choose life is to accept pain.*

Ernest Hemingway's classic novel *"The Old Man and the Sea,"* echoes the notion that we need purpose in our lives. And since nothing worthwhile is ever easy in life, chasing purpose invites some pain along the way.

That's why Santiago, Hemingway's elderly fisherman, says to himself, "My big fish must be somewhere."

The lesson in *"The Old Man and the Sea"* is that the journey through life is the reward. The key is to live with courage and integrity. To have a purpose.

The late author David Foster Wallace gave a memorable commencement speech in 2005 to Kenyon College. The speech was titled *"This Is Water."*

Like Richard Paul Evans's book *"The Walk,"* Wallace's speech *"This Is Water"* warns against living a walking dead or "default setting" kind of life.

So, what exactly is a "default setting" kind of life?

You can be shaped, or you can be broken

With time and a little bit of life experience, a lot of us start to suffer from what David Foster Wallace describes as "blind certainty, a close-mindedness that amounts to an imprisonment so total that the prisoner doesn't even know he's locked up."

Our arrogance is sometimes blind to us. We celebrate the stuff we're right about and disregard or ignore our mistakes.

We think we are the center of the universe. This self-centeredness is kind of our "default setting", according to Wallace. After all, we are the center of all our experiences. Yes, there may be other people and things going on, but it's all filtered through our senses.

Wallace argues that "learning how to think really means learning how to exercise some control over how and what you think. It means being conscious and aware enough to choose what you pay attention to and to choose how you construct meaning from experience."

The reality is that much of adult life consists of boredom, repetition, disappointments, and frustration. It's the traffic jams, long lines at the grocery store, elevator music at the dentist's office, laundry you forgot to do, and a million other daily indignities.

Our natural default setting is to make everything about us. So, when the elderly woman holds up the grocery store line to study her coupons, we take it personally. She's delaying us from getting home.

But what if we took a moment to realize that the elderly woman is the center of her world. And in her world, she's on a fixed income because her husband died unexpectedly. Her children don't visit her, and those grocery store visits provide a few precious minutes of social interaction.

"You can be shaped, or you can be broken. There is not much in between. Try to learn. Be coachable. Try to learn from everybody, especially those who fail. This is hard... How promising you are as a

Student of the Game is a function of what you can pay attention to without running away." — David Foster Wallace, Infinite Jest

There is actually no such thing as atheism

According to David Foster Wallace, "in the day-to-day trenches of adult life, there is actually no such thing as atheism. There is no such thing as not worshipping. Everybody worships. The only choice we get is what to worship."

It's one thing to worship a god, spiritual deity, or noble truth that pulls us out of our self-centeredness and into the service of others.

Unfortunately, many choose to worship money, looks, power, or intellect. Doing so doesn't usually end well. Such false gods, according to Wallace, "...will eat you alive."

We see the destruction of people worshiping false gods all the time. Politicians addicted to power at the expense of ethics. Aging actors abusing plastic surgery to grasp at distant youth. Entrepreneurs who would sell their own mother to make a buck. And academics so impressed with their credentials they can't see how pompous they are.

If we're honest, we've all fallen under the spell of these false gods at one time or another in our lives. But if we ever want to get past the deadness of default living, we need to find a true purpose. Deeper meaning.

In his commencement address, Wallace drives home the point:

"If you worship money and things, if they are where you tap real meaning in life, then you will never have enough, never feel you have enough. It's the truth. Worship your body and beauty and sexual allure and you will always feel ugly. And when time and age start showing, you will die a million deaths before they finally grieve you.

Worship power, you will end up feeling weak and afraid, and you will need ever more power over others to numb you to your own fear. Worship your intellect, being seen as smart, you will end up feeling stupid, a fraud, always on the verge of being found out. But the insidious thing about these forms of worship is not that they're evil or sinful, it's that they're unconscious. They are default settings."

To care about other people and to sacrifice for them

People usually seek higher education in universities to become educated, gain marketable skills, and grow personally. They believe that a university diploma is a ticket to a better life.

It's true that people with higher education generally go on to get better jobs than less educated folks. But the point of higher education used to be about more than just money, prestige, or getting a corner office. It was supposed to be about becoming a well-adjusted person.

There are lots of highly educated people out there, working in elegant offices, who have fallen into a default life. They're unhappy and don't know why. The false gods they worship haven't given them true purpose or fulfillment.

The problem is that true freedom is not found in wealth, looks, status, or power. If we are to find true happiness and freedom in our lives, we need to look outside of ourselves.

David Foster Wallace wraps up his commencement speech with the following:

"The really important kind of freedom involves attention and awareness and discipline and being able truly to care about other people and to sacrifice for them over and over in myriad petty, unsexy ways every day.

That is real freedom. That is being educated and understanding how to think. The alternative is unconsciousness, the default setting, the rat race, the constant gnawing sense of having had, and lost, some infinite thing."

Take care of your children. Think of your spouse before yourself. Help your neighbor carry in her groceries. Be there for those in need.

Do these things, and you'll sleep well at night. You'll live an authentic life and experience the kind of freedom that only comes from caring about others more than yourself.

Chapter Thirty

My Best Answers to 9 Life Questions from a Reader

Last year I almost made a major mistake with my website blog.

As a full-time writer and artist, I look for ways to simplify and streamline my creative process. Accordingly, I considered axing blog comments from my website.

Poking around the Internet I noticed a lot of top bloggers who don't include comments from readers. Bloggers like James Clear, Michael Hyatt, and Seth Godin.

Best-selling author and marketing guru Neil Patel wrote a whole blog post about the pros and cons of blog comments. Stuff like social proof versus spam, and reader engagement versus moderation time.

In the end, I decided to retain blog comments on my website because I learn a great deal from readers. They share stories and provide feedback that inspires me to write better blog posts.

Such was the case with one reader, who politely asked if I would answer nine questions about life. The questions were great prompts for me to share my best life wisdom.

What follows are the questions and answers. I took the liberty here to update and expand on my answers, but the essence is the same.

I hope they're helpful to you.

What's the one quality that has helped you the most and everyone should have?

Persistence. People tend to give up too easily. Many of the accomplishments I'm most proud of in my life were the result of persistence.

"You don't start out writing good stuff. You start out writing crap and thinking it's good stuff, and then gradually you get better at it. That's why I say one of the most valuable traits is persistence." — *Octavia E. Butler*

There is a caveat. If your goals have changed, or your health is threatened or suffering, persistence may not make sense.

For example, Simone Biles, the American gymnastics star, stepped down from the Olympic competition. Her head was no longer in the game, and she feared injuring herself.

Some agree with her decision, others do not. In the end, only you can decide what's best for yourself. But when it comes to important goals, healthy persistence is invaluable.

What are a few books you suggest everyone read?

This is an impossible question for two reasons. First, I'm a book lover, and it's hard to name just a few books.

Second, books affect people differently, due to our unique backgrounds, cultures, and experiences. Nevertheless, here are few books that helped me grow or moved me.

Man's Search for Meaning by Viktor Frankl. I learned that we can't control what happens to us, but we can control how we respond.

Deep Work: Rules for Focused Success in a Distracted World by Cal Newport. Deep work is a superpower few people possess because they're addicted to smartphones and devices. Conquer deep work, and you'll accomplish much.

Letters to a Young Poet by Rainer Maria Rilke. Rilke teaches us how to survive as sensitive observers in a harsh world. An excerpt from the book:

"Perhaps all the dragons in our lives are princesses who are only waiting to see us act, just once, with beauty and courage. Perhaps everything that frightens us is, in its deepest essence, something helpless that wants our love."

Too Soon Old, Too Late Smart: Thirty True Things You Need to Know Now, by Gordon Livingston. Dr. Livingston argued that *"any relationship is under the control of the person who cares the least."* In my 26-year law enforcement career, I found this to be true in countless domestic calls.

The Obstacle Is the Way: The Timeless Art of Turning Trials into Triumph by Ryan Holiday. Holiday is a devoted student of the Stoics (people like the Roman Emperor Marcus Aurelius). The Stoics dealt with life objectively. They saw things as they were, not as they wished them to be. We can learn a lot from this approach.

To Dance with the White Dog, by Terry Kay. In this poignant story, a kind old man's wife dies and then a white dog appears in his life. Loss is a reality in life, but maybe miracles are too?

Here's a line from the book, illustrating Kay's poetic writing:

"Always there was a moment — a quick slip of time — when the sun broke free of the trees and bled from its yolk, spilling in red-orange rivers over the silk."

Tuesdays with Morrie: An Old Man, a Young Man, and Life's Greatest Lesson by Mitch Albom. What would you do if you learned a beloved teacher of yours was dying? And what final lessons might that teacher have for you?

Bird by Bird: Some Instructions on Writing and Life by Anne Lamott. This book is funny and full of wisdom, like this bit of advice:

"Almost all good writing begins with terrible first efforts. You need to start somewhere."

The Year of Magical Thinking by Joan Didion. I learned a lot about loss, thanks to wisdom in the book like this:

"I know why we try to keep the dead alive: we try to keep them alive in order to keep them with us. I also know that if we are to live ourselves there comes a point at which we must relinquish the dead, let them go, keep them dead."

What's one powerful piece of advice for living a fulfilling life?

Learn to see through the eyes of others. Embrace empathy.

Doing so will make you less judgmental, more understanding, and kinder. Failing to do so may make you egocentric and selfish.

What's one piece of important financial advice?

Less is more. Become a minimalist and learn to save/invest your money. The death of my parents, and having to deal with all their accumulated stuff, taught me a lot. Do you own your things, or do they own you?

What are your regrets and how do you avoid regrets?

Comparison is the thief of joy. I regret comparing myself to others when I was younger. What works for others doesn't always work for you. It's okay to admire others, but don't envy them.

Focus on personal improvement, embrace emotional maturity, and pursue your passions. The rest will take care of itself.

What's one thing you learned the hard way?

There are no second chances to make a good first impression. Opportunities I squandered for lack of preparation taught me that success rewards the prepared.

"It is not often that a man can make opportunities for himself. But he can put himself in such shape that when or if the opportunities come he is ready." — Theodore Roosevelt

What's one thing that should never be forgotten?

Love is the most powerful thing in the universe. And it costs nothing to give.

What's one thing we must not think twice about spending?

Time with loved ones. Because someday, one of you won't be there anymore.

How do you tackle a dilemma? How do you make tough decisions with your heart and mind?

Problems and dilemmas require logic and thoughtful focus, so we don't fall prey to confirmation bias. But we must also consider our hearts, and what we can live with and without.

When I joined my local Rotary club, I was given a little card with the Rotary "4-Way Test" printed on it. It's an excellent template for handling challenges and dilemmas.

Here are the four questions printed on the card:

Is it the truth?

Is it fair to all concerned?

Will it build goodwill and better friendships?

Will it be beneficial to all concerned?

Thanks to the above nine questions from a blog reader, I was inspired to think about and share my best life advice. Some folks may disagree with my answers, and that's fine.

The point is that if we are to live fulfilling lives, we should be thinking about such questions.

Read broadly, interact with quality people, love with all your heart, and life just might bring you joy and fulfillment.

Chapter Thirty-One

The Monsters Will Come in Your Life: Here's How to Vanquish Them

When I was ten years old, something in the backyard knocked on the window to my bedroom.

It was around midnight, and it startled me awake. I scrambled out of bed, ran down the hall into my parent's bedroom, and shook my father's shoulders.

"Dad! Something's outside my bedroom! It knocked on the window!"

My father, groggy-eyed, squinted at me and said, "Oh Johnny, it's probably just a dream." He crawled out of bed and walked me back down the hall to my bedroom.

"Fear tastes like a rusty knife and do not let her into your house."
— *John Cheever*

Dad opened my bed covers and told me to go back to sleep. He leaned over to tuck me in.

And that's when the second knock on my bedroom window happened.

I live in that atmosphere

We lived in the hills of Los Gatos, California, surrounded mostly by oak trees and woods. Deer, raccoons, and assorted wildlife were common visitors on our property.

But they didn't knock on windows.

Dad reacted quickly, fetching his flashlight and World War II Colt M1911 semi-automatic pistol. I remember my mother was awake from all the commotion.

"What's going on, John?" she asked my father.

"Stay inside, I think someone is in the backyard," he said.

Looking back, Dad should have called the police and stayed inside, but he was a former United States Marine with a strong personality. His instinct was to immediately confront the situation.

Dad went quickly out through the side door of our garage, where he would be able to surprise anyone in the back yard.

My mother and I peered through the bedroom window, following the light stream of Dad's flashlight. After a few minutes, Dad came back into the house.

"There was nothing," Dad told us, adding, "I walked around the entire house. Not even shoe prints in the dirt beneath your window."

"Life is full of awe and grace and truth, mystery, and wonder. I live in that atmosphere."— Dion DiMucci

"So, what knocked on Johnny's window?" my mother asked.

"I don't know." It was all my father could say, but to a ten-year-old boy, the incident confirmed that monsters and ghosts must be real.

Children fear to go in the dark

With time and maturity, I outgrew my belief in monsters. Unexplainable things happen, I concluded, like the mysterious knock on my bedroom window.

Fast forward several years, and I was now a university student back home for summer break. I stayed in the upstairs guest room since my childhood bedroom was occupied by my 95-year-old maternal grandmother, Mary.

Mary's health had declined, and she was no longer able to live alone in her apartment, so my mother began taking care of her.

During the first week I was back home, Mary collapsed in the bathroom. Mom was unable to lift her and screamed for help.

My father and I carried Mary to the bedroom and laid her down. Dad sat beside her, holding her hands.

"Men fear death as children fear to go in the dark; and as that natural fear in children is increased by tales, so is the other." — *Francis Bacon*

He asked Mary how she was doing, and she faintly said, "I'm fine." Right after that, her eyes seemed to change. They looked distant and cloudy.

Dad checked Mary's pulse. Then he asked my mom to bring him a small mirror, which she ran and brought back.

Dad held the mirror in front of Mary's mouth, but there was no sign of breath. I felt strange. Fearful. Like something in the room had changed.

It was my first encounter with the real monster. Not the kind of monster you see in a Frankenstein movie or childhood nightmare, but the kind that whisks souls away.

The monster known as death.

Everything that I do is in honor of him

Following my university years, I entered the law enforcement profession and saw plenty of death, up close. Messy suicides, automobile accidents, and murder victims.

But in these incidents, I never saw the death monsters. Because they weren't personal. But in the back of my mind, I could sense the death monsters lurking.

In later years, my father's heart problems led to bypass surgery, and I always feared he'd succumb one day to a heart attack. But it didn't happen that way.

In his mid-eighties, Dad descended into the fog of dementia. I think this hazy landscape in his mind became a playground for the monster. I could never see the monster outright but sensed its presence during Dad's confused conversations.

Near the end, we called hospice. Dad was still alive, but he seemed to be melting away into a haunted landscape. It frightened me, like the stabbing fear I felt as a boy when something unseen knocked on my window.

"The loss of my father will always sting. But now, everything that I do is in honor of him and celebrates his life." — Adrienne C. Moore

The day Dad died I was with him, holding his hands. Telling him how much I loved him. Saying that, if he was tired, to go ahead and sleep.

Dad's breathing was uneven and slow. Much like with my dying grandmother, the room felt odd. I think it was the monster, not visible but hovering expectantly.

It was getting late. I said goodbye to my father and left him in the care of the hospice nurse. She called me a few hours later to say that Dad passed away.

It's so much darker when a light goes out

Sooner or later, the monsters will come into your life. They often condition us with test runs. The death of pets, for example.

But nothing prepares you for the big encounters. Like this last January. Once again, I found myself holding a parent's hands, in a hospice setting.

"It's so much darker when a light goes out than it would have been if it had never shone." — John Steinbeck, The Winter of Our Discontent

My 89-year-old mother's body had had enough of Parkinson's disease. Her twisted and frail body was unconscious but still breathing. The hospice nurse assured me that hearing is the last sense to go.

So, I spoke to Mom. I told her, "I've got you. You're okay. We love you. Rest now."

I sensed that the monster had her, too. It must have been so hard for her to finally let go. To give in to the monster.

How we choose to live

How do we vanquish this monster called death? How do we face something so big and scary and final?

The answer begins in how we choose to live. The sacrifices we make for the ones we love. How we care for them.

I took care of my mother all through her elderly years. There were endless doctor appointments, grocery trips, Sunday visits, and more.

Of course, the years of taking care of my mother coincided with some of the busiest years of my professional career. And I was raising a teenage son.

Doing the right thing and making sacrifices for loved ones is often inconvenient. It's understandable at times to feel frustrated.

But here's the deal:

The investment you make in caring for loved ones is proportionate to how successfully you will vanquish the monsters later in life.

All the memories of surprising my mother with trips to the coffee shop, and the laughs we shared at doctor visits, protected me from the death monster.

The death monster may have bitten me a few times, but nothing fatal. The wounds and loss linger, but so does the love. And the love, I've found, is bigger. It eclipses the death monster.

Part of defeating the death monster is acceptance. Hating death doesn't change the outcome, but it might change you.

"Whoever fights monsters should see to it that in the process he does not become a monster. And if you gaze long enough into an abyss, the abyss will gaze back into you." — Friedrich Nietzsche

Death, once it happens to someone you love, is a monster you don't want to fight. Doing so can bring bitterness and a dark heart. You risk never healing.

Yes, fight illness in yourself and your loved ones. Seek the best doctors. Take care of your body. But once death arrives, accept the path of grief.

Carry the loss with you. Rejoice in the memories. Be thankful for the sacrifices you made. And live your life. Those we loved and lost would want us to be happy.

In these ways, you can vanquish the monsters. You can defang them.

The wounds and loss may linger, but love will prevail. And love is the most powerful force in the universe.

Chapter Thirty-Two

The Most Important 3 Words to Ask Yourself Before Pursuing a Goal

Wouldn't it be nice to experience greater fulfillment in life?

Everyone has aspirations and dreams, but they don't always think things through. Worse, they don't stop to examine their underlying motivations, and where they might lead.

I'll bet you know people who are unhappy in their careers. They complain about their bosses, the commute, office politics, and more. Maybe this applies to you?

"How did I get into this mess?" you might ask yourself.

The answer often has to do with money, the expectations of others, and unexamined goals. We chase dollars over contentment, do what others want for us, and fail to reflect on what we really want for ourselves.

Or we romanticize some dream job but fail to reflect on how such a job would change our life. We focus on the perceived good and ignore the bad.

I'm too real for this sh**

The R&B singer Summer Walker has over 3 million followers on Instagram, and her official music video *"Body"* has over 14 million views. A lot of aspiring singers and fame-seekers would kill for this kind of exposure.

So, what does Summer Walker say about fame? Namely, that she's tired of the phoniness. An article in Thrive Global explored "the bitter spoonfuls of stardom" that Walker is facing.

An excerpt:

"To paraphrase, Walker told her 1.6 million Instagram followers that she's exhausted with the false-I cloaks that the music industry drapes over its artists. She added that while people under the spotlight put a lot of effort into concocting phony images of themselves, they are lazy about doing the much-needed self-work in discovering who they really are behind all the smoke and mirrors of fame. Walker, in her own words, said, 'I'm too real for this sh**.'"

Too real for this sh**. That's an important insight into how the dream sometimes conflicts with reality.

A lot of famous people are polished, carefully branded, and marketed products. Sometimes the real person behind the image loses sense of who he or she truly is.

We go blindly on our way

The actor Jim Carrey has made a fortune with his comedic talent. Yet he has battled depression and unhappiness. Carrey once said:

"I think everybody should get rich and famous and do everything they ever dreamed of so they can see that it's not the answer."

So, what is the answer?

It probably varies for everyone because we're all made up of different passions, abilities, and backgrounds. But part of the answer starts by asking a question consisting of three words: *To what end?*

For example, your parents keep telling you to study law or medicine. "You'll make a nice living," they say. Or your boyfriend discourages you from pursuing photography. "You'll be broke," he warns.

The question you should ask is, "To what end?" A career in law or medicine might indeed bring a good income, but will it bring contentment? A photography career may not be lucrative, but it might feed your soul.

"Without reflection, we go blindly on our way, creating more unintended consequences, and failing to achieve anything useful." — *Margaret J. Wheatley*

People often romanticize their dreams instead of examining unintended consequences.

You think being a rock star sounds great. But to what end? What's the underlying reason you want it? If it's just for fame and fortune, that can be a shaky reason.

On the other hand, if you are a born singer and songwriter, and you want to move and inspire people with your music, that's something different. You know that despite the challenges, the end game means you'll be fulfilled and content with your work.

Who or what is driving me in this direction?

Writer Amy K. Hutchens, in an article for Entrepreneur.com, notes:

"We can set a lot of goals, we can think a lot of thoughts, we can behave in all sorts of ways, but ultimately, to what end? Where will this decision lead you?"

You can save yourself a lot of time, energy, and grief by asking "To what end?" Take the time to reflect and think about what brings you the greatest contentment.

Without contentment, wealth and fame can be a burden, just as poverty and irrelevancy can be a burden. Contentment comes from doing things we enjoy, not romanticized delusions of grandeur.

In her article, Amy K. Hutchens went on to write:

"Too often, entrepreneurs set goals or outcomes and never ask themselves why. Unpacking your decision and taking a hard look at how it will fuel or complete you is important to your long-term peace. Discerning how this choice might make you feel along the way will influence whether your journey is more pleasurable or painful. So ask yourself: Where am I going? Why am I going? Who or what is driving me in this direction? How do I want to travel down this path?"

Journalist Joe Geiger, in an article for the Richmond Times-Dispatch, also embraces the "To what end?" line of thinking. He writes:

"When considering taking any action in business or in life, I have for years asked myself, 'To what end' do I want to do this? I have found the question helpful in making sure that there is a compelling reason for the action being considered.

This is not to say that there is no place for emotionally driven actions. Such action is the goal in music, painting, sculpture, and many other artistic endeavors. However, in most business and life situations, emotional reactions do not advance the situation toward a specific goal."

A sense of identity, fulfillment, and meaning

When I was a young police sergeant, I used to moonlight as an editorial cartoonist for two local newspapers. I enjoyed my law enforcement career and helping people, but I used to fantasize about being a full-time cartoonist.

One day I applied for a full-time, staff editorial cartoonist position at a large newspaper in another state. I ignored the fact that newspapers were dwindling around the country, and the position would be far less secure than my police job.

"We live in an age where our career becomes a key playground through which to derive a sense of identity, fulfillment, and meaning.

A job is no longer just a way to pay the bills." — Adele Barlow, *Leaving Law: How Others Did It and How You Can Too*

I didn't stop to ask myself "To what end?" What happens if I get the position? It will mean less income and benefits than my police job. My family would have to relocate. I'd be far away from all my friends.

Fortunately, I didn't get the position. Even if I had, I realized I no longer wanted the position. I was seduced by the fantasy of the job more than the reality.

I asked myself, "To what end?" I realized that I didn't have to work for a newspaper to be a cartoonist. I could freelance and still enjoy my law enforcement career, and the financial security it provided my family.

Turns out I enjoyed a 26-year career in law enforcement, and then retired early to write, paint, and draw cartoons full-time. Sometimes dreams work out, just differently than you thought.

Many people lose the small joys

You can save yourself a lot of time and energy by asking the question "To what end?" Serious reflection allows you to see the pros and cons of whatever decision you're grappling with.

"Many people lose the small joys in the hope for the big happiness." — Pearl S. Buck

In his book, "*The 7 Habits of Highly Effective People*," Stephen Covey advised that you "Begin with the end in mind." Understand the consequences of your decisions.

Ask yourself, "To what end?" You'll save a lot of time and energy, avoid making bad decisions, hold fast to the small joys of life, and find the contentment you deserve.

Chapter Thirty-Three

How to Turn Apartness Into Your Creative Asset

Do you know what it feels like to be different or outside of a particular group?

Most of us, sooner or later, experience the feeling. Exclusion at the hands of others is never fun.

Near the end of my 7th grade school year, the private school I attended announced its closure. My father arranged for my transfer to another private school.

The new private school was exclusive and catered to well-to-do families. The first day of my 8th grade school year was disorienting and stressful.

The teachers were pleasant, but my fellow students were cliquish and unfriendly. I complained about it to my mother, who told me that kids are immature. Of course, adults can be immature, too.

"I don't really understand this. When you have so many people, each one inevitably fascinating, why would you limit yourself to only those like you?" — Jodi Picoult, Off the Page

I only knew one other boy at the school. Like me, he transferred from our old school. We lunched alone together for a few weeks, feeling like social lepers. But then he became absorbed in a small group of boys he knew from his neighborhood.

And so, I ate lunch alone.

Make the world a little less cruel and heartless

Physical education class was the worst. Team captains selected players, and I was among the dregs who were chosen last. Not because I lacked ability, just status.

One lunch break, I tried humor to break the ice. I took the plastic spoon for my peach cup and hid it under my shoe. Then I turned to a few kids lunching near me and said, "Hey, have you guys seen my contact lens? I dropped it."

The kids looked at me weirdly. Then I stood up and crunched on the spoon beneath my shoe. The kids sat speechless, staring at me for a second, and then they went back to chattering amongst themselves. Epic fail.

I decided humor was not a viable path to making new friends. So, I resigned myself to eating lunch alone.

I told my father about the failed spoon joke at school, and how I didn't like the other kids. Then I asked him what I was doing wrong.

"Just be yourself, Johnny. Don't worry about the other kids. Let the best of who you are shine," my father said.

"It's not our job to toughen our children up to face a cruel and heartless world. It's our job to raise children who will make the world a little less cruel and heartless." — L. R. Knost

Each recess and lunch, I found refuge in the library, where I enjoyed reading books and drawing cartoons in my binder. In fact, I increasingly escaped into my artwork to pass the time.

A teacher noticed my creative abilities and often chatted with me in the library. She learned that, in addition to my drawing talents, I played the piano and liked to sing. She suggested I join the cast of the school's annual holiday music production.

At first, I declined since I didn't know anyone. But somehow the teacher got me to sign up, and before I knew it, I was selected to be a dancer. My assigned partner was a lovely Iranian girl who boarded at the school.

She blushed and so did he

Thanks to the musical production rehearsals, I became friends with my dance partner and a few of the other performers. Being from Iran, my dance partner shared her own feelings of awkwardness and exclusion. We became kindred spirits.

The rest of my 8th-grade year improved. I had a few students from the musical production to hang out with, and especially my new Iranian friend.

In December, shortly before graduation, the holiday musical was held. My parents attended, and it was a big night for me. There was thunderous applause, and afterward, I introduced my dance partner to my parents.

Pictures were taken, and my new friend hugged me tightly. We chatted excitedly, sometimes finishing one another's thoughts. I remember feeling a little flutter of affection in my heart.

"She blushed and so did he. She greeted him in a faltering voice, and he spoke to her without knowing what he was saying." — *Voltaire, Candide*

I learned a lot that 8th-grade year. I stopped trying to win friends with lame jokes. I accepted my apartness and used it to focus on reading and drawing in the library. My creativity was noticed by a teacher, which led to my participating in the musical production.

If you use your apartness to hone your creative skills and unique talents, doors can open for you.

They recognized in each other "an apartness"

Most people have read the book or seen the movie *"To Kill A Mockingbird,"* by the late Harper Lee. It's a remarkable story about racial injustice and the destruction of innocence.

Harper Lee was a tomboy growing up. Many readers assumed that she patterned the novel's narrator, Jean Louise Finch (nicknamed "Scout") after herself. When asked, Lee denied this, saying she identified more with her novel's reclusive character Arthur "Boo" Radley.

Charles J. Shields is an American biographer of mid-century American novelists and writers like Harper Lee and Kurt Vonnegut. Shields wrote the following about Harper Lee:

"Harper Lee and Truman Capote became friends as next-door neighbors in the late 1920s, when they were about kindergarten age. From the start, they recognized in each other 'an apartness,' as Capote later expressed it; and both loved reading. When Lee's father gave them an old Underwood typewriter, they began writing original stories together."

Just as I found companionship in the 8th grade with an Iranian girl who shared my feelings of apartness, Harper Lee found similar solace in her friendship with Truman Capote.

Capote was ridiculed as a boy for his lisp and advanced vocabulary. He and Harper Lee loved to read. The two escaped their feelings of alienation by writing and acting out stories together.

Harper Lee and Truman Capote turned their apartness into creative escapism. Both would go on to become successful novelists. Lee's novel *"To Kill a Mockingbird"* was immediately successful, as was Capote's non-fiction novel *"In Cold Blood"* which detailed the 1959 murders of four members of the Herbert Clutter family in the small farming community of Holcomb, Kansas.

Nobody is born to blend in

When my son was little, he bounced around to a few different schools. As a result, it was difficult for him to make friends. Much like me when I was his age, he retreated to the school library to draw.

I remember worrying about him, hoping he would be spared the feelings of apartness that I felt. Hoping he'd learn that it's okay to be unique.

Fortunately, thanks to my wife's help, my son embraced reading and his creativity. His amazing drawings were appreciated by a few other boys in his school, and they became friends. My wife and I affectionately dubbed them "The Nerd Herd."

"For a really long time, I thought being different was a negative thing. But as I grew older, I started to realize we were all born to stand out; nobody is born to blend in." — Halima Aden

My son became interested in martial arts, eventually earning his black belt. Looking back, I'm glad he was not part of the popular crowd in school. As a result, he developed a strong interior life, fueled by good books and creativity.

My son is now 23 years old, completing his university computer science degree, and serving as a United States Air Force reservist. He still interacts with his old "Nerd Herd" buddies, spends time with his girlfriend, and has developed quiet confidence and self-assuredness.

Going against the grain of society

Your apartness in life doesn't mean you won't succeed or find your way. There are lots of people who are different or unconventional, yet they go on to successful careers and lives.

"I think being different, going against the grain of society is the greatest thing in the world." — Elijah Wood

Here are three tips for how to leverage your apartness.

Skill development. Harper Lee and Truman Capote knew they were unique. Instead of trying to fit in with the popular kids, they read books, fed their minds, and wrote stories together. The most popular kids at their high schools are likely forgotten today, but Lee and Capote are both famous writers.

Birds of a feather. It's often not hard to find a kindred spirit, you just have to pay attention and look around. Harper Lee and Truman Capote recognized that they were both unique. My Iranian dance partner shared my feelings of apartness at school. My son's "Nerd Herd" buddies banded together to play video games, take up archery, and overcome those awkward teen years to-gether.

Help someone else. Harper Lee traveled with and helped Tru-man Capote for several years as he researched and wrote *In Cold Blood.* I joined the Rotary Club during my law enforcement career, to help others. My son volunteers at his girlfriend's work to lend a hand. Volunteerism, and helping others, can build your confidence and enrich your life. Especially if you feel apart from others.

If you feel an apartness in your life, don't give up. Hidden in whatever makes you different may be the key to your future.

Harper Lee and Truman Capote used their apartness to read books and write stories. Their apartness became a creative asset.

My lunchtime drawing attracted a teacher, who led me to the school musical production. My son's apartness, and drawing in the school library, attracted the attention of like-minded boys, and the "Nerd Herd" was formed.

Look at your unique talents and abilities. Focus on developing your skills, find kindred spirits, and help others. Don't worry about blending in. Go against the grain of society a little, and the world will be your oyster.

Chapter Thirty-Four

Love and Sacrifice: Why the Days Are Long But the Years Are Short

Yesterday I was stuck in the service department at my local Chevy dealership, waiting for them to fix my truck's headlight. A home improvement show blared on the flat-screen TV, but everybody around me seemed hypnotized by their smartphones.

I settled into a corner chair and pulled a book from my backpack. Out of habit, I always take a book with me to appointments.

As I became absorbed in what I was reading, the shrieks of a little girl broke my concentration. Looking up, I saw a frazzled woman leading her energetic daughter to the available chairs across from me.

The woman looked tired. She was on her phone speaking to someone about a rent problem, daycare issues, and her work. She collapsed into the chair and let her daughter distract herself at an adjacent table of magazines.

The woman finished her phone conversation, leaned back, and sighed. I lowered my book and saw the little girl grinning at me.

Every cliche about kids is true

I glanced at the mother, who then looked my way. I smiled and said, "Mine's 22-years-old now. He's bigger and taller than me. I don't know what happened. I guess it's because we kept feeding him."

The woman giggled and said, "Well, this one can put away the mac 'n' cheese, that's for sure."

"Yeah, they love any kind of food that's orange in color," I said.

The woman looked at her daughter and said, "Sweetie, don't chew on that magazine, you don't know where it's been." Then she looked back at me, shaking her head.

"I feel for you," I said. "I remember trying to juggle everything with my son. Appointments. Park visits. The birthday parties and parent/teacher conferences."

"It's exhausting," she said.

"Yeah, it is. But someone once told me something about raising kids that I never forgot," I said with a smile.

She leaned over a little. "What's that?"

"The days are long, but the years are short."

She sat there a few seconds, processing what I said. Then she smiled and said, "Yeah, I like that, cause it's true, right?"

"Absolutely," I said. "There were times I barely got through the day. Occasionally I was impatient. Or exhausted. I remember falling asleep at home with my son when we were watching *Toy Story*. But looking back, the years flew by. And now I miss it."

"When your son was little?" she asked.

"Yeah, when he was a little devil, dragging me to the park. Picking up his spilled cheerios. Burying his dead hamster. You miss the toys, the laughter, the discoveries. There's a lot of magic in childhood."

"Every cliche about kids is true; they grow up so quickly, you blink and they're gone, and you have to spend the time with them now. But that's a joy." — Liam Neeson

We both sat there a few moments watching her daughter. Then I softly said it again. "The days are long, but the years are short."

Nobility of character

It wasn't long after our chat that the service manager approached the woman to tell her that her vehicle was ready.

The woman seemed a little less frazzled now. Maybe my piece of wisdom was helpful. She picked up her daughter, purse, and paperwork.

"Tonight you, me, and Daddy will have some of that ice cream we got," she said to her daughter. The little girl squealed with delight.

"To be a good father and mother requires that the parents defer many of their own needs and desires in favor of the needs of their children. As a consequence of this sacrifice, conscientious parents develop a nobility of character and learn to put into practice the selfless truths taught by the Savior Himself."— James E. Faust

The woman turned back to me, before walking away. She smiled and said, "Thank you."

"You're welcome," I said with a wave. The truth is, I think our little interaction helped me more than her. Because it took me back to those early days with my son.

Back to all the joys and hopes and stations of life. From potty training and braces to martial arts classes and high school graduation.

There's a poignant song and video by the country music singer Trace Adkins titled *"Then They Do."* It reflects on how raising kids can wear us out. We think about how nice it will be when they grow up. And then they do.

If you want to be a good parent, then the days will be long. Because you sacrifice for your kids. You put yourself second. You place virtue above your own wants and needs.

Being a good parent is certainly a worthy goal. Good parents usually raise good children, which benefits society.

But what if you want to be more than a good parent? What if you want to be a good person, too?

To find peace with ourselves

Society is fixated on happiness. A great deal of self-help and personal development content focuses on finding happiness. The things that supposedly bring us happiness are good looks, wealth, and fame. But do they?

Why is it that so many Hollywood stars self-destruct with divorces, drugs, and alcohol? The following quote by the actor Jim Carrey has probably become stale from overuse, but it's still worth considering:

"I think everybody should get rich and famous and do everything they ever dreamed of so they can see that it's not the answer."

Why is it that, for many people, once they achieve their dream or career pinnacle, they find they're not happy? TEDx speaker and marketing expert Leonard Kim, in a blog post responding to the above Jim Carrey quote, wrote:

"What I found to be a healthy alternative to the answer of all our dreams is to become happy with who we are. To live in the moment. To stop worrying about the future or living in the past. To shed ourselves of our expectations, both of ourselves and others. To forgive the ones who wronged us, most importantly ourselves. To find peace with ourselves. Then, most importantly, to think of all the things we are grateful for and blessed to have in our lives, even as simple as the roofs over our heads, or even the ability to breathe in fresh air."

Author David Brooks, in his book *"The Second Mountain: The Quest for a Moral Life,"* explores how the struggle for personal advancement only brings temporary happiness.

People reach the top of their first mountain (i.e., professional career), look around, and find they're unsatisfied. They ask themselves, "Is this all there is?"

And so, they climb down the mountain and begin searching for their second mountain. As the Amazon.com intro to Brooks' book explains:

"And so they embark on a new journey. On the second mountain, life moves from self-centered to other-centered. They want the things that are truly worth wanting, not the things other people tell them to want. They embrace a life of interdependence, not independence. They surrender to a life of commitment."

The second mountain is about finding deeper meaning in your life. Becoming "other-centered" instead of "self-centered." One way to do this is by pursuing virtue in your life.

In other words, learning to become a good person.

We've damaged our souls

If we live our lives with virtue, then we strive to do the right thing, like sacrificing for our kids. We don't hurt others to get ahead. We live by the Golden Rule.

We understand that success and happiness wrought from unvirtuous behavior is a kind of Pyrrhic victory. We think we've won when really, we've damaged our souls.

"There is but one rule of conduct for a man: to do the right thing. The cost may be dear in money, in friends, in influence, in labor, in a prolonged and painful sacrifice; but the cost not to do right is far more dear: you pay in the integrity of your manhood, in honor, in truth, in character. You forfeit your soul's content and for a timely gain, you barter the infinities." — Lucius H. Bugbee

In today's society, happiness has become our god at the expense of virtue. We see it everywhere. The university admissions scandal. The recent West Point and Dartmouth cheating scandals.

In the end, the cheaters are only cheating themselves. If we fail to put in the hard work, we deny ourselves the knowledge and experience that comes with it.

When we do the right thing, it may take longer to reach certain goals. But we protect our character. We reach our second mountain faster.

My conversation with the woman in the Chevy dealership was all about raising kids. How the days are long, but the years are short. But it was also about love and sacrifice. About doing the right thing. Living with virtue.

Don't be afraid to love and sacrifice in your life. Accept that sometimes the days will be long, and the years will be short. Don't put happiness above virtue. Keep an eye on your second mountain. Do these things, and you will be at peace with yourself, and inspire others.

Chapter Thirty-Five

How One Act of Kindness Can Rekindle a Loved One's Memory

On the morning of May 6th, my iPhone buzzed on the nightstand, awakening me. I fumbled for my reading glasses, sat up, and looked at the glowing screen.

It was a calendar reminder, with the words, "Dad's birthday." I leaned back on my pillow, slid off my glasses, and closed my eyes.

Dad passed away in 2004 at the age of 83. I was with him the day he died, holding his hands. He was unconscious, but the hospice nurse said he could still hear me.

"A couple of years before he died, I kissed my father goodbye. He said, 'Son, you haven't kissed me since you were a little boy.' It went straight to my heart, and I kissed him whenever I saw him after that, and my sons and I always kiss whenever we meet."— *Terry Wogan*

I spoke softly in Dad's ear, reminiscing about the past, family vacations, and how well everyone was doing. And then I said,

"Dad if you're tired, rest. Sleep. You've earned it. We'll all be fine. We love you."

Two hours later my father slipped away.

A tree is known by its fruit

My father was an administrative law judge, former United States Marine, bibliophile, intellectual, and an imposing figure. He stood six feet tall and weighed over 200 lbs.

Dad had a kind of magnetic presence and authority when he walked into a room. He could be driven and purposeful, but beneath all of this was a gentle and kind man.

Dad was always helping people, especially the elderly. There was the homeless man named Mr. Strollo, who was hit by a car. Dad witnessed the accident, brought Mr. Strollo home to recuperate, and helped with his legal representation.

Another time Dad rescued a stranded family whose car broke down on the freeway. He brought them home to dinner, found them lodging for the night, and took them to the garage the next day.

"A tree is known by its fruit; a man by his deeds. A good deed is never lost; he who sows courtesy reaps friendship, and he who plants kindness gathers love."— Saint Basil

This is the gift of good fathers because their children pay attention to actions more than words. Dad's endless examples of love and kindness to strangers rubbed off on me. It's partly why I became a police officer.

Do your little bit of good

It occurred to me that this May 6th would have been Dad's 100th birthday. How I wish he was still with us.

Later in the morning, in my office, I held a framed picture of my father. I could see my smiling reflection in the glass of the photo as if I was a ghost happily greeting him. I took a photo of the picture and texted it to my sister.

My text read, "Dad's 100th birthday today! Hard to believe. Hope you have a great day!" I like to leave my sister encouraging messages, and she does the same for me. Perhaps we're emulating a little bit of the good that Dad taught us.

"Do your little bit of good where you are; it's those little bits of good put together that overwhelm the world." — Desmond Tutu

My sister was at work and later tried to call me, but I had taken my wife to a doctor's appointment and was unable to answer her call. My wife is recovering from breast cancer surgery, and I attend all her appointments.

After the doctor's visit, my wife and I went to lunch at a nearby Mexican restaurant. My wife's recovery is going well, and she celebrated with a pineapple margarita.

Behind us, the hostess seated two cheerful, middle-aged women. One of the women was carrying a brightly decorated gift bag with the words "Happy Birthday!" written on it.

The brightly decorated bag reminded me of a special little girl I saw years ago in a different restaurant, while away with friends on vacation.

Their echoes are truly endless

The restaurant was in a lovely setting along the California coast. My friends and I were staying in the area and decided to enjoy some fine dining together.

It was a higher-end restaurant, where the food and service were impeccable. Everyone at our table was laughing, enjoying the hors d'oeuvres, cocktails, and conversation.

I noticed a young family entering the dining room. A father, mother, and approximately ten-year-old girl in a pediatric wheelchair.

The little girl was wearing a beautiful dress with a frilly collar and brightly colored bows in her hair. She had big, expressive eyes.

The little girl was moving her arms and head somewhat uncontrollably, leading me to believe she might have cerebral palsy. I tried not to stare, but what attracted my attention was not the girl's movements, but the mother's loving attention.

I continued enjoying dinner with my friends but couldn't help but admire the way the young mother helped her daughter with her meal, her sippy cup, and discretely wiping her mouth.

Now and then, the mother would whisper something in her daughter's ears, and the daughter would burst out laughing. So much so other diners would crane their necks to see what was going on.

Something about the whole scene moved me. It must be hard to take a special needs child into a fine dining restaurant and attend to her while trying to enjoy your dinner and drinks. Especially while people are staring.

I wished people would have stood up, said a toast of admiration for the mother and daughter, and then burst into applause. But then I got an idea. I slipped out a piece of notepaper and wrote the following note:

Please forgive my anonymous intrusion. You have a beautiful daughter, and the way the two of you interact reflects the kind of love all families should celebrate. Thank you for showing the rest of us what a remarkable mother looks like, and for inspiring me to be the best father I can be.

As my friends and I got ready to leave, I ordered an ice cream dessert and asked our server to deliver it to the beautiful family with the little girl. And I asked that the server include my note.

"Kind words can be short and easy to speak but their echoes are truly endless." — Mother Teresa

I was outside the restaurant when the ice cream and note arrived for the family, but I caught the mother's reaction. She opened the note, then put her hand up to her mouth. She looked around the restaurant and then handed the note to her husband.

I could tell she was crying, and her husband was smiling. Then the mother leaned over, kissed, and hugged her little girl.

Dad always told me that acts of kindness should expect no reward, but I admit I felt good inside. Like I found a way to shine a little grace in that family's life.

You are making the world

Fast forward to the Mexican restaurant, and the women with the birthday bag. When we finished our meal, I quietly asked our server if I could pick up the bill for the women dining next to us. "Don't tell them until after we're gone," I said. Our server smiled and obliged me.

As my wife and I got up to leave, I asked the dining women, "So whose birthday is it?" and one of them said, "It's mine."

"Well happy birthday!" I said. "Today would have been my father's 100th birthday. He was a kind man. If he were here, he'd probably buy you lunch."

The women laughed and said, "Well thank you."

This time there was no outside window to see the reaction of the women when the server told them their meal was paid for, but that's okay.

It was really a birthday gift for my father. To honor his legacy of kindness. To let him know his son learned well.

And if I'm honest, maybe it was a little gift to myself. Because this act of kindness, on my father's 100th birthday, rekindled the memory of Dad. It was like I felt a bit of his spirit.

"Every minute of every hour of every day you are making the world, just as you are making yourself, and you might as well do it with generosity and kindness and style."— Rebecca Solnit

Sharing random acts of love and kindness with strangers fills your soul with peace. It brightens people's lives. Gives them hope. It's a great way to honor loved ones who taught you well and keep their memory burning bright in your soul.

Chapter Thirty-Six

The Flower of Your Life Will Wither Without Care

The deer trail was slightly overgrown, and I had to navigate past a thicket of poison oak and huge webs from orb-weaver spiders. When you're an adventurous kid, it's amazing the things you'll tolerate outdoors.

The backyard of our home in the hills of Los Gatos, California, opened to the deep woods. Entering this shadowy world beneath the tree foliage felt like leaving the wardrobe into magical Narnia.

"One day, you will be old enough to start reading fairytales again."
— C.S. Lewis, The Chronicles of Narnia

As a ten-year-old boy, I knew little of the challenges and turmoil of adult life. My world was family, school, friends, drawing, and the magic of the woods. I loved to discover new trails and stand still as deer grazed in the nearby grass.

My deer trail adventure through the woods led to a grassy clearing, where a dilapidated greenhouse greeted me. The remote property lacked any "No trespassing" signs, and curiosity got the best of me.

It had not yet surrendered its dignity

The exterior of the structure appeared to be molting layers of green, cracked, peeling paint. Many of the glass windows were missing or shattered in their tired, rustic panes.

Weeds licked at the base of the structure, and meandering vines consumed portions of the walls. Just like the wrinkled skin and protruding veins of elderly people, the splintered exterior of the greenhouse exposed its advanced years.

Still, for a young boy exploring, the greenhouse held its charms and mysteries. It may have been old, but it had not yet surrendered its dignity.

"One's dignity may be assaulted, vandalized and cruelly mocked, but cannot be taken away unless it is surrendered." — Michael J. Fox

I stepped inside, spying rows of terra cotta pots that held desiccated remnants of long-neglected plants. What a splendor they must have been in their day, brightening the interior with the kind of soft cheer only flowers possess.

A nearby worktable, rickety but still upright, held a half-empty wine bottle beside two dusty glasses. Perhaps there was more rainwater than wine left in the bottle.

I imagined someone preparing to enjoy the wine but being called away. Perhaps to attend to a child or other adult responsibility.

And then I wondered why they never came back? Why did they abandon the wine and the greenhouse?

Only the forgotten are truly dead

There were a few old magazines strewn about, their covers faded from sun exposure. Miscellaneous gardening tools and a tipped-over wheelbarrow cluttered one corner.

And then I saw it. An old, French easel, with a dried-out palette and brushes beside it on a workbench. There were a few faded canvasses, with nearly phantom marks of incomplete floral studies. A coffee can and an empty turpentine bottle lay nearby.

I imagined that an old woman used to visit the greenhouse to garden, paint, and escape the burdens of life.

Or maybe it was an elderly gentleman, who found the solitude of the greenhouse a perfect environment to fuel his creative passion?

I stood very still in the Greenhouse. There was a slight breeze and the late afternoon light told me I should get home soon. I felt like the Greenhouse was melancholy but happy for my visit. Like it no longer felt forgotten.

"Only the forgotten are truly dead." — Tess Gerritsen, The Sinner

Each breeze felt like a whisper, or perhaps a prayer, that some-day life would return to this forgotten place of refuge, beauty, and art. Most people tell you that buildings are inanimate objects, but I'm not so sure. Maybe they have their own souls? Perhaps they miss us when we leave them?

Keep alive the dream in the heart

In our home, my father had a beautifully framed excerpt from the author and theologian Howard Thurman's *"Keep Alive the Dream in the Heart."* It opens thusly:

"As long as a man has a dream in his heart, he cannot lose the significance of living. It is part of the pretensions of modern life to traffic in what is generally called 'realism.' There is much insistence upon being practical, down to earth. Such things as dreams are wont to be regarded as romantic or as a badge of immaturity, or as escape hatches for the spirit."

What dreams of the heart led to the construction of that old greenhouse? Someone who valued plants, art, solitude, and maybe the conviviality of wine, built that place.

I'll bet they returned to the greenhouse often. Because they knew that we have needs beyond money and status. They understood that our hearts and spirits require tending. The flower of our lives will wither without care.

All the sadder, I felt, that the greenhouse was now in disrepair and seemingly forgotten. If we abandon the things that nourish us, our lives suffer. We need our beautiful places, hopes, and dreams.

As Howard Thurman's *"Keep Alive the Dream in the Heart"* notes:

"Men cannot continue long to live if the dream in the heart has perished. It is then that they stop hoping, stop looking, and the last embers of their anticipations fade away."

Hold fast to dreams

As luck would have it, I found myself a few years later trudging through the woods behind our home. There was a neighbor girl who caught my fancy, and her family invited me to a pool party.

The deer trails were now overgrown, and I nearly got lost. But then I found the clearing, and there was the old greenhouse. It was still in sad shape, but I caught a glimpse of movement from within.

Moving closer, I crouched by an oak tree to get a better look. There was a woman inside the greenhouse, painting on the French easel. A few healthy- looking plants and colorful flowers populated several of the terra cotta pots.

Then I heard a child laugh, and the woman lifted a little boy and sat him on the worktable beside her. They spoke to one another, but I couldn't make out what they said.

It made me happy to think that the woman returned to the greenhouse. To tend to the flowers in her life and share the joy with her child. To rekindle what dreams still smoldered in her heart.

"Hold fast to dreams For when dreams go Life is a barren field Frozen with snow." — *Langston Hughes*

As I quietly made my way past the greenhouse, I could hear their laughter in the distance. Maybe it was the afternoon breeze, but I'd swear I heard the greenhouse let out a sigh of happiness.

How about you? Have you neglected the greenhouse in your life? Have you forgotten your dreams? Have you lost the significance of living?

It's never too late to go back. Your greenhouse is patiently waiting. Yearning to bring joy back into your life, so that the flowers in your soul will never wither.

Chapter Thirty-Seven

Why Grace Is Found in the Mundane

My mother was a Parkinson's patient. Her tremors made it difficult to eat, and she was unable to walk.

As she aged, Mom needed to go to doctor appointments more frequently. Fortunately, she lived in the same town where I worked, and I was able to take her to appointments.

Getting Mom to the doctor was a production. I had to take time off work because the whole affair was time-consuming.

I'd arrive at her apartment in the assisted living center and help her into her wheelchair. We'd stroll down the long corridors to the parking lot, where I lifted her up and into my vehicle.

Then I would wrestle with her wheelchair until it was folded up and in the back of my Dodge Durango. Next, I'd strap her seatbelt on. This always resulted in Mom's perfume rubbing off on my suit, which stayed with me the rest of the day.

Mom was a chatty person, and she talked non-stop from the moment I picked her up, throughout her appointments, until I dropped her off back at her apartment.

Mom's hearing declined, so she tended to talk loudly, especially in waiting rooms. It was impossible to have a quiet, private conversation.

"I hate the waiting room. Because it's called the waiting room, there's no chance of not waiting. It's built, designed, and intended for waiting. Why would they take you right away when they've got this room all set up?"— Jerry Seinfeld

I remember some days when I loathed the thought of taking my mom to another appointment because the process was exhausting.

I complained about it to a coworker one day, and she said something life-changing:

"Why don't you use those appointments as a chance to get to know your mom better?"

The suggestion made a lot of sense. I used to bring work-related paperwork to my mom's appointments. Other times I'd bring a book or try to respond to emails on my phone. All of it was futile because Mom wanted to talk.

I would always chat with Mom, but I never thought about using this precious time with her more wisely. Why not take my coworker's advice, and get to know Mom better?

The invisible woman

It wasn't long before I found myself in another waiting room with Mom. It was the dentist's office. But this time I brought no books or paperwork. Instead, I brought questions.

"How did you and Dad meet?" I asked Mom.

"It was on a train in New York. Your father was working on Wall Street, and I was a young model at Barbizon," she began. And for the rest of our visit and the ride home, I listened to the history of my parents.

Thus began a new period in life when I got to know my mother better. I took advantage of the time together at appointments to ask questions and hear her stories.

We spoke about aging. Mom acknowledged the difficulties of growing old, especially for a woman who was once a beautiful, professional model.

When she was young, she turned the heads of young men. "You lose that with wrinkles and aging. People stop paying attention to you," she once told me.

Her comments echoed an article in *The Atlantic* by Akiko Busch. An excerpt:

"The invisible woman might be the actor no longer offered roles after her 40th birthday, the 50-year-old woman who can't land a job interview, or the widow who finds her dinner invitations declining with the absence of her husband. She is the woman who finds that she is no longer the object of the male gaze — youth faded, childbearing years behind her, social value diminished. Referring to her anticipated disappearance on her upcoming 50th birthday, the writer Ayelet Waldman said to an interviewer, 'I have a big personality, and I have a certain level of professional competence, and I'm used to being taken seriously professionally. And suddenly, it's like I just vanished from the room. And I have to yell so much louder to be seen … I just want to walk down the street and have someone notice that I exist.'"

The thing is, Mom was anything but invisible. She never lost her sense of fashion and style, and she was famous for colorful outfits and loads of decadent jewelry. Most of all, her upbeat personality and sense of humor charmed everyone.

Beauty in the mundane

Photographer Anthony Epes wrote an article in Petapixel.com about finding beauty in the mundane. He defines mundane as "the everyday, ordinary, or banal."

Epes explains that *"it's easy to take amazing shots of amazingly beautiful places. Although we can always do something fresh, or unique or interesting with our subjects, you're bound to get something awesome with, for example, a great location and a great sky."*

Then Epes adds:

"But to create something beautiful, or find beauty in the mundane? That's a skill that is fantastic to have and one that's worth developing because it will help your photography as a whole."

The same is true with how we approach the mundane appointments and waiting rooms of life. There is beauty to be found there if we use our time wisely.

Some of the most enjoyable and informative conversations I've had occurred in waiting rooms. I remember encouraging a woman in the Veterinarian's office once, and it led to a wonderful conversation.

Most importantly, it was my mother's seemingly mundane doctor and dentist appointments that helped me know her better. Sometimes she'd tell stories and our laughter became infectious.

One woman in the waiting room said with a smile, "You two are having a lot more fun than the rest of us." Soon we roped the woman into our conversation, and she shared a few of her own memories.

We forget the big picture

Most of the people I see in waiting rooms are either glued to their cell phones or mesmerized by the superficial daytime programs on the television.

I used to be embarrassed by Mom's loud talking in waiting rooms, but I grew to love it as a counterbalance to the TV noise. Also, it showed others that meaningful conversation is a better choice than mindless scrolling on one's cell phone.

"Sometimes you have to disconnect to stay connected. Remember the old days when you had eye contact during a conversation? When everyone wasn't looking down at a device in their hands? We've become so focused on that tiny screen that we forget the big picture, the people right in front of us."

— *Regina Brett*

"Why don't people put away their cell phones, shut off the TV, and talk to one another?" I used to think. Everyone is a walking history book, with stories and lessons to offer.

But instead, we languish in silence, denying ourselves the enrichment that strangers with adventures and anecdotes can share. Or we accompany loved ones to appointments and then ignore them as we wait.

There is grace to be found in the mundane. Waiting rooms only hold us captive if we fail to take advantage of the downtime.

What better place than a waiting room to learn more deeply about the ones we love. Or to engage a stranger, and maybe learn a new life lesson.

A partisan for conversation

At the age of 87, my mother's body finally decided it had enough. The day she died, I was blessed to be with her. Holding her hands. Stroking her hair. Telling her how much she was loved. She slipped away peacefully.

Thank God I listened to my coworker's advice and used all those doctor and dentist appointments to get to know my mother better. Now I have so many cherished stories and memories.

Of course, good conversation is available outside of mundane appointments. It's just a matter of making room for *them.*

"I am a partisan for conversation. To make room for it, I see some first, deliberate steps. At home, we can create sacred spaces: the kitchen, the dining room. We can make our cars 'device-free zones.' We can demonstrate the value of conversation to our children. And we can do the same thing at work."— Sherry Turkle

There is grace to be found in those mundane appointments and waiting rooms. Take advantage of the opportunity.

If you're with a loved one, ask questions and then listen intently. If you engage a stranger, do the same thing.

You might just discover a little bit of magic, make some new memories, and be forever thankful that you spent your time so wisely.

Chapter Thirty-Eight

What a Little Soul Taught Me About Being Grateful

I'm allergic to cats. They make me sneeze and wheeze. The problem is something called Fel d 1, which is a glycoprotein produced by salivary and sebaceous glands in cats.

When my wife Nicole and I first met and began dating, I was introduced to her loyal cat. His name was Einstein, and she raised him from a kitten. The two of them were a package deal.

I had an ex-wife and a young son. All Nicole had was a cat. She used to joke that I came to the relationship with baggage, whereas she only had carry-on.

I fell in love with Nicole, and despite a few visits to my allergist, I grew to love Einstein, too. We enjoyed Einstein for many years before old age and illness claimed our purring friend.

The loss was hard on Nicole. She and Einstein had been through a lot together. She swore off getting another cat since she could never replace the special bond she had with Einstein.

There was a palpable absence in the house. We missed his little chatter and the way his spirit seemed to bring warmth to any room.

"I love cats because I enjoy my home; and little by little, they become its visible soul." -Jean Cocteau

I loved Einstein, but the selfish side of me wouldn't miss the sneezing and allergy medications. Before long I was breathing easier, and life marched forward.

Mine had me trained in two days

In 2016, I retired early from my law enforcement career to pursue writing and artwork full-time. We moved from California to Nevada, since my son chose the University of Nevada, Las Vegas to pursue his computer science degree.

A few years passed. We enjoyed the company of our two dogs but came to realize that we missed the Zen-like presence of a cat in our home. Call me a glutton for punishment.

We tried several times to find a rescue cat who would tolerate our dogs. I made several visits to the SPCA. I brought one cat home, but she was scared to death of our dogs, hid under our bed, and tended to bite.

Nicole loved the size and beauty of Maine Coon cats and found a breeder who had an adorable grey kitten available. It had to be a grey kitten since Einstein was grey in color.

Before long, we were the proud companions of a Maine Coon kitten. I say "companions" because you don't own a cat, the cat owns you.

We named our new kitten "Skye" and wasted no time adding scratch bars and cat towers for Skye to play on. He had his own toy box filled with bells, balls, and assorted toy mice.

It wasn't long before Skye was running the show. He enjoyed tormenting the dogs, batting them in their muzzles, and playing with their tails.

"I had been told that the training procedure with cats was difficult. It's not. Mine had me trained in two days."-Bill Dana

Skye had me trained to pour him a spoonful of fresh, heavy cream every morning. And sometimes in the evenings, too.

You'll miss the scenery

My law enforcement career was demanding, and I was away from home a lot. Especially the last ten years of my career, when I was chief of police. Most of my interaction with Einstein was in the evenings, and a little bit on the weekends.

It was different with Skye. Working from home every day in my studio office, Skye became my constant companion. He liked to sit or nap on my desk. Sometimes he'd play with the typewriter keys or knock my fountain pen on the floor.

I began to think of him as my editor and creative confidante. I had conversations with Skye. He often chattered back. But mostly he'd give me a steady, knowing gaze.

As I labored over articles, artwork, and self-imposed deadlines, Skye would look up at me with such inner peace. His sweet eyes seemed to be saying:

"Why are you so ambitious? Why don't you slow down? You might reach your destination faster, but you'll miss the scenery. The small moments. The splendid quietude of being present in the moment. Here, watch me. I'll show you."

And then he would curl up in a ball and fall asleep.

Expressions of love

Nicole used to joke that Skye became my cat because we spent so much time together. But the truth is, I spoiled the hell out of that cat. So, he knew I was an easy mark.

I bought Skye the best, heavy cream I could find. I carried him around in the backyard, so he could sight-see. I'd take breaks to play with him.

But it was Nicole who did the hard work of grooming Skye. His long hair was prone to matting, and his nails needed to be clipped.

Skye would mildly protest these grooming sessions, but soon he was purring in Nicole's arms. They often enjoyed the early mornings together.

"I have felt cats rubbing their faces against mine and touching my cheek with claws carefully sheathed. These things, to me, are expressions of love." -James Herriot

Skye was not really a lap cat, but he sometimes melted into Nicole's lap. Once, he even gently caressed Nicole's face. I recorded the touching moment on my iPhone.

Nothing to get excited about

Skye knew how to live. He took luxurious naps. He played with the dogs. He alerted us when he wanted his dinner. He waited for Nicole to finish her popsicle so he could play with the wooden stick.

Skye loved to bang on our bedroom door and almost learned how to open the handle. I nick-named Skye "Kitty Kitty Bang Bang."

"Having a bunch of cats around is good. If you're feeling bad, you just look at the cats, you'll feel better because they know that everything is just as it is. There's nothing to get excited about. They just know. They're saviours."-Charles Bukowski

Skye loved to watch birds on his special mat in the "catio." He seemed to be reminding me that there's more to life than ambition and working. One must smell the roses and make time for nature.

The most precious thing there is

Skye came to us with a strange little cough, and during a vet visit, it was discovered that his heart was a bit enlarged. On those rare occasions that he ran through the house, he wheezed a little.

Skye seemed to prefer relaxation, staring out the windows, and deep thought over-exercise.

The biggest lesson I learned from Skye is that happiness and joy reside in the quietude of life. Those easy evenings with family on the couch. The silent mornings on the patio, sipping coffee and watching the hummingbirds and verdins. Or feeling the sunshine on our face in the garden.

It's when we stop aspiring, striving, worrying, and competing that we begin to slow down and settle into the present. Into the divine comfort of the moment.

"Time isn't precious at all, because it is an illusion. What you perceive as precious is not time but the one point that is out of time: the Now. That is precious indeed. The more you are focused on time — past and future — the more you miss the Now, the most precious thing there is." — Eckhart Tolle, The Power of Now: A Guide to Spiritual Enlightenment

The other thing that Skye taught me was to be grateful. To appreciate our health, family, comforts, and all that we have. His little soul was utterly true and uncomplicated. No pretense, just love of life, family, and the simplicity of daily living.

"I have lived with several Zen masters — all of them cats." — Eckhart Tolle, The Power of Now: A Guide to Spiritual Enlightenment

I think Einstein had the same lessons for me, but back then I was immersed in my professional work and too self-consumed to listen. Too busy being ambitious.

Maybe Einstein used divine clairvoyance to conspire with Skye and teach me to slow down, live in the present more, and stop endlessly racing with my creative ambitions.

Because it can all be over in an instant.

What dies inside us

On a Monday evening, Skye jumped on the kitchen counter, sauntered over, and gently head-butted me. His way of requesting a spoonful of heavy cream, which I promptly accommodated. Satisfied, he chirped his familiar trill and wandered off.

Later, my son urgently called us from his room. "It's Skye," he yelled, "he's not moving!"

Nicole and I raced into the bedroom to find Skye lying on the floor, unresponsive, his eyes open and fixed. Nicole listened and could hear a faint heartbeat. We scooped him up and raced to the veterinarian's office.

Maine Coon's are known to have cardiac issues. Sometimes, their enlarged hearts simply stop, and when they do, they break our hearts.

The veterinarian was unable to do anything. After only one amazing year of joyful companionship, Skye slipped away.

I have enjoyed and lost other animals in my life, but none have left such a profound sense of loss. Skye was very special to me.

"Death is not the greatest loss in life. The greatest loss is what dies inside us while we live." -Norman Cousins

I see and hear Skye's ghost all the time. His paw poking under the bathroom door. A faint meow from the washroom. A feline shadow disappearing under the furniture.

It's remarkable how much Skye's sweet little soul touched our hearts, and I don't believe I'll ever get over his loss.

But I'm also deeply grateful. Grateful that we had such a joyful, loving year with our furry Zen master. Grateful to find happiness and joy in the quietude of life. Grateful to be reminded that family and love are what matter most.

For such a little soul, Skye, you taught us a great deal. We miss you terribly, but we are grateful you came into our lives, and we will love you in this life and the next.

Rest in peace, Kitty Kitty Bang Bang. Rest in peace.

Chapter Thirty-Nine

This Is How Ghosts Make You Sick

Sometimes I spot a flock of birds, departing in mass from the branches of a barren winter tree. It always feels like a sad event to me.

Where once the birds seemed to provide warmth and company to the tree, now they are gone. Like departing souls of those we have loved and lost.

The branches, stripped of their leaves, are abandoned and alone now. Not unlike people, still of sound mind and limbs, but devoid of warmth and color.

Trees need only wait until Spring, and their leaves return. So do the birds, to build nests and begin life anew.

The question is whether we can wait until Spring, after the birds have flown from our souls. After the hardships and loss of loved ones, can we endure the winter long enough for the promise of Spring, with its gifts of renewal and hope?

The answer is yes, we can make it to Spring. We may miss the birds who have flown away, but to carry on, we must make peace with their ghosts.

Fighting epic personal battles

A few years back, the Irish philosopher Peter Rollins was a guest on Pete Holmes's *"You Make It Weird"* podcast. In their illuminating conversation, Rollins talked about ghosts.

Rollins defined ghosts as *"a presence of an absence. The echo of something gone."* He said that we are all haunted houses. And then he shared the following wisdom:

"We are all full of ghosts. People that we've hurt and people we have loved and people we have lost. And all of these things are in us. And we've got two options. We either push them down and try to forget about them and drink and party or we make peace with our ghosts. For me the option for having a full life is to make peace with our ghosts."

In an interview in Dumbo Feather magazine, Rollins notes:

"If you randomly picked someone on the street and asked about their life, you would realise they were fighting epic personal battles. Everyone, in different ways, has fought battles and confronted traumas of various kinds. Even people whose lives have been relatively peaceful have struggled and suffered. It's amazing that we can get anything done when we realise that."

The trick to dealing with our ghosts is to face them. It's easier to run, deny, or hide from uncomfortable things in our lives, but they never go away. In fact, when we ignore the ghosts, they tend to make us sick.

Rollins explains:

"We don't really realise it, but then we have an outburst of anger for no reason, we burst into tears over some stupid film on television. Or we have migraines, bad backs, fatigue. We go to the doctor's thinking it's just a bad back! 'Can you fix me?' But they can't find anything wrong, because sometimes your bad back is telling you something else. It's telling you that you're not looking at something, that you're running from something. That you're not wrestling with your ghosts and making peace with them."

The little sparks

In the interview, Rollins mentions his reading of Simone Weil. Weil was a French philosopher, mystic, political activist, and author. Her book *Gravity and Grace* is a collection of her writings, exploring the topics of affliction, politics, love, and more.

She describes the world of gravity as the world of physical laws and internal laws. She explores violence, war, and suffering. But then she talks about grace, and how we cultivate it.

Gravity reflects the weight of the world, and the pressures bearing down on your shoulders. Your worries, concerns, and regrets.

Grace reflects love and hope. It's the bright spot in your life. Your ghosts tend to keep you in the darkness, and it's your job to open the windows. Let the light shine in. Feel the fresh breeze on your face.

Receiving and giving grace in this world warms your heart. It helps you to vanquish the ghosts in your life. It reminds you that the past doesn't define the future.

Peter Rollins defines grace as:

"The little sparks, the little explosions within the world of gravity that invite us to repay war with peace, fire with water, hatred with love."

The infinite call of the other

If we slow down and pay attention, there is grace all around us. It's when you get a letter from a long-lost friend, out of the blue. Or a child hands you a flower. Or someone helps an elderly woman carry her groceries.

Rollins calls these moments of grace "the infinite call of the other." And it's up to us to respond to those calls and pay it forward.

It may be the lonely woman sitting across from you on the bus. Or the weary cashier in your local grocery store. If we are truly our brother's keeper, then why not commit little acts of grace to lift their spirits?

Taking the time to ask how someone is doing, visiting an elderly person, or simply smiling and thanking a service person, all spread grace in this world. Such acts help you make peace with your ghosts. They help fasten you to the present, turn your focus to others, and reduce worry about the past.

We are condemned to freedom

Jean-Paul Sarte once said, *"We are condemned to freedom."* As Rollins explains in the Dumbo Feather article:

"You have to take responsibility for what you do or don't do. And no one will tell you exactly what the best way is to respond to your neighbour. You do it in fear and trembling. Cause none of us — whether we go to our religious tradition or to a fortune teller or tarot cards or a horoscope — can escape the responsibility for what we do."

We are always in a battle between gravity and grace. Between the hardships and indignities of daily living versus those moments when the light shines down upon us.

If we are to defeat the ghosts in our personal haunted house, then we can't settle for passivity. Doing nothing changes nothing. We must do the work of confronting our ghosts. Making peace with them.

How do we do that? For some, professional therapy may be the first step. For others, we can start taking better care of ourselves. We can forgive ourselves for past mistakes. We can forgive the ones who hurt us, too. There is grace in forgiveness.

Living in the past won't move us forward. Worrying about the future doesn't help much either. These are the places where ghosts lay in wait, ready to dispense stress and illness.

Start living in the present more. Help others. Embrace the grace found in daily living. The company of your partner. The joy of your children. The smiles found upon the faces of strangers.

This is how we win the battle between gravity and grace. This is how we release the ghosts in our haunted house. In this way, we can live again and spread some grace in the world.

Chapter Forty

Do You Know What Kills More Dreams Than Failure?

Microsoft founder Bill Gates once gave a speech in Beijing, China. A boy named Jia Jiang listened to the speech and was impressed. So much so that he wrote down a plan to become a successful entrepreneur. He even planned to buy the entire Microsoft company someday.

Dreams don't always work out as planned. Jiang and his family emigrated to the United States when he was 16 years old. He ended up working in the marketing department of a company. He was unhappy in his work and still wanted to become a successful entrepreneur.

Jiang left his corporate job and embarked on his entrepreneurial dream. Unfortunately, his first efforts ended in rejection. But he realized that worrying about rejection was a bigger obstacle than rejection itself.

Jiang decided that he needed to find a way to cope with rejection without letting it destroy him. He came up with a "100 days of rejections" experiment, which he filmed and chronicled on his website.

Why not?

Jiang's crazy experiments included asking for a "refill burger" much like people ask for a soda refill (he was denied). He knocked on a stranger's door and asked if he could plant some flowers in their back yard. When the person said no, Jiang asked "Why not?"

The person said the dog would destroy the flowers, but suggested he ask the neighbor. Jiang asked the neighbor, and she was thrilled to have flowers planted in her backyard. Jiang learned that respectfully asking "Why not?" can sometimes lead to other opportunities.

One of Jiang's more famous experiments was asking a Krispy Kreme employee to make donuts in the shape of the Olympics logo. Much to his surprise, the employee accommodated him and then gave him the donuts for free. Jiang learned that people are kinder than we realize, and sometimes grant the most preposterous wish.

Jiang went on to do Ted talks about his rejection experiments, and he authored the best-selling book *"Rejection Proof."* His work sheds light on an important lesson:

It's not failure that kills our dreams, it's fear.

What we truly are

A lot of people talk themselves out of the risks and efforts that could bring them success. Their fear of failure, ridicule, or rejection prevents them from even trying.

Where would J. K. Rowling be today if she gave in to her self-doubt and fear of not making it as a writer? The manuscript for Rowling's first book, *Harry Potter and the Philosopher's Stone*, was written in Edinburgh cafes while Rowling and her daughter lived on government benefits.

The Harry Potter book was rejected by twelve publishers before being picked up by Bloomsbury. Today, J. K. Rowling is worth around 1 billion dollars.

"It is our choices, Harry, that show what we truly are far more than our abilities."— Harry Potter and the Chamber of Secrets

Consider the choices you make. Do they bend towards calculated risk-taking? Do you sidestep fear and try new things, or do you stick with what's safe and comfortable?

Deliberately choose discomfort

Failure is seldom what's keeping you back. It's fear. And fear can disguise itself in lots of unproductive ways. Here are a few examples.

Perfectionism

Are you the kind of person that lines your ducks up in a perfect row before you embark on a new project? Does everything have to be perfect in your art studio before you can begin painting?

Perfectionism is a kind of fear. You resist starting and waste time getting everything ready.

"You'll always miss 100% of the shots you don't take." -Wayne Gretzky

Maybe you conduct endless research or seek out the most expensive tools when they're not necessary. There's nothing wrong with trying to do everything perfectly but sometimes done trumps perfect.

It's better to dive into your new project with the tools at hand and upgrade later if you experience some success.

Ridicule and shame

Nobody likes to be made fun of or laughed at, but in many ways, our fear of ridicule and shame is far worse than the actual ridicule and shame. The more well-adjusted and self-confident you become, the more you realize that people laughing at you is short-lived. They quickly forget and move on in their lives.

People like Jia Jiang have figured out that rejection, embarrassment, and ridicule are a part of life. Ambitious and successful people tolerate these uncomfortable moments because each failure is instructive. However embarrassing or mortifying, each failure moves us closer to the prize.

Procrastination

Human beings are designed to conserve energy. We don't like to seemingly waste our time on unpleasant tasks. We fear how such tasks will make us feel. In this sense, procrastination is a form of fear. Fear of discomfort. Maybe even a fear of success.

This is why we settle onto the couch and watch Netflix instead of jumping on the treadmill for a vigorous workout. We take the path of least resistance. But then, as we're watching those attractive and physically fit action heroes on Netflix, we start to feel bad about our own fitness.

Don't let the fear of discomfort prevent you from doing hard things. Consider the wisdom of decorated Green Beret Jason B. A. Van Camp, in his book *"Deliberate Discomfort: How U. S. Special Operations Forces Overcome Fear and Dare to Win by Getting Comfortable Being Uncomfortable."*

Van Camp writes:

"When you make the courageous decision to deliberately choose discomfort, you prove to yourself that you are no longer satisfied with the way things are and you won't tolerate it any longer. You're ready for change, for growth. You are ready to accept and embrace suffering because you want a better life for yourself, your family, and/or your business."

Learned helplessness

Past experiences are powerful. When the experiences are good, they can empower us to try new things and risk. When the experiences are bad, they can immobilize us with inaction and fear.

Learned helplessness is a condition in which someone suffers from a sense of powerlessness. It's often caused by a traumatic event or persistent failure to succeed. It is a major source of depression in people.

Overcoming learned helplessness will vary with different people. Some folks may need professional help, to deal with past trauma and/or abuse.

For others, an optimistic (versus pessimistic) mindset will help greatly. Start with baby steps, pushing yourself each day to try new things and risk a bit more.

Enlist family or friends for moral support. Ignore internal, defeatist self-talk. Remember that embarrassments and failures are survivable and will move you closer to your goal.

Ignorance

When we fail to educate ourselves, it's easier for fear to hold us back. Ignorance makes us succumb to fear-based narratives running through our minds. The antidote is education. The more you learn about the thing that scares you, the easier it will be to defeat.

I used to be afraid of flying. Everything about air travel made me anxious and afraid. My mind would run wild with thoughts of mechanical malfunctions. Each ringing bell in the plane, and every bump of turbulence, caused a near panic attack in me.

To combat my aerophobia, I educated myself. I read about how planes work, how safe they are, and how to manage my anxiety. I learned to recognize the triggers that set me off and ways to calm down. By eliminating my ignorance, I became a much more confident air traveler.

My fear of air travel nearly prevented me from flying to Idaho to study landscape painting with an acclaimed artist I admire. Same for my trip to Tennessee, where I attended an intensive workshop on writing and blogging. Fortunately, my wife convinced me to take those trips, and they proved essential to my creative growth.

By overcoming my ignorance, I was able to fly, and attend educational events that moved me closer to my dreams.

The secret of life

Fear kills more dreams than failure. Failure is no picnic, but at least it teaches us lessons. We learn to do things differently. We learn to try better approaches.

"He who is not every day conquering some fear has not learned the secret of life." -Ralph Waldo Emerson

When we overcome our fear, we free ourselves to try. To risk. To experiment. We might fail, but at least we learn what doesn't work. In this way, we grow and move forward.

Take a page from Jia Jiang and get more comfortable with rejection. Follow J. K. Rowling's example and don't give up. Twelve publishers said no to Rowling's Harry Potter book, but the thirteenth publisher said yes. Now Rowling is a billionaire.

Follow Green Beret Jason B. A. Van Camp's advice and *"deliberately choose discomfort."* Resist the path of least resistance, punch fear in the face, view failures as learning moments, and chase your dreams.

Someday the self-help writers might share your success story in their articles.

Chapter Forty-One

This Is What He Did After the Plane Crash

Roger Berlind was a successful man, despite several setbacks in his life. He majored in English at Princeton University and was involved in the Triangle Club, which put together musical productions.

Berlind served in the U. S. Army until 1954. He was a fluent pianist who played by ear. He pursued songwriting but was unable to sell his music to publishers.

Despite knowing little about the world of finance, he interviewed for various positions on Wall Street. After many rejections, a firm finally picked him up.

Berlind would go on to create a small investment firm with friends. The firm later became swept up in a merger, followed by more deals. Berlind eventually became a chief executive and was successful.

But then his entire world fell apart.

Swept down by wind shear

Helen Berlind and three of her four children were on an Eastern Air Lines Boeing 727 non-stop flight from New Orleans to New York's Kennedy Airport. Her flight encountered a severe electrical storm.

The plane's captain attempted to land at JFK but entered a microburst often found in severe thunderstorms. Microbursts consist of severe and localized winds capable of knocking down a plane. Microbursts contain wind shears, which vary in speed and direction.

An article in baruch.cuny.edu described what happened next:

"As the Boeing 727 approached the runway, it was swept down by wind shear towards a row of lights. Its left wing was torn off by the lights in a matter of seconds and soon the impact of the ground shattered the plane into pieces. The explosion caused debris to fly in the surrounding area of Rockaway Boulevard. Flight 66 traveled from New Orleans to Queens, New York, with 124 people on board, eight of which were crew members. All but 11 people perished in the crash."

Tragically, Helen Berlind and her three children perished in the crash.

Roger Berlind was devastated. He quit his Wall Street job to take care of his toddler son, who had not taken the fateful trip with his mother and siblings.

There is a thin line

What do you do when your entire world crumbles? When tragedy or unexpected loss happens, how do you go on? What do you do next?

"There is a thin line that separates laughter and pain, comedy and tragedy, humor and hurt." -Erma Bombeck

In the case of Roger Berlind, he suddenly found no meaning in his Wall Street work. As he later told the Wall Street Journal, *"I wasn't in any shape to do anything useful at the firm, and I didn't want to be there."*

Berlind's obituary in the Wall Street Journal explained what Berlind did next:

"Reverting to his early love of show tunes and theater, he began investing in Broadway productions and soon found himself hooked. Over more than four decades, he had a role in producing more than 100 plays and musicals and won 25 Tony Awards. His hits included 'The Book of Mormon,' 'Amadeus,' 'Sophisticated Ladies,' and 'City of Angels.'"

Berlind remarried and lived to be 90 years old before succumbing in 2020 to a heart attack in his sleep. He survived the crushing loss of his first wife and three children by turning to his love for music and theater.

How much did they first pay you to give up on your dreams?

There's a lesson in Roger Berlind's life about how to overcome tragedy and reinvent yourself. Sometimes you must look to the past to remember the things you were passionate about. The dreams you gave up on, still yearning for expression.

In the outstanding movie *"Up in the Air,"* George Clooney stars as a hatchet-man hired by companies to fire people. He's training a young, new coworker (Anna Kendrick) and together they break the bad news to an employee.

Clooney's character reminds the man they're firing that he can reinvent himself and revive an old dream. Clooney's character looks at the man's personnel file and notes that he once trained to become a professional chef. But somehow the current job kept the man from pursuing his culinary dreams. He asks the man, "How much did they first pay you to give up on your dreams?"

An article in Forbes contains the following, eloquent paragraph:

"We plot our lives carefully, toiling in relative obscurity, constructing private narratives of hope. We tinker and tweak with the script of our lives — shaping and reshaping it — as we face and overcome life's challenges, and strive to reach and surpass its milestones."

No matter how well we've planned and built our lives, adversity and tragedy can turn everything upside down. You can be on top of the world one minute and in hell the next.

Life is not an accident

Don't think it can happen to you? Just ask former basketball star Jay Williams, who used to play in the NBA for the Chicago Bulls. At one point people were calling him "Chicago's second coming of Michael Jordan."

But then he crashed his motorcycle into a light pole resulting in major, career-ending injuries. What followed were years of depression and demoralization.

Until he found a way to reinvent himself.

Williams realized that by sharing his story with others, he could heal. He could rebuild his life. His book, *"Life Is Not an Accident: A Memoir of Reinvention,"* details his journey from tragedy to reinvention.

An article in Forbes.com had this to say about Williams' book:

"Williams' book celebrates the critical importance of learning to accept change. 'This is about learning the process of letting go,' he told me. 'I had to allow myself to fall in love with something else. These are issues that everybody has in life.'"

Today Williams will tell you that his tragedy taught him how to live.

Perhaps the same thing happened for Roger Berlind. Maybe the loss of his wife and children, crushing as it was, allowed Berlind to reignite an old dream. To rekindle his passion for music and theater.

The familiar rhythms of work

We often define ourselves by our careers. In a way, careers are a form of self-expression. But careers can be changed, and there are many forms of self-expression.

Jay Williams' form of self-expression was basketball until the motorcycle accident ended it. Then, he wrote a memoir and became a public speaker and sports analyst on TV. He found another form of self-expression.

Of course, not everyone changes careers or reinvents themselves after adversity or tragedy.

Sheryl Sandberg was the Chief Operating Officer for Facebook and author of the book *"Lean In."*

Sandberg's husband, Dave Goldberg, died in a gym accident in 2015. He fell off a treadmill and hit his head, although an autopsy later revealed the cause of his death was a coronary arrhythmia.

In another book by Sandberg titled, *"Option B: Facing Adversity, Building Resilience, and Finding Joy,"* she describes what it was like telling her children that their father had died. An excerpt:

"The screaming and crying that followed haunt me to this day — primal screams and cries that echoed the ones in my heart. Nothing has come close to the pain of this moment."

Despite this gut-wrenching experience, Sandberg remained in her position at Facebook and even found comfort in the familiar rhythms of work.

In the end, we will all face adversity and loss in our lives. Remember that you will get through it.

You might pick up the pieces and continue in your current career and life, like Sheryl Sandberg. Or you might reinvent yourself in a new profession, like Roger Berlind and Jay Williams.

A few tears might be shed. It won't be easy. But hang in there. Remember what Jay Williams said, how his tragedy taught him how to live. You'll figure out how to go on living, too.

Chapter Forty-Two

This Is How to Dance With Loss

The dispatcher's voice startled me. It was 3AM and I was parked in a lonely, empty lot in the north end of town. I liked parking there because it was quiet, and I could get my reports done.

"Code 7 at Oak Tree Villa," the dispatcher continued over the radio. In other police agencies, Code-7 meant "lunch break." Unfortunately, in my department's radio vernacular, it meant "dead body."

Oak Tree Villa was our town's only retirement and assisted living community. A local firefighter once called it "Croak Tree Villa," which was awful but not inaccurate. Cops and firefighters often refer to retirement/assisted living communities as "God's waiting room."

"After you find out all the things that can go wrong, your life becomes less about living and more about waiting." — Chuck Palahniuk, Choke

I drove the short five miles across town and arrived at Oak Tree Villa. It was summer, and the crickets were in full song as I navigated the pathway to the front entrance.

So many roads to choose

Fire personnel were already there, as their station house was nearby. Inside the lobby, I was greeted by Karen, who often worked the night shift.

"Hey John," she said, "Thanks for coming over. It's Mr. Benson, in room 209. One of our night shift staff found his apartment door ajar and went in to check on him. Looks like he passed away in his sleep."

I thanked Karen and made my way back to room 209, where the fire guys greeted me and confirmed that Mr. Benson had been dead for several hours. They packed up their gear and soon I was alone in the apartment.

I radioed dispatch, and arrangements were made for the Sheriff-Coroner's office to respond. To pass the time, I strolled around Mr. Benson's apartment.

You can learn a lot about someone by the photographs and pictures in their homes. In Mr. Benson's apartment, there were many framed pictures on the walls and desktops.

There were some black and white wedding photos of Mr. Benson and his wife. They looked happy. Eager for life to unfold. The photo reminded me of the old Carpenters song and the following verses:

We've only just begun to live
White lace and promises
A kiss for luck and we're on our way
(We've only begun)
Before the risin' sun, we fly
So many roads to choose
We'll start out walkin' and learn to run
(And yes, we've just begun)

Other pictures captured family trips, children, and holiday festivities. By all accounts, Mr. Benson enjoyed a rich family life. But time's relentless march was also evident in the photos. I could see how the years aged Mr. Benson and his wife.

Waiting is the most difficult bit

It's a solemn thing, to stand watch over the recently departed. To take in their photos, mementos, and personal effects. Sometimes I felt like I was trespassing, a voyeur into the private world of another person. But really, I was a temporary guardian, until arrangements were made, and the family could respond.

I couldn't help but wonder what it was like for Mr. Benson, in his late stage of life. Was he lonely? I later learned that his wife died a few years ago, and his adult children lived in the neighboring county.

Was Mr. Benson waiting patiently for death, to be with his wife again? How did he deal with the loss of his wife?

"I've learned that waiting is the most difficult bit, and I want to get used to the feeling, knowing that you're with me, even when you're not by my side." — Paulo Coelho, Eleven Minutes

Loving ghosts

One of the Oak Tree Villa staff members, named Maria, came by the room to ask about Mr. Benson's next of kin. I told her that my police department had contacted the Sheriff's Office in the next county and that Mr. Benson's adult children were notified. One of his sons was enroute.

"I've been admiring all these amazing pictures of his family," I said to Maria.

"Yes, he loved his family. When his wife died a few years back, it was hard on him," Maria said, adding, "He also lost two brothers over the years." Maria pointed to one of the pictures of Mr. Benson with two other elderly men.

"I can't imagine losing your brothers, and then your wife," I said to Maria.

"He told me once that the pictures of his wife and brothers were like loving ghosts, keeping him company in his old age," Maria said.

I thought about the many other death calls I responded to at Oak Tree Villa. There were always family pictures and framed photographs on the walls. Loving ghosts, standing watch with the remaining loved one, until the end.

Grace is what matters in anything

Old age is hard enough to navigate, but throw in the loss of loved ones, and even the strongest people can crumble. Experiencing loss earlier in life can be equally devastating, as we grapple with sorrow and thoughts of what could have been.

"Grace is what matters in anything — especially life, especially growth, tragedy, pain, love, death. That's a quality that I admire very greatly. It keeps you from reaching out for the gun too quickly. It keeps you from destroying things too foolishly. It sort of keeps you alive." -Jeff Buckley

In my law enforcement career, I saw death up close and personal. I dealt with suicide calls, fatal accidents, and medical emergencies ending in death.

One of the hardest things to do in police work is a death notification. Knocking on someone's door, waiting for it to open, knowing you're about to destroy someone's world.

These experiences were challenging, but they helped me think about my own life and loved ones. I thought about how precious time was. How I wanted to invest in my family.

So how do we dance with loss? How do we console our broken hearts, and mend our shattered spirits? Here are five suggestions, my love letter of hope for the broken among us. A little bit of cop wisdom.

Memories

Make memories whenever you can. Don't put off family vacations. Visit your parents often. Turn off the TV and take your kid to the park.

Nearly every funeral I've ever attended shared pictures and photos of the good times. Family trips. The laughter. The cherished memories. These memories will help sustain us when loss comes into our life.

"God gave us memory so that we might have roses in December."
-James M. Barrie

Forgiveness

People are going to wrong you in this life. Perhaps you've wronged a few, yourself. Of course, when it involves family, our hearts ache even more.

"Holding on to anger is like grasping a hot coal with the intent of throwing it at someone else; you are the one who gets burned."
-Buddha

When we let go of anger and learn to forgive, we bestow a tremendous gift on another person. But we also unburden our own hearts.

Some may not accept your forgiveness, and others may not forgive you. But whenever possible, forgiveness will soften the pain of loss.

Friendship

Never take for granted the healing power of friends. Other family members can be leaned on, but often they're struggling with grief too.

The greatest gift of friendship is simply being there when you're needed. Showing up. Listening. Hugging. Helping with little things (meals, laundry, etc.) when loss shatters the normal cadence of our lives.

"A real friend is one who walks in when the rest of the world walks out." -Walter Winchell

Remember too that friendship is reciprocal. The friend you lean on today may need to lean on you tomorrow.

Movement

Loss has a way of immobilizing us. Our normal routines, work, habits, and passions are all put on hold. Our bodies might rebel with weight loss, anxiety, depression, and malaise.

The very thing we feel least like doing, moving, is often exactly what we need. Studies prove that exercise combats depression and improves our mental health. Grief is not depression, but exercise seems to help both.

In an article for Self.com, author Rachel Tavel shared how running helped her cope with the loss of her father:

"Running has become a time when I can feel my dad's presence instead of isolating myself in his absence. It's an active, moving meditation during which I can release emotions that have nowhere else to go. Sweat and tears aren't the same, but there is something cleansing about releasing both — especially together."

When my father passed away years ago, I found long walks with my dog to be therapeutic. The fresh air and scenic park allowed me time to reflect, and the movement of walking helped loosen the tension of loss.

Hope

My favorite song by country music artist Garth Brooks is *"The Dance."* Here are a few of the lyrics:

"And now, I'm glad I didn't know
The way it all would end
The way it all would go
Our lives are better left to chance
I could have missed the pain
But I'da had to miss
The dance"

The dance of life is exquisite. It's such a gift. To love and receive love. We can hide from love, but we would be cheating ourselves.

Love gives us hope. It shows us that there is goodness in this world. Maybe even a hint of the divine. And love is not just for people. Animals give and receive love too.

Inviting, giving, and receiving love in our lives means that there will be loss someday. That's the deal.

Grief is never easy, but it's a reflection of what we had. With the help of memories, forgiveness, friendship, movement, and hope, loss eventually gives way to gratitude. We become thankful that we got to dance with the love we lost.

In Mr. Benson's bedroom, there was a small frame with a quote by the British poet Alfred Lord Tennyson, that echoes the message of Garth Brooks' *"The Dance"* song.

"Tis better to have loved and lost than never to have loved at all."
-Alfred Lord Tennyson

I hope you can avoid loss for as long as possible in your life. But one day, when it arrives, hang in there. The pain reflects the love. Remember that you got to enjoy the dance, and the love in your heart is a flame that never burns out.

Chapter Forty-Three

You Can Reinvent Your Life and Be Happy

Certain things stay with us our entire lives, like immutable guideposts that reflect our deepest passions.

For me, it has always been the blank page, awaiting marks from my drawing pen or words from my laptop computer.

As a young boy, I often escaped to the blank pages of my sketchbooks. They became worlds of creative joy and discovery. They remain so now, in my fifth decade.

Whether drawing, painting, or writing, the blank page (or canvas) is home to my creative being. It's where the swirling dreams, ideas, and artistic expressions come alive.

Creating artwork and writing have always brought me great fulfillment and joy. Being a creative was my destiny, even though most of my adult professional life was in law enforcement.

We become tempted to fill the emptiness

My parents supported my artistic nature but suggested a conservative career route, since being a full-time artist can be financially challenging. Accordingly, I obtained undergraduate and graduate degrees in criminal justice administration and pursued a career in police work.

I enjoyed helping people and the adventure of my law enforcement career. I steadily promoted to new positions and spent the last ten years as chief of police.

But the creative muse was always whispering in my ear, like the voice of my old self calling from the past.

"When we have waited a long time for what we really want, we become tempted to fill the emptiness with unworthy substitutes. Don't." — Jackie Viramontez

Despite my law enforcement success, I missed who I used to be. That creative, easy-going young man who loved to draw and write.

As a police chief, I sometimes used to paint on my lunch breaks.

I realized that my time away from work should not be wasted on unworthy distractions. Rather than playing golf or attending wine parties, I began prioritizing free time for my artwork.

I created a website for my art, took vacation time to attend painting and writing workshops, and stayed up late to paint and write. At work, I often used my lunch breaks to paint or draw cartoons.

These efforts resuscitated the spirit of my old, creative self, and kept me sane at work.

You get to decide

Most people have to be pragmatic to make a living. Writing poetry, gardening, pottery, painting, and other creative pursuits seldom generate enough income to support yourself or a family.

But if you're going to revive the person you were meant to be, you have to re-orient your life. You have to say no to discretionary distractions and buy time for your passions.

"You get to decide where your time goes. You can either spend it moving forward, or you can spend it putting out fires. You decide. And if you don't decide, others will decide for you." -Tony Morgan

It can be challenging, but it's possible. With sound time management and reprioritization, you can revive the person you were meant to be.

The key is to become a pragmatic juggler, balancing work, family, and passions. Understand that it's okay to politely say no to things that prevent you from becoming the person you were meant to be.

You might reach a point where your passion can become a full-time career. For some, this is great. But for others, it's better to keep your passion apart from your financial livelihood. A monetized passion can quickly turn into a grind, killing the joy of it.

Is this everything I wanted for myself?

It would have been easy to continue my career as a police chief. I was making an excellent income, was established in my profession and community, and worked with amazing people. I was comfortable.

Yet I knew that my police career wasn't everything I wanted for myself. I knew I had reached a point where I had to transition into becoming a full-time writer and artist. I had to revive the person I was meant to be.

An article in Lifehack.org notes:

"When we stay in a certain lifestyle or situation for a long time, we have a tendency to just continue on without thinking too much about it. But when we begin to ask the questions 'Is this everything I wanted for myself? Could things possibly be different somehow?' we open ourselves to the possibility of something new. Things can, and always do change. We just need to recognize it."

There are always options for people looking to make a change in their lives. If you're lucky enough to know exactly what you want to do with the rest of your life, then the next step is to start planning.

Talk things over with your loved ones. Research what it would take to make a change. Weigh the financial costs. Explore the possibility of re-locating. Talk to people already doing what you want to do. In short, do your homework. Make a plan.

The other thing is to be honest with yourself. Do you have the skills and talent to do the thing you always dreamed of? If not, then restructure your schedule to develop those skills.

Seek the best instruction, find mentors, and get comfortable with practice. Rare and valuable skills take time to develop.

Put yourself into newness

For many people, they know they need a change in their lives, but they don't know what that change might be. Or perhaps they've outgrown old passions.

If this is you, then it's time to experiment and try new things.

The article in Lifehack.org explains:

"If you are beginning to recognize some unhappiness or malcontent, change things up. While this is not always easy, change things to the best of your ability. You will gain a new perspective on things that maybe you had no real idea about. You may end up walking a mile in another person's shoes. You may end up walking a mile in no shoes at all. By simply putting yourself into newness, however, you are at the very least exposing yourself to possibility and new ideas. Change is as good as a holiday."

By taking the time to experiment and explore new things, you just might land on something new that truly excites you. This is one way to reinvent yourself. Put yourself into newness.

Never stop learning

I already know that writing and creating artwork are what I was meant to do. But that doesn't mean I can rest on my laurels.

"There is no end to education. It is not that you read a book, pass an examination, and finish with education. The whole of life, from the moment you are born to the moment you die, is a process of learning." -Jiddu Krishnamurti

To grow and sharpen the quality of my creative expression, I must keep learning.

The Lifehack.org article suggests:

"Never stop learning, never stop discussing, never stop peacefully exchanging thoughts and words and opinions. Your new self is constantly an amalgamation of all of your old selves combined with the greatness you continue to expose yourself to. And always remember that you are exactly where you are supposed to be, right now."

I read regularly, take on-line courses, and continually try to hone my creative skills. You can do the same thing. And if you can't afford to pay for online courses, there are plenty of free instructional videos online. If you want to reinvent your life and be happy, you need to never stop learning.

I could never do that

Negative past experiences and discouragement from others can injure our self-confidence and ambition. Don't let this happen. The past does not get to define the future, you do.

Ilene Strauss Cohen Ph.D., in an article for PsychologyToday. com, notes:

"We think, 'I could never do that!' or 'I could never make that happen!' If you truly believe that, you'll never accomplish your goals. Open up your mind, and believe in yourself. There will be many people who tell you that you can't do it. It's up to you to prove them wrong."

People tend to favor the familiar over the unfamiliar. The devil we know over the one we don't. The problem with this is that personal growth requires some courage and discomfort. When we stick with the familiar, we limit ourselves and our potential.

"Courage is your natural setting. You do not need to become courageous, but rather peel back the layers of self-protective, limiting beliefs that keep you small." — Vironika Tugaleva

Stop telling yourself you're not good enough, or you don't deserve it, or that you don't have any ability. Imagine if you shut off these negative, self-limiting beliefs and just went for it. Sure, you might fail here and there, but odds are you'll also succeed.

Stop trying to change everyone else

People are unique. We may share similarities, but everyone has their own likes, dislikes, tastes, preferences, biases, etc.

It's a waste of time trying to change other people, and what gives you the right in the first place? Learn to focus on improving you and stop worrying about everyone else.

There's nothing wrong with treating people well and trying to make them happy. So long as you understand that ultimately, it's not up to you to make other people happy. It's up to them.

Dr. Cohen, in PsychologyToday.com, observes:

"You can't change another person, so don't waste your time and energy trying. I think this is the biggest factor that pushes people to hold onto unhelpful behaviors, like the need to please. We think, 'If only I do everything for everyone, they'll never get mad at me.' Wrong!"

If you want to reinvent your life and be happy, you can't put yourself at the mercy of everyone else. You must set your own goals and dreams and work toward them unapologetically. Others may share their opinions of your dreams, but only you get to decide how to act.

This doesn't mean you should abdicate your responsibilities in life. You still must show up for work, be a loving spouse, provide for your children, etc. There's a difference between being selfish and focusing on self-improvement.

God grant me the serenity

There's a lot of wisdom in the opening lines of Reinhold Niebuhr's serenity prayer:

"God, grant me the serenity
to accept the things I cannot change,
the courage to change the things I can,
and the wisdom to know the difference."

You can reinvent your life and be happy. You can revive the person you were meant to be.

Start by developing rare and valuable skills. Try new things, never stop learning, get rid of self-limiting beliefs, stop trying to change others, and remember the serenity prayer.

Do these things and you'll be on your way, with the wind at your back, and your dreams anxiously awaiting your triumphant arrival.

Chapter Forty-Four

Here Is the Antidote for Modern Life

Corbett Barr is the co-founder and CEO of the website Fizzle.co, which helps people earn a living doing something they love.

I discovered Fizzle.co a few years back when I first started blogging and writing online. I used to read their posts but eventually moved on to other content.

Apparently, I was still on one of the Fizzle.co email lists, because I received a recent email from Corbett Barr. In the email, Barr wrote that he was "starting over" and had deleted all the content on his social media accounts. He also plans to delete most of his old blog posts.

Barr's email explained why he's doing this digital house-cleaning:

"Essentially, I want to make digital room for who I've become, and who I intend to be. Much of the old content isn't serving the new me."

This resonated with me since I've been re-evaluating my own online presence, social media habits, and creative work. As Barr notes in his email:

"It's not natural for every thought or scribble you've produced to exist publicly for everyone to see for all time. I don't think we've come to terms with that yet, nor do we know how it is affecting all of us."

Solitude can be used well by very few people

I've come to recognize that much of our online connections are superficial, and social media sites cater to our vanity. What is the point in sharing photos of our latest workout or dinner meal?

"Solitude can be used well by very few people. They who do must have a knowledge of the world to see the foolishness of it, and enough virtue to despise all the vanity." -Abraham Cowley

Should our self-esteem cling to how many likes or followers we attract? Shouldn't we be seeking deeper experiences? Can we escape from the popups, shallow tweets, click-bait piffle, and digital self-absorption?

It was during these questions that I stumbled upon a beautiful short film entitled, *"Nobility of the Air."* The film is all about Paul Manning, a professional falconer in Hampshire, England.

While the rest of the world is glued to flashing updates on digital screens, Paul Manning is out in the breathtaking countryside of Hampshire, England, with his majestic birds of prey.

As Manning notes in the film:

"Falconry is a wonderful antidote to modern life. We live our entire lives with an 'I want a fix now and I'll buy it.' A relationship with a bird of prey is the complete opposite, it has to be selfless. You have to put the bird of prey first. You have to think about the bird of prey and its needs before your needs."

We are very bad at scale

Our modern lives are meant to be far more than YouTube videos, click-bait distractions, and Zoom chats. Such things are rabbit holes, keeping us from deeper connections and pursuits.

Real-life is about getting out there and experiencing things. Spending hours alone practicing and pursuing a passion until you achieve mastery. Helping others, connecting, and talking in person. Yes, this is harder right now in a pandemic, but not impossible.

Perhaps this is why I love painting outdoors. Every time I pack my paintbox and trudge out into the desert or woods, I feel a sense of freedom and exhilaration. The solitude and creative focus provide a kind of transcendence, far beyond what digital life can offer.

Even in my art studio, engrossed in drawing or painting, I enter a delicious zone where time seems to standstill.

Such experiences are the antidote for modern living. They rescue us from our self-absorption and the frequently shallow charms of social media and the Internet. They can be found in gardening, hiking, painting, woodworking, recording music, and many more analog pursuits.

The author Helen MacDonald, in her magnificent book *"H is for Hawk,"* eloquently reminds us how our self-absorption keeps us from seeing so much more.

"We are very bad at scale. The things that live in the soil are too small to care about; climate change too large to imagine. We are bad at time, too. We cannot remember what lived here before we did; we cannot love what is not. Nor can we imagine what will be different when we are dead. We live out our threescore and ten, and tie our knots and lines only to ourselves. We take solace in pictures, and we wipe the hills of history."

— *Helen Macdonald, H is for Hawk*

Never limit your mind

For falconer Paul Manning, transcendence is found in the nobility of his hawks, soaring above the glorious landscape. Helen MacDonald found it too, with her goshawk. For me, transcendence is found in the creative arts, where ink and paint come together to help me express my artistic vision.

"Never limit your mind; it is capable of great intelligence; or your heart; it is capable of extraordinary kindness; or your soul; it is capable of remarkable transcendence." — *Matshona Dhliwayo*

How about you? Are you tired of the online noise, digital clutter, and blinking distractions of modern life? Do you crave something deeper? Why not restructure your time, to make more room for the people you care about and the creative pursuits that quicken your heart?

There is more to life than endlessly documenting our lives online and following the social media updates of others. Corbett Barr figured this out, which is why he deleted everything and is starting over.

Maybe we should all start over? It just might be the antidote for modern life.

Chapter Forty-Five

Do You Make These Mistakes at Work?

There were people in my law enforcement career who seemed determined to fail. Despite mentoring, instruction, gentle correction, and discipline, they consistently chose the low road.

What's the low road? An appetite for excuses, blame, and underperformance. An aversion to personal responsibility.

"If you could kick the person in the pants responsible for most of your trouble, you wouldn't sit for a month." — Theodore Roosevelt

Not long after being promoted to the rank of police sergeant, I was sent to a supervisory school. There, among many subjects, I learned the art of performance appraisal. How to honestly evaluate subordinates and provide constructive, actionable feedback.

Most employees wanted to improve, and they were open to useful feedback. Some, unfortunately, resisted.

This was frustrating to me because I had taken the time to build rapport with them. I always pointed out their good qualities and successes at work. In short, I developed trust with them. Yet they refused to own their mistakes or change behavior.

Striving for mediocrity

I watched a fair number of bright and promising employees repeatedly shoot themselves in the foot, thereby killing their prospects for broader career development and promotion.

"No one gets ahead by striving for mediocrity." — Glenn C. Stewart

It was frustrating to see employees with great potential who succumbed to mediocrity and the path of least resistance. Sometimes they were lazy. Other times, they became invested in a perceived wrong. Whatever the reason, they consistently fell short.

There's no judgment here, just disappointment that I was unable to help these employees. Heck, I've made some of the same mistakes in my career, but eventually changed course.

Here are some of the mistakes you want to avoid at work.

Inconsistency

You've probably heard or read the advice, "Under promise and over deliver." Sounds reasonable, but according to research, it's not very good advice.

People value others who deliver on their promises but don't care that much if they over-deliver on their promises. An article in Eurekalert.com used the following example:

"If you are sending Mother's Day flowers to your mom this weekend, chances are you opted for guaranteed delivery: the promise that they will arrive by a certain time. Should the flowers not arrive on time, you will likely feel betrayed by the sender for breaking their promise. But if they arrive earlier, you likely will be no happier than if they arrive on time, according to new research."

I don't see much harm in overdelivering on promises, but what's most important is CONSISTENCY in meeting your promises. Employees who can be counted on to consistently follow through on assignments are golden.

In my career, there were always a handful of employees who became indispensable, go-to people because they consistently followed through on assignments.

Other employees sporadically achieved great things, but they were inconsistent. If you want to stand out at work and not shoot yourself in the foot, worry less about being an occasional superstar and focus more on consistently doing good work.

Emotional immaturity

I could write a book about this one. Emotionally immature employees take things personally, often play the martyr, and fail to take responsibility for their actions.

Such individuals cannot work around their feelings to achieve positive outcomes. They expend more energy resisting or fighting things they don't want to do or disagree with, rather than getting their work done.

I recall one employee who worked very hard at finding loopholes in our minimum standards of performance. He often did the least work possible and blamed others for his low productivity. The effort he put into resisting work was far more than simply doing his job. He was eventually fired.

"Maturity: Be able to stick with a job until it is finished. Be able to bear an injustice without having to get even. Be able to carry money without spending it. Do your duty without being supervised." -Ann Landers

Focus on doing an honest day's work for a day's pay. Don't shoot yourself in the foot by letting your emotions get the best of you.

Negativity

There will always be things in life to complain about. No doubt, you know people in your work who grumble endlessly about everything. Ask yourself, how much fun are they to be around?

Better to be the little train that could than the negative one who quit.

Successful, well-adjusted people don't waste energy on negativity. They work around setbacks and obstacles. They don't quit. They focus on the goal, not the challenges.

"See if you can catch yourself complaining, in either speech or thought, about a situation you find yourself in, what other people do or say, your surroundings, your life situation, even the weather. To complain is always nonacceptance of what is. It invariably carries an unconscious negative charge. When you complain, you make yourself into a victim. When you speak out, you are in your power. So change the situation by taking action or by speaking out if necessary or possible; leave the situation or accept it. All else is madness." — Eckhart Tolle, *"The Power of Now: A Guide to Spiritual Enlightenment"*

Don't be one of those negative souls at work, bringing everyone down. You'll only shoot yourself in the foot. Optimism can be a force multiplier, whereas negativity can become a cancer at work.

Gossip

People love to talk about other people, especially when it's negative. They'll even do it via text messages.

I knew a young banker named Wayne who shared the following story. He was at work when his boss arrived, a bit late. Wayne received a text from a co-worker, speculating that their boss had "tied one on again," the night before.

Wayne's boss had a problem with alcohol, and everyone knew it. Wayne texted back to his co-worker, stating, "Yep, the boss is late for work again. I'll bet she's still drunk."

Unfortunately for Wayne, he accidentally used a group text in his response. Not long after, his boss called Wayne into her office. Wayne was mortified. He felt terrible.

Wayne felt even worse when his boss apologized for being a poor example and admitted that she was struggling with her alcohol addiction.

"Great minds discuss ideas; average minds discuss events; small minds discuss people." -Eleanor Roosevelt

Who are we to talk about others behind their backs? Do we think we are superior to them? Is it fair to judge when we know little about their backgrounds, circumstances, and struggles?

If you want to shoot yourself in the foot at work, gossip about other people. It won't take long before others and even your supervisor will figure out that you're a gossip. And then they'll think less of you.

Impatience

We live in an instant gratification world. As a result, we've become more impatient.

We can order food and have it immediately delivered to our home. With a few clicks and swipes on our phones, we can purchase goods and have them delivered, or hail a ride to take us anywhere we want.

Technology has made our lives easier and brought many conveniences. As a result, we forget that most things of value in life take time to achieve.

If you want an athletic body and six-pack abs, it's not going to happen overnight. It will take many months of regular training and an improved diet.

If you want to make more money, you'll have to invest time and energy in developing rare and valuable skills. That means furthering your education, practicing, and applying your new abilities in ways that get you noticed. All of which takes time and sacrifice.

"A certain amount of impatience may be useful to stimulate and motivate us to action. However, I believe that a lack of patience is a major cause of the difficulties and unhappiness in the world today." -Joseph B. Wirthlin

Impatient employees shoot themselves in the foot because they're not willing to put in the time and make the sacrifices necessary to grow. Developing patience within yourself will serve you well, in dealing with other people and learning new skills.

All we have is our character

There are many other mistakes you can make at work, like dishonesty, backstabbing, etc. In the end, all we have is our character. Our reputations hinge on our work ethic and how we treat others.

Don't shoot yourself in the foot with inconsistency, emotional immaturity, negativity, gossip, and impatience.

Embracing hard work, decency, and virtue will take you far in the workplace, and other areas of your life. Best of all, you'll become a role model for others, which is how we make the world a better place.

Chapter Forty-Six

This Is What an Octopus Can Teach You About Life

Over the last few years, I have posted tons of blog posts and thousands of comments online. I enjoy writing and consider it a privilege to have people read and follow my work.

I illustrate all my articles and stories, which adds additional time and energy to the research and writing I put into each published post. It's a labor of love, but sometimes the things we love can wear us out.

What should we do when career or creative burnout creeps into our souls? Some folks go on vacation, hoping they'll catch their second wind. Others make a career change or alter their artistic direction.

For acclaimed nature filmmaker Craig Foster, he took a different approach to his career burnout. He sought refuge along the Western Cape of South Africa, freediving beneath the rough waters into the magical kelp forest below.

What Foster found in the kelp forest and seafloor not only cured his career burnout, it filled his heart with a deeper appreciation of nature, people, and especially family.

All thanks to an encounter with a speckled, intelligent octopus.

Where life feels okay again

My creative burnout started to settle in over the last few months. I began to question the value of my work. "Is it worth the energy and time?" I thought to myself. "Should I just go back to painting?" I wondered.

Perhaps my creative angst reflects our altered lives, thanks to the COVID pandemic. Or maybe I'm navigating a mild, mid-life crisis?

"In my early fifties, I was going through a phase where few things felt right and I was trying to figure out those that did. It was not uncommon. In your twenties, you pursue your dreams. By your late thirties and early forties, you hit a certain stride. Then you hit your fifties, you get your first annoying thoughts of mortality, you begin more serious questioning of not just the meaning of your life but of what's working, what's not working, and what you still want, and all of a sudden you don't know which way is up. You thought you knew but don't. You just want to get to where life feels okay again." — Dick Van Dyke, My Lucky Life in and Out of Show Business

Whatever the cause of my malaise, I retreated to the television the other night to mentally escape for a while. My wife joined me, and we began scrolling through channels in search of something decent to watch.

That's when we found the Netflix documentary "*My Octopus Teacher.*" "This looks interesting," I said to my wife. "Sure, why not," she said.

Without a doubt, the documentary turned out to be poignant and memorable experience.

Respect and joy

Craig Foster is no stranger to the rough waters off the Cape of South Africa, having swum and free dived there in his youth.

So, it was natural that he returned to those waters, to escape his career burnout.

During one of his free dives, Foster encountered a strange-looking tangle of abandoned seashells, balled up on the ocean floor. Suddenly they all fell apart, revealing an octopus that used her suckers to camouflage herself with the seashells.

Foster was intrigued by the intelligence of the octopus. Apparently, octopi are incredibly smart, as noted in this excerpt from a New York Times article:

"Cephalopods behave in ways that certainly suggest they're highly intelligent. An octopus named Inky, for example, made a notorious escape recently from the National Aquarium of New Zealand, exiting his enclosure and slithering into a floor drain and, apparently, out to sea."

Foster decided to return the next day and learn more about the octopus he encountered. On a subsequent dive, he found her den beneath a seabed rock (later in the documentary we learn how Foster knew the octopus was female).

At first, she was cautious. But eventually, she reached out with one arm from beneath the rock and gently touched Foster's hand. It didn't take long for her to figure out that Foster was not a threat, and soon the two were swimming together.

Sometimes she would swim onto Foster's hand, and ride to the surface with him so he could inhale more air. Often, Foster would follow along and watch her hunt small fish and crabs.

Foster's beautifully filmed and narrated documentary shows us how clever his octopus friend is. How she entwines herself in kelp to sneak up on prey and uses seashells as armor against a pyjama shark attack.

"The bond that links your true family is not one of blood, but of respect and joy in each other's life." -Richard Bach

Foster's many underwater excursions with his octopus friend remind him how fragile life can be, and how beautiful. He begins to think about the important things in his life, like his young son, Tom.

Foster's octopus friend teaches him that he is a part of the environment, not just a visitor. So many important realizations, all thanks to a small octopus.

Strength to body and soul

Most octopi only live a year or two, but that didn't prevent Foster from falling in love with his cephalopod friend. Every day he discovered new things about her.

For example, octopi can be playful. One day Foster found her happily flailing her arms at fish swimming above. Foster realized she was not hunting but playing.

"Everybody needs beauty as well as bread, places to play in and pray in, where nature may heal and give strength to body and soul."
-John Muir

Then, inexplicably, she stopped and swam over to Foster, latching on to his chest in an extended octopus hug. To see such trust and affection between a sea animal and a human being is incredibly moving.

Foster found himself completely absorbed about his octopus friend, and the world she lived in. He wondered if she dreamed, and if so, about what? He invited his son Tom on dives, so that he could meet the octopus and share in the experience.

What Foster found was a renewed appreciation for the ocean environment, and most importantly, his relationship with his son.

Had it not been for Foster's career burnout, he would never have escaped to the underwater world where a new friend awaited him. Thanks to his octopus pal, Foster deepened his relationship with his son, and found renewed direction and purpose in his work.

The question is, how do the rest of us find such meaningful breakthroughs to overcome burnout? Where do we find our octopi?

How to overcome burnout and live again

You don't have to dive the rough waters along the Cape of South Africa to overcome career or creative burnout. Here are six strategies that you might find useful.

Get outdoors

Never underestimate the power of fresh air and nature to restore your spirit and perspective. Whether it's a weekend camping trip, fishing at the lake, hiking in the woods, or frolicking along the beach, the outdoors will reinvigorate you. Getting outside and away also gives you time to think and reflect on where you are and where you're headed.

Say no

Nobody likes to disappoint others, so we often say yes to things when we should say no. Other people will always spend your time for you if you let them. Learn to politely say no to discretionary commitments that keep you away from family, passions, and a healthy work/life balance.

Self-care

A poor diet, lack of exercise, and little sleep create a recipe for stress and burnout. The same goes for relying on alcohol. Drinking is an easy escape, but often eats up free time and can lead to hangovers and demotivation.

Prioritize passions

During the busiest years of my law enforcement career, I made my artwork a priority. I gave up golf to buy more time for landscape painting on my weekends. Your creative passions feed your soul, so guard them closely. Also, if you're burned out with your creative passion, experiment with related or even different pursuits, to see what quickens your heart.

Escape plan

If you want to break out of prison, you need a sound escape plan. And being in a lousy job is a lot like being in prison. Make a list of your talents and abilities. Then, research related or different jobs that are a good fit for you. Before you apply for that new job, learn all you can about it. Who is the boss? What are their challenges and strong points? The more you know about a prospective employer, the better you'll do in an interview.

Lean on love

When we're burned out in life, learning to lean on the ones we love is crucial. Craig Foster's little octopus leaned into him for a big hug. Your loved ones can help you cope, plan, make changes, and escape burnout. But you must talk to them. Let them in. Take advantage of their advice.

Craig Foster's octopus documentary came along at a good time. It inspired me to reevaluate the things I'm working on and learn to listen to my heart more.

My wife and I have two trips planned for next year, and I'm rearranging my schedule to put more emphasis on personal fitness. I've also been busting out my oil paints and brushes more, to deepen my artistic abilities.

All this from the wisdom of a little octopus.

Chapter Forty-Seven

What Happened to the Gift of Empathy?

The parking lot of our local supermarket was crowded when I pulled into an empty stall. All manner of people were coming and going, adjusting their face masks, and juggling groceries.

I sighed, realizing it would be crowded and busy inside. I turned off the engine and leaned back in my seat. Sometimes I enjoy sitting quietly in my car, safely cocooned from the bustle and frenetic pace of life. I seem to need such moments now and again, to mentally check out and daydream.

There was an older model car adjacent to me that had seen better days. The paint was faded and scratched, and the bumper dented. Within sat an elderly woman in the driver's seat. Like her car, she too was an older model.

The problems of aging present an opportunity

Her hair was thin, curly, and gray. She was looking down at her lap, and her thick glasses clung to the tip of her nose. Her skin was somewhat pale and wrinkled.

I thought maybe she was reading or checking her phone, except that she seemed unfocused. At one point, she closed her eyes for nearly a minute. Then she raised her head and stared out the windshield for a while.

Eventually, she opened the door to her car, slowly climbed out, and started to pull on a red vest with a name tag. That's when I realized she worked at the grocery store.

What had she been thinking about in her car? Was she psyching herself up to face another long shift at work? Was she reminiscing about the past when the bloom of youth was still within her? Or was she mourning the loss of a spouse?

"The problems of aging present an opportunity to rethink our social and personal lives in order to ensure the dignity and welfare of each individual. -Daisaku Ikeda

She had a tired yet kindly face. As she ambled by my car, I felt a pang of sorrow for her. I thought of impatient shoppers, and how they often treat cashiers and clerks as if they barely exist.

Part of me wished I could tell the woman that everything will be alright, but sometimes I wonder if that's true.

Between the pandemic, political division, and social unrest, the world feels a bit unmoored. Like things are unraveling. It reminds me of the poet Yeat's verse, *"the centre cannot hold,"* in his poem *"The Second Coming."*

For the center to hold these days, we need more love and compassion.

Love and compassion are necessities

When I was about thirteen years old, there was an automobile accident near our family home. We lived in the hills of Los Gatos, California, and there was a sharp turn in the roadway above our house.

A young man in a GTO was driving too fast to negotiate the turn and flipped his car. My father heard the crash, and the two of us ran down the driveway and up the street to investigate.

Our neighbor, a man named Jonce Thomas, came running up the street as well. Jonce was an authentic cowboy and a barrel racer. He had a stable on his property, and sometimes let my friend and I ride his horses.

Jonce was also a self-made man, who built a successful construction company. Despite his success, he was kind and humble.

Jonce found the young man lying beside the overturned car. The young man was injured, but conscious and breathing. A neighbor already called for police and an ambulance, and Jonce sat down beside the young man.

"Can I offer you a smoke, son?" Jonce said, adding, "Sometimes it helps calm the nerves." True to his cowboy image, Jonce was a heavy smoker. He pulled out his pack and slipped a cigarette between the young man's lips.

Jonce lit the cigarette, and the young man took a few puffs and managed to say, "Thanks, man." I remember Jonce putting his calloused hand on the young man's shoulder, and saying, "You just hang in there, son, help is on the way. You're going to be okay."

"Love and compassion are necessities, not luxuries. Without them humanity cannot survive." -Dalai Lama

My dad ran back to our house and returned with a wool blanket, which he placed over the young man, to lessen any shock from setting in. The actions of Jonce and my father left an impression on me.

Namely, that it's important to take care of one another in this life. To have empathy and kindness, even for people you don't know. Because they're struggling too. With the same fears, losses, and challenges in life.

The better off we are

One time Jonce came over to visit with my parents, and he stayed for dinner. During conversation, he shared a story about how he bought his Lincoln Continental.

Jonce, in his usual jeans, boots, and cowboy hat, had strolled into a Cadillac dealership. The salesmen gave him a once over and decided to ignore him. They assumed this humble cowboy couldn't afford a new Cadillac.

"The least amount of judging we can do, the better off we are."
-Michael J. Fox

Since the salesmen were unhelpful, Jonce went across the street to the Lincoln dealership, where the sales staff were kind and helpful. He bought his new Lincoln Continental and waved his cowboy hat out the window as he drove past the Cadillac dealership.

"You should have seen the look on those boys' faces," Jonce told my parents with a chuckle.

Grown men don't cry

There's a poignant Tim McGraw song titled, *"Grown Men Don't Cry"* which was a big hit in 2001. It was written by composers Tom Douglas and Steve Seskin, who based the song on personal experiences.

Explaining the lyrics, Tom Douglas shared the following in an interview with the Tennessean.com:

"I was going to get doughnuts early one morning for my son's third-grade class at the Oak Hill School. I rushed in because I should have gotten the doughnuts the night before. As I rushed in, I literally saw a lady talking on a payphone and a very distressed situation. She had a little boy who was weaving himself in and out of his mother's legs and she was weeping. This was, I guess, 2000 or 1999, and they still had payphones. The little boy was weaving himself in and out of his mother's legs, mascara tears running down her face. They looked like the shape of an ice cream cone melting. I rushed in to get the doughnuts and rush back. I saw them in a rusted red Corvair with newspapers and soup cans littered in the car."

We've probably all seen moments like this in our lives. Walking past others who are down on their luck. Douglas went on to say:

"In a moment I thought, 'I could give 'em 10 bucks. I could tell them where a Union Mission is, or I could just drive off in my black, new Chevy Suburban.' And that's what I did. I did nothing, and I was so ashamed that I let something kind of insignificant get in the way of a real life experience."

Courage to display it

What happened to the gift of empathy in our lives? Have we forgotten why we exist? Yes, we have families to love, careers to pursue, and passions to embrace. But they're not the only reasons why we exist.

We are also here on this earth to make it a better place. To love thy neighbor, regardless of his or her political party. To look out for one another. Try to spread a little more light, instead of darkness.

We seem to look for the worst in one another rather than the best. We gossip and judge instead of listen and care. We're so busy typecasting others we become blind to the things we share.

"I think we all have empathy. We may not have enough courage to display it." -Maya Angelou

Everyone wants to be loved. To find a good job. Chase passions. But increasingly, these things have become threatened by our worst instincts.

Angry presidential tweets won't move the needle any more than looters burning down the neighborhood. What we need instead is a path back to our humanity. Back to kindness, patience, and consideration.

Dignity and respect

In a quiet moment, I was able to see the humanity in a grocery store employee parked next to me. I saw the exhaustion in her eyes. I felt it. I would have given her a hug of encouragement, but we're still dealing with social distancing.

The composer Tom Douglas felt the humanity of a woman crying in a phone booth, with her little boy wrapped around her legs. But he failed to do anything about it. Instead, he just got in his Suburban and drove away.

Here in the United States, if we want to thrive again as a nation, we can't allow ourselves to get in the Suburban and drive away. We need to judge less and be a little more like those Lincoln salesmen who treated Jonce Thomas with dignity and respect.

We must resuscitate the gift of empathy, double down on kindness, and remember that the reason why we exist is to love one another and make the world a better place.

Chapter Forty-Eight

Are You Aware of the Good Bones in Your Life?

What does it mean when someone says that a house has good bones? According to an article in moving.com, it means the following:

"In general, a home with 'good bones' is considered to be a good home with the potential to be a great home. It typically describes a fixer-upper or some sort of neglected house (think: diamond in the rough) that features quality, well-made construction — hence the good bones meaning."

Realtors know that not every house is in perfect condition. While the overall structure of the house may be sound, there are often flaws and needed improvements.

"Every spirit makes its house, and we can give a shrewd guess from the house to the inhabitant." -Ralph Waldo Emerson

Buyers weigh the shortcomings of a house against its good bones and then negotiate with the seller. Of course, the positive aspects of a house may extend beyond its underlying structure.

Proximity to good schools, neighborhood crime, and the weather are all factors in deciding on a new home. But beyond external factors and fixable flaws, what we all want is a house with good bones. A sound structure we can rely on.

Improve it anyway

In 2016 Maggie Smith wrote a poem entitled "Good bones." Take a moment to read it:

Life is short, though I keep this from my children.
Life is short, and I've shortened mine
in a thousand delicious, ill-advised ways,
a thousand deliciously ill-advised ways
I'll keep from my children. The world is at least
fifty percent terrible, and that's a conservative
estimate, though I keep this from my children.
For every bird there is a stone thrown at a bird.
For every loved child, a child broken, bagged,
sunk in a lake. Life is short and the world
is at least half terrible, and for every kind
stranger, there is one who would break you,
though I keep this from my children. I am trying
to sell them the world. Any decent realtor,
walking you through a real shithole, chirps on
about good bones: This place could be beautiful,
right? You could make this place beautiful.

She wrote the poem in a coffee shop on a yellow legal pad. Little did she know how much her poem would resonate with people during the difficult year of 2016.

Three days before Smith's poem was published in a literary journal, a gunman shot and killed 49 people at the Pulse night club in Orlando. Smith's poem seemed to capture the troubled mood of people in 2016, and "Good bones" spread across the Internet and social media.

No doubt the poem resonates with people today, as we navigate a world-wide pandemic, social unrest, and political division.

How do we tell our children about the bad things in life? The pain, suffering, injustice, and disillusionment.

Smith's poem grapples with these questions, but it's not meant to be pessimistic. Smith states in a Washington Post article that she doesn't think she could write a poem about the world being beyond repair. She states:

"My hope is that the poem is a call to improve it anyway."

Your character is what you really are

Individuals are a lot like houses. Some of us are in pretty good shape, while others are fixer-uppers. People can overlook small flaws, so long as our underlying bones are good. A sound foundation trumps a bad paint job.

Like houses located in a good school district or near the ocean, we too may have positive, external qualities. Perhaps we are financially well off or highly respected in our field.

"Be more concerned with your character than your reputation, because your character is what you really are, while your reputation is merely what others think you are." -John Wooden

But in the end, it's our bones that matter more than amenities. Our sturdy character and reliable word. This is what attracts people of character. Superficial people fall for appearance or money, but those with depth look for good bones.

The cracks in my life

Realtors will tell you how important "staging" is to sell a house. A new paint job, basic landscaping, decluttering, and open windows to let the light in can go a long way in making a house more attractive to buyers.

But then there's the home inspection. An expert comes in to look more deeply at the house. It's foundation, roof, electrical, and more. Basically, the bones of the house.

All the fancy furniture, new paint, and flower beds can't make up for a cracked foundation or systemic electrical flaws. Bad bones are bad bones, in houses and people.

Like the twice-divorced man in the Ferrari, who doesn't want to tell you he's a cheater. Or that he's mortgaged to the hilt, and his sports car is a lease. As the cowboys say, he's "all hat and no cattle." No good bones.

"I let people see the cracks in my life. We can't be phony. We've got to keep it real." -Charles R. Swindoll

Well-adjusted people aren't afraid to let you see their superficial flaws, because they know that their character is sound. They know they've got good bones.

A house into a home

Some people are lucky. They are raised by amazing parents and families that show them love and teach them character. Their personalities and ethics are built upon a sound foundation. And thus, they have good bones.

Others are less fortunate and must endure retrofits and costly rebuilds. But if their hearts truly desire, they can have good bones too.

Beyond our good bones, there are external good bones in our lives as well. Namely, our health, loved ones, and passions. Sometimes we get lost in ambition or superficial desires and lose sight of these good bones in our lives.

If this is you, take a moment to consider your life without good health, loved ones, and your cherished passions. I give thanks each day that I am healthy, loved by my family, and able to pursue my writing and artwork.

"Gratitude unlocks the fullness of life. It turns what we have into enough, and more. It turns denial into acceptance, chaos to order, confusion to clarity. It can turn a meal into a feast, a house into a home, a stranger into a friend." -Melody Beattie

Gratitude for the external good bones of your life will strengthen the good bones of your character. We make our lives beautiful by inviting gratitude into our hearts. By truly seeing the good things in our lives.

Yes, there will be hardships and pain. Just as a house endures wear and tear, so do we (physically and emotionally). But a strong foundation, our good bones, will sustain us through life.

Home is where the heart is, and when you've got good bones, people will be drawn to you like a warm fire in a country cottage. May your good bones remain sturdy, and that fire within your hearth forever burn bright.

Chapter Forty-Nine

This Is the Damage of Labels

When I was a young man attending university, I applied to be a resident assistant in the campus apartments and dormitories. Resident assistants receive free room and board in exchange for providing counseling and event planning for students living on campus.

I got the job, which thrilled my father since he was footing the bill for my education. Unfortunately, I only lasted one year as a resident assistant.

I started strong, organizing dorm events, and counseling students who were struggling with personal problems. But, as I neared the end of the school year, I started to burn out on the job.

The residential life coordinator, Roger, (who was a friend of mine as well as my boss), sat me down one day and gently delivered the bad news. I would not be hired back next year.

Roger assured me that I was not being fired. Rather, they simply decided not to renew my contract next year. Still, I knew the truth. My performance had declined, and it cost me the job.

Change makes us grow

At the time, I viewed the situation as bad news. I was hesitant to tell my father, but when I finally mustered the courage to call him, he surprised me.

"Don't worry about it, Johnny," Dad told me, adding, "There's often good and bad in things like this."

"Well, I don't see much good. Obviously, I didn't do a good job, and now it's going to cost you more money next year," I said.

"That may be true, but you'll learn from this experience. And part of me didn't want you to take the job, anyway. I wanted you to enjoy your university experience and focus on your course-work." Dad said.

"The good and bad things are what form us as people... change makes us grow." -Kate Winslet

Turns out, Dad was right. The next year at university was spectacular. Free from the responsibilities of my resident assistant job, I was able to join the campus newspaper as their editorial cartoonist.

I also took up swimming, martial arts, and weightlifting with my friends. I doubled down on my academic work and graduated with distinction. It was a great year, and I learned to think differently about the "good and bad in things" as my father put it.

The label we put on people, events, and experiences isn't always the whole story. What's good or bad often depends, and sometimes it can be relative.

Fate had other ideas

Heather Lanier is the author of *"Raising a Rare Girl: A Memoir."* When Heather was pregnant with her daughter, she focused on having a Superbaby. She swallowed mercury-free capsules of DHA and filled her grocery carts with organic fruits and veggies.

She prepared meticulously for an unmedicated birth and listened to a natural birthing program of self-hypnosis. Later, after thirty-six hours of labor, her daughter Fiona was born.

As much as Lanier planned for a Superbaby, fate had other ideas. Lanier's daughter Fiona was born with an ultra-rare chromosomal condition called Wolf-Hirschhorn syndrome, which results in developmental delays.

"If there is a meaning in life at all, then there must be a meaning in suffering. Suffering is an ineradicable part of life, even as fate and death. Without suffering and death, human life cannot be complete."
-Viktor E. Frankl

For a while, Lanier was gripped by despair over her daughter's seemingly tragic condition. But then her perspective changed. In a TED talk about her daughter, Lanier said that:

"...reality is much more fluid, and it has much more to teach. As I started to get to know this mysterious person who was my kid, my fixed, tight story of tragedy loosened. It turned out my girl loved reggae, and she would smirk when my husband would bounce her tiny body up and down to the rhythm. Her onyx eyes eventually turned the most stunning Lake Tahoe blue, and she loved using them to gaze intently into other people's eyes."

Lanier learned that there were different ways of perceiving things. Where an occupational therapist described Fiona's eyes as neurologically dull, Lanier viewed her daughter's eyes as a calm, attentive presence.

Lanier decided that labels are damaging. Instead of declaring her daughter's condition a bad thing, she realized she had another choice. As Lanier states in her TED talk:

"I could drop my story that neurological differences and developmental delays and disabilities were bad, which means I could also drop my story that a more able-bodied life was better. I could release my cultural biases about what made a life good or bad and simply watch my daughter's life as it unfolded with openness and curiosity."

Good or bad, hard to say

We tend to label things in life as good or bad. If we hear that a work colleague's baby has Down syndrome, we whisper with others about the unfortunate outcome. Or we try and spin the good, saying how people with intellectual disabilities are so simple, pure, and here to teach us something.

Lanier questions our assumptions about what makes a life "good" or "bad." She urges us to stop fixating on labels and solutions for whatever we deem not normal. Rather, we should take life as it comes.

"When we label a person tragic or angelic, bad or good, we rob them of their humanity, along with not only the messiness and complexity that that title brings, but the rights and dignities as well."
-Heather Lanier

In Lanier's Ted talk she opens with an ancient parable about a farmer who lost his horse. The farmer's neighbors tell him, "Oh, that's too bad." And the farmer said, "Good or bad, hard to say."

Days later, the horse comes back with seven wild horses. The neighbors say, "Oh, that's so good!" The farmer shrugs and says, "Good or bad, hard to say."

The next day, the farmer's son rides one of the wild horses, is thrown off, and breaks his leg. The neighbors say, "Oh, that's terrible." And the farmer says, "Good or bad, hard to say."

Later, officers come knocking on village doors, looking for men to draft into the army. They see the farmer's son and his broken leg and pass him by. The neighbors say, "That's great luck!" And the farmer says, "Good or bad, hard to say."

What makes us most beautifully human

So it is with our lives. Things happen. Good or bad, hard to say. I lost my job as a resident assistant, which freed me the following year to have the best university experiences ever.

Think about your own experiences. Perhaps some that seemed awful at the time, led to good things later? Maybe this is the yin and yang of life.

Heather Lanier is raising a rare little girl. The experience is beautiful, complicated, joyful, frustrating, and more. It's not good or bad. It's life.

In a Wall Street Journal article, Lanier notes:

"A better life isn't one that steers clear of the most pain, managing to arrive at the end with the eulogy, 'He had it easy,' or 'She was the least scathed person I know.' This belief in the virtue of the 'happy' and suffering-free life sterilizes and shrinks us, minimizing what makes us most beautifully human."

Why would we want to run away from what makes us beautifully human? All of us have warts and imperfections. But we have our talents and charms, too.

Let's spend less time assigning labels and more time enjoying all that life has to offer. Neither good nor bad, it's all part of life and our human condition.

Lanier ends the Wall Street Journal article with the following, elegant observations:

"The point of this human life, I believe, is love. And the ridiculous and brave and risky act of love turns my heart into taffy, stretches it across the broad spectrum of human feeling. I hurt, I long, I exalt, I rejoice. And yes, my chest sometimes aches from the work of raising a rare girl. But the ache in my chest is a cousin of joy."

Chapter Fifty

What Monks Know About Better Living

When I awoke today the birds outside were in full song. There's a mockingbird who is a regular. He's been busy trying to attract a mate, often singing and dancing atop a nearby streetlight.

The house finches and verdins chirp and flit about in the courtyard as I leash my two dogs for our morning walk. The hummingbirds zoom around my wife's citrus garden, but also frequent the red feeder outside our kitchen. I call it their local pub.

It's early, but the fountain in our courtyard is on. The trickling of water is soothing, as I take in the sweet scent from our blooming lemon tree. It's very peaceful.

"The final wisdom of life requires not the annulment of incongruity but the achievement of serenity within and above it." -Reinhold Niebuhr

Some measure of isolation

We live in the desert of southern Nevada, in a Dell Webb type development. There are palm trees and rolling golf courses that bring greenery to the desert landscape.

Our sunrises and sunsets can be quite spectacular. Around dusk, my wife and I sit out by our pool and watch the bats as they fly erratically, eating tiny gnats and dipping into our pool for a sip of water.

Often, we sit in silence, taking in the sights, sounds, and calm grandeur. There's quietness, too, when I walk the dogs. We stroll to the rhythm of our footsteps. A dashing rabbit here and there might quicken the pace and cause tails to wag, but overall, there's a kind of stillness with our walks.

Sometimes I see passers-by listening to music or podcasts on their smartphones. I prefer to turn my phone off or leave it at home. I don't want technology to intrude on the solitude.

"Mechanization best serves mediocrity." -Frank Lloyd Wright

The dog walks remind me to slow down and enjoy the outdoors. I notice little details every day. Like the painted rocks with words of encouragement that someone is leaving along the footpaths.

I rather prefer some measure of isolation and solitude to the frenetic pace of modern life. Even on my dog walks, I tend to avoid people. I select obscure routes less likely to encounter others.

It's not that I'm anti-social. I enjoyed the limited social engagements I had before the pandemic upended our lives. But since retirement in 2017, I've largely retreated to my art studio/office, to read, write and create art.

"Be a loner. That gives you time to wonder, to search for the truth. Have holy curiosity. Make your life worth living." -Albert Einstein

Maybe this preference for solitude and quiet is a corrective following years of a very public life serving as a police chief. Back then, my schedule was an ocean of daily appointments, phone calls, meetings, and relentless emails. I was over socialized, and always had to be "on."

Since retirement, I've transitioned to becoming a full-time writer and artist. I'm blessed to able to work from home and embrace a quieter life.

Where many seem to be struggling with the pandemic quarantine, I've found home isolation, and the lack of social commitments, freeing. It's allowed me to become more contemplative and connected to the rhythms of family life.

As a result, I've thought a lot about the lifestyle choices we make, and the consequences of them.

It's not the answer

Why are so many people addicted to busyness? Why do we find it so hard to be alone with ourselves? Why do we get uncomfortable with silence, and feel the urge to interrupt it with talking? Are we looking in the wrong places to find happiness?

"There are times when good words are to be left unsaid." -The Rule of St. Benedict

Power, sex, and money seem to drive a great deal of modern life. While it's true that people need to make a living and provide for their families, there's more going on that just that. A lot of people want to be rich, beautiful, and famous. What is it inside themselves they are trying to ameliorate?

Contemporary media and the entertainment industry fuel these aspirations for affluence, good looks, and celebrity. Technology, particularly social media, amplifies such goals.

The irony is that for the few who achieve it all, they often find themselves unfulfilled. As the actor Jim Carrey famously stated:

"I think everybody should get rich and famous and do everything they ever dreamed of so they can see that it's not the answer."

In my law enforcement career, I saw plenty of unhappy people. Officers in our police department regularly responded to apartments and modest homes to deal with domestic disturbances, addiction issues, infidelity, suicides, mental health problems, and broken people along the margins of society.

Interestingly, our officers dealt with the same issues and problems in the affluent side of town, too.

I remember responding with other officers to an attempted suicide call. The home was a spectacular, multi-million-dollar property. We had to break into the house and a barricaded bedroom to find the nearly comatose women. She was young, attractive, and seemed to have everything one could wish for. Yet she was deeply unhappy.

If power, sex, and money don't reliably bring happiness or personal fulfillment, what does?

The answer might come from an unlikely source: Benedictine monks.

All these superficial pleasures in life

Father Christopher Jamison is the former Abbot of Worth, a Benedictine monastery in Sussex, England (he has since been appointed Abbot President of the English Benedictine Congregation).

Father Jamison is the author of *"Finding Sanctuary: Monastic Steps for Everyday Life."*

In 2005 Father Jamison and several other monks participated in a United Kingdom TV series titled *"The Monastery."* It chronicled the experience of several men of varying backgrounds selected to spend forty days and nights in the monastery.

The men had to embrace the 1500-year-old Benedictine practice of silence, obedience, and humility. They attended masses and counseling sessions with the monks.

One of the participants, Tony Burke, used to work in the world of advertising and production of television trailers for sex chat lines. Of all the participants, Burke experienced the most profound personal changes.

After the completion of the series, Burke quit working in the sex industry and continued to make frequent visits to the monastery.

As Father Jamison said at the beginning of the TV series:

"We find that people say to us that they've got more and more of all these superficial pleasures in life, and yet at a deeper level they're not happy. We believe that what we're offering is in fact the answer to that dissatisfaction with life."

A pause in a relentless continuum

In his book Finding Sanctuary, Father Jamison explains that the word sanctuary *"has two meanings: the primary meaning comes from the Latin root Sanctus, meaning 'holy.' So, the first meaning is 'a sacred space,' and deriving from this comes the secondary meaning: 'a place of refuge,' a place where someone on the run can escape to."*

Busy people often talk about "getting away on vacation." They long for an escape from their busy lives. The problem is that vacations may be temporary places of refuge, but they are generally not sacred spaces. Sacred spaces are something more. They connect us to the deeper things in life.

As one woman in Father Jamison's book said:

"I have started to understand that sanctuary is not just time out, a pause in a relentless continuum, but an opportunity to do some intense listening, made oddly unique through the company of others."

In other words, the starting point for finding sanctuary in your life is the *"quality of your day-to-day dealing with other people."* As Father Jamison notes:

"You cannot mistreat people one moment and then find sanctuary the next. Finding sacred space begins with the recognition of the sacred in your daily living."

Whether one is religious or not, Father Jamison unveils a Benedictine approach to finding sanctuary in your life. He likens it to building a house, which begins with the door. And the door signifies "virtue."

According to Father Jamison:

"Virtue is the recognition of the sacred in daily life. As we open the door of virtue in our personal and working lives, we will open the way into a sanctuary of peace for ourselves and for others. We are enabled to lead a unified life with the same values at home and at work, a life that is transparent and has nothing to hide."

The seven monastic steps

Once we walk through the door of virtue, we step on the floor, which equates with the first monastic step for everyday life: **Silence**.

Benedictine monks know that outside silence fosters inner silence. Distractions inside your head are often noises inside your heart. By laying down a carpet of contemplation, prayer, and meditation, you can inch closer to that sacred place inside yourself.

"Silence is a true friend who never betrays." -Confucius

Getting comfortable with silence takes time. At first, busy thoughts will intrude. Father Jamison says that fostering silence is like gardening. The weeds are your mental distractions. You pull them out, but they return. It's frustrating, but you must keep weeding if you want the flowers (voice of God, sacred thoughts, or deeper meanings).

The second monastic step is **contemplation**, which reflects the walls of the house we are building for our sanctuary. The great aim of Benedictines is to pray constantly. In other words, keeping the memory of God alive in their hearts.

"Slow down and live in the moment. Take the time to reflect on what you have done and where you are headed."- Jil Ashton-Leigh

Benedictine monks view reading as part of contemplation and meditation. In the Christian tradition, this involves reading of sacred texts like the Bible. However, non-religious individuals can benefit greatly from contemplation and meditation as well.

Choosing a quiet space each day, learning to breathe rhythmically, clearing your mind, and slowly reading meaningful texts can calm your spirit, and bring you closer to an inner sanctuary.

The third monastic step in building the roof of our sanctuary house is **obedience**. This is not meant to be blind obedience. It's all about listening. The word obedience derives from the Latin word "oboedire" which means not only to obey but also to listen.

"Blind obedience is a sign of weakness. Faithful obedience is a sign of strength."-Bob Lonsberry, A Various Language

A lot of us think we are free but fail to recognize ways we are not. We dress in ways that follow popular fashion. We parrot political views from news networks we follow. We are often held hostage by the popular culture instead of our own hearts.

Obedience means learning to listen to other people and not just yourself. It's about learning to set aside your desires to consider the desires of others and then finding a community to accommodate one another.

Through obedience, we develop a conscience and learn to consider the wider world of other people's feelings. If we only follow our feelings in life, we can run into problems.

The fourth monastic step is building the ladder of **humility**, which takes us to the roof and shelter. It comes from the Latin word "humus" which means earth or soil. It's about being realistic, honest, and truthful. It's what we mean when we say someone is "down to earth."

From a Biblical viewpoint, Adam and Eve ate the forbidden fruit because of their egos. They defied God, instead of being humble and human. Similarly, people today often act out of pride rather than humility.

"With pride, there are many curses. With humility, there come many blessings." -Ezra Taft Benson

We struggle with temptation and wanting to be the center of the universe. We find it hard to be down to earth. In Christian theology, humility involves avoiding the seven deadly sins of pride, envy, gluttony, greed, lust, sloth, and wrath.

How much more sanctuary would you have in your world if you embraced humility and resisted these seven deadly sins?

The fifth monastic step is building **community**. It means more than just being around other people. Groups are not communities.

The word community is used all the time these days. "She's part of our school community," or "He's part of our local community." The problem is that true community involves a deeper, reciprocal arrangement.

"The person who tries to live alone will not succeed as a human being. His heart withers if it does not answer another heart. His mind shrinks away if he hears only the echoes of his own thoughts and finds no other inspiration." -Pearl S. Buck

True community focuses on individuality more than individualism. Individualism is about doing your own thing in your own way, whereas individuality brings your contributions to the community, and vice-versa. The latter is about fostering good communication. There's an honest back and forth, and nobody is left behind.

Ideally, communion with other people should be like communion with nature. We should focus on the sacred. The humanity in others, and their unique gifts and contributions.

As we nearly complete our sanctuary house, we must consider the inner furnishings. These reflect the sixth monastic step, which is **spirituality**.

There are many modern spiritual movements. Some people find spirituality in nature. Spirituality allows us to move past the superficial things in life. To ask deeper questions about life's purpose and meaning.

"Spirituality is a brave search for the truth about existence, fearlessly peering into the mysterious nature of life." -Elizabeth Lesser, The New American Spirituality

In classic religions like Christianity, it's about being set free from the idolatry of people, objects, and techniques. It's about freedom from, what Father Jamison calls *"the constantly shifting sands of human desire. In classic religion, you do not pick and choose, you learn a whole way of life."*

Practicing a particular faith tradition, or seeking your own spirituality, helps connect you to deeper meaning, faith, and purpose.

The seventh and final monastic step in finding sanctuary is **hope**. Hope is often in short supply, especially in this time of a pandemic that has taken the lives of many and sickened others. Not the mention the economic hardship that people are facing around the world.

Yet, hope is possible. The demanding work of building your own sanctuary is how you achieve hope. Because a sturdy inner sanctuary will hold the wolves at bay. You'll have a sense of order in your life. A peaceful retreat in your heart, which invites the serenity that hope always brings.

"Hope is important because it can make the present moment less difficult to bear. If we believe that tomorrow will be better, we can bear a hardship today." -Thich Nhat Hanh

A kind of inner peace

You don't have to become a monk to live a better life. But if sculpting your abs, buying more things, chasing more likes on social media, and focusing only on yourself have not brought you peace, then maybe a few monastic steps could help?

When asked once if he was happy, Father Jamison answered, "I'm not unhappy." From all the videos I've watched and accounts I've read about monks, none of them seem to be unhappy. In fact, they radiate a kind of inner peace infrequently seen in the rest of society.

Try to look past the superficial pleasures in life. Build that door of virtue, and then work through the seven monastic steps of silence, contemplation, obedience humility, community, spirituality, and hope.

Do this, and chances are you'll live a better, more fulfilling life.

Chapter Fifty-One

How to Get Your Life Off Autopilot

"You need to get out of the house more," my wife declared one evening as I was enjoying a good book.

"Why do you say that?" I asked. "I'm quite happy in my art studio. Besides, I visit the gym, enjoy coffee with the boys, and take lots of walks with the dogs."

"Babe, we live in Vegas," she said. "You should explore more. See new things. Besides, I found the perfect event for you."

Nervous, I put my book down, turned to her, and said, "What would that be?"

"There's a Las Vegas typewriter club," she said. "I found them on Facebook, and they're having a meet up soon. You should go."

"Sounds interesting, but I don't have a working typewriter. The Underwood you got from your mom needs a new ribbon or something," I said, pleased with having found a reasonable excuse.

My wife's expression was not cheerful, so I added, "But what the heck, I guess I can go check it out."

Find out who you are

Truth be told, I wasn't enthusiastic about the typewriter meet up. A loner at heart, I'm not much of a joiner, but I know such experiences can be enriching and lead to meeting fascinating people.

The next day my wife was at work and texted me pictures of two working typewriters she found online for sale. She asked which one I preferred, and I picked the compact little 1933 Corona №4.

A few days later, UPS delivered my new (old) Corona, just in time for the typewriter meetup that afternoon. We bought some fancy typewriter paper, and I was all set.

I hadn't typed on a typewriter since my university days, but I always loved the clickety-clack sound of the keys and pleasing physicality of the device, with its carriage return lever, spools, and type bars.

"At the typewriter you find out who you are." — Tom Robbins

Like it or not, my same old routine of working from home, going to the gym, and walking the dogs was about to be interrupted.

Little did I know what adventure lay ahead.

We're so comfortable we're miserable

Speaking of adventure, consider the endurance athlete and NY Times bestselling author Dean Karnazes. His long-distance running has taken him all over the world.

Karnazes has pushed his body and mind to unbelievable limits. His website notes:

"Among his many accomplishments, he has run 350 continuous miles, foregoing sleep for three nights. He's run across Death Valley in 120-degree temperatures, and he's run a marathon to the South Pole in negative 40 degrees. On ten different occasions, he's run a 200-mile relay race solo, racing alongside teams of twelve."

You don't become an ultimate athlete like Dean Karnazes unless you learn to do one thing: ***Embrace discomfort***

The repetitious nature of our work lives, comfy recliners at home, television, and social media distractions all cocoon us into a safe, mediocre comfort zone. We like what's easy and familiar.

The problem is that easy and familiar won't move you forward. Discomfort does. The discomfort of hitting the gym when you don't feel like it. The discomfort of putting yourself in unfamiliar social settings (like a typewriter meet up in Las Vegas).

Discomfort is how we grow.

Outsideonline.com posted a fascinating interview with Dean Karnazes, who shared the following insight:

"Western culture has things a little backwards right now. We think that if we had every comfort available to us, we'd be happy. We equate comfort with happiness. And now we're so comfortable we're miserable. There's no struggle in our lives. No sense of adventure. We get in a car, we get in an elevator, it all comes easy. What I've found is that I'm never more alive than when I'm pushing and I'm in pain, and I'm struggling for high achievement, and in that struggle, I think there's a magic."

Despite being happy and content with my life of reading, writing, and creating art in my studio, the truth is that I became a little stale. I found my comfort zone and lost my sense of adventure.

Fortunately, my wife knows me better than I know myself sometimes. Which is why she encouraged me to get out of the house and attend the typewriter meetup.

Sisters of perpetual indulgence

I drove north on Highway 15 and took the Sahara exit to downtown Las Vegas. The typewriter meetup was to take place in a photography studio. It was an area of town I was unfamiliar with, and it felt a bit sketchy.

I drove past graffiti walls, an adult entertainment club, a few shuttered businesses, and several guys with tattoos hanging around buildings and corners. I found out later I was in the Arts District of Las Vegas.

The Las Vegas typewriter club's Facebook page provided an address for the meetup and warned that the photography studio was a bit hard to find.

I parked my car and slung a backpack containing my new typewriter over my shoulder. The main building in front of me included a business called "Las Vegas Oddities." Apparently, it's the go-to place if you're in the market for unique collectibles such as animal bones, herbs, and occult supplies.

After some exploration, I found the photography studio, but the door was locked, and no one was there.

To kill time, I strolled upstairs. The first business I encountered was called *"The Nunnery: Holy Order Sin Sity Sisters of Perpetual Indulgence."*

You can't make stuff like this up.

According to their website:

"The Sisters of Perpetual Indulgence, founded in San Francisco in 1979, have become a worldwide movement, with orders of queer nuns springing up across the planet fighting for the promulgation of omniversal joy and the expiation of stigmatic guilt. The Holy Order Sin Sity Sisters are the Sisters of Perpetual Indulgence of Las Vegas, founded June 2005."

The Sin Sity Sisters' mission statement includes the following:

"We work to raise money for our Sisters AIDS Drug Assistance Program (SADAP); fight for queer rights and visibility; do safer sex outreach; and strive diligently to keep our sense of humor, never taking ourselves so seriously that we forget to have fun."

Looking around, it was clear to me that the clusters of buildings housed an eclectic mix of Indie, hipster, and alternative lifestyle businesses.

A surreal experience

I gazed downstairs, and the photography studio, "Photo Bang Bang," was now open. I was greeted at the door by the owner, Curtis Joe Walker. Behind him, I could see an old typewriter and knew I was in the right spot.

Curtis gave me a tour of the photography studio, and I was impressed by his photography work (especially his retro, Lomography instant photography).

The photo studio was a surreal experience, containing different themed rooms that photographers rent by the hour for creative work. Rooms include a 3-wall Cyclorama, a clock tower, a medieval dungeon, a haunted house, and endless props.

We set my old typewriter down, and Curtis helped figure out why the spools were not working properly. He offered different typing papers to experiment with.

I started plinking away on my 1933 Corona №4 while Curtis gave an impromptu studio tour to a couple who popped in. Then, a tattooed woman in leather arrived and settled into the adjacent haunted room to work on a typewriter there.

I spent over an hour typing some fun letters to my wife, thanking her for pushing me out of my comfort zone. Photo Bang Bang was the last place I expected to find myself in Las Vegas, but the experience was an eye-opening, fun adventure.

You'll never get better

Many of my accomplishments in the past were the result of getting comfortable with discomfort.

For example, during graduate school, I worked long shifts as a security guard. I pulled all-nighters studying for exams and spent weekends in the school library doing research.

At times I was tired and uncomfortable, but the master's degree I achieved served me well my entire career.

I trained for years in the martial arts, often driving to the dojo after working a graveyard shift as a young police officer.

Jujitsu was the martial art I studied, and the intense grappling and throws caused many scrapes, bruises, and injuries. Sometimes, I just lay on the dojo mat, exhausted.

Once I was thrown so hard the impact of landing on the mat threw my heart into super ventricular tachycardia. It took an ambulance ride and emergency room injection to correct my heart rhythm.

Despite the injuries and discomfort of my martial arts training, I gained many things, such as self-confidence, the ability to defend myself, strength, stamina, and greater focus.

"If you're never able to tolerate a little bit of pain and discomfort, you'll never get better." — Angela Duckworth

Think of the hard things you accomplished in your life. Consider the discomforts you endured to reach a goal, gain new skills, obtain a certificate or degree, or achieve a promotion at work.

It's the hard knocks in life, the discomforts, and challenges, that shape us. Allowing yourself to remain stuck in the same old routines and cycles will not move you forward. They'll just keep you on autopilot.

Your comfort zone is not your friend. Yes, it might guide you away from dangerous, unwise things. But often, it will prevent you from stretching yourself. It will insulate you from discomfort, which is often the price of admission for personal growth.

Mindless repetition and mediocrity

An article in Huffpost.com made the following observation:

"Have you ever paused to consider the ease at which you follow daily, weekly, and annual routines? Most people wake up at the same time, eat similar things for breakfast, wear the same rotation of clothing, arrive at work at the same time, grab lunch with the same people, watch the same shows at night...yada, yada, yada."

While habits, consistency, and routines can accelerate achievement in areas like exercise and creative work, they can also lull us into a rut of mindless repetition and mediocrity.

The Huffpost.com article goes on to note:

"Routines like these become so familiar that we often lose track of the fact that we're just cruising through life. Despite the fact that we live in an enormous universe with seven different continents, nearly 200 different countries, more than 7 billion people, thousands of languages, and hundreds of thousands of unique experiences, we stick to what we know. Then we wonder why we feel stuck, stale, and stagnant."

An article in Forbes.com mentions Jacquelyn James, director of research at the Sloan Center on Aging & Work. According to the article, James *"argues that being engaged in new and exciting activities can provide a host of benefits as we mature."* She goes on to state:

"As we get older, it is more important to find things to do that light up our lives...Our minds are central to this effort and thrive when we are finding new things for them to do. Whether it's acquiring a new skill or language (very high on the list of mental acuity benefits), joining a new group, and meeting new people, or finding ways to continue using existing skills, successful aging and longevity are built upon patterns of lifelong learning."

Try new things

Work, sleep, and eating make up most of our days, leaving precious left-over time for leisure pursuits. If we don't get intentional about how to wisely spend our free time, we'll fritter it away on less meaningful things. Or worse, we'll stay lost in our comfort zone.

Hamster videos on YouTube and political rants on Facebook might make for an easy diversion, but they don't stretch your mind in new ways that help you grow.

In contrast, new experiences release dopamine in our brains and create new neurons and neural connections. The more challenging the experiences, the better.

If you want to want to get your life off autopilot, then you need to get comfortable with discomfort, and do the following: ***Try new things.***

Thanks to my wife, I got out of my comfort zone and attended a typewriter meet up in the arts district of downtown Las Vegas. It was an entertaining adventure. I learned more about my new typewriter and got creatively inspired by Curtis Joe Walker's amazing, old-school photography.

When was the last time you tried something new? Usually, it's laziness or fear that prevents us from venturing beyond our comfort zones. We imagine worse case scenarios when most often a new experience will enrich us.

Trying new things will amplify your creativity. Visiting Photo Bang Bang, viewing Curtis's work, and exploring the Las Vegas Arts District have ignited all kinds of creative ideas for my writing and artwork.

Trying new things will make you more well-rounded. Ask anyone who travels frequently. New experiences can release dopamine and create new neural pathways in the brain.

A Huffpost.com article on neurogenesis and neuroplasticity noted:

"Traveling promotes neurogenesis by exposing your brain to new, novel, and complex environments. Paul Nussbaum, a neuropsychologist from the University of Pittsburgh explains, 'Those new and challenging situations cause the brain to sprout dendrites.'"

You don't have to take big, expensive trips to try new things. There are simpler ways to get out of your comfort zone, such as:

Change or vary the people you talk to. Meeting new people will open you up to new ideas, perspectives, and experiences.

Change the things you read or view. If you read spy thrillers, switch things up and try a science fiction novel. If you watch FOX news, switch to CNN, and challenge your views (and vice versa).

Put yourself in different environments. Go on a micro-adventure, as I did with the typewriter meetup. It doesn't have to cost much to explore new places.

Life is too short to stay huddled in your protective little comfort zone. The more you try new things and get comfortable with discomfort, the more you will grow.

You don't have to become Dean Karnazes and run an ultra-marathon. You don't have to join the Sin Sity Sisters or buy an antique typewriter and hang out with hipster photographers.

All you have to do is try new things. It's a powerful approach to improving your life, and I'll wager you'll be happy with the results.

Chapter Fifty-Two

The Art
of Emotional
Wintering

We were watching TV in the living room when it happened.

Dad lurched forward in his reading chair. He was perspired and a little out of breath. My mother looked at him from the couch and said, "John, are you alright?"

"I think it's my heart," he said.

It was a flurry of activity after that. Dad tried to stand up, and my mother asked me to help guide him to the couch. Then she ran to the kitchen phone and dialed 9-1-1.

I was 13 years old and scared to death. Dad looked up at me from the couch and said, "Keep a stiff upper lip, Johnny." Typical Dad, always stoic.

Paramedics arrived quickly, despite our home being tucked away in the mountains. The street we lived on was "Hidden Drive."

Later, at the hospital, there were tense conversations as my father laid out worst-case instructions for my mother. "Cremation and an inexpensive urn," he said. "Don't let them talk you into pricey caskets. Sell the Lincoln and get an affordable car."

Watching a beloved parent dance with death leaves an impression. Nothing is certain in life.

Anything can happen.

Those who have endured, feared, striven, and lived

Dad's heart attack was a wake-up call. He was a Type A personality. Driven. Sometimes impatient.

As an administrative law judge, Dad handled stressful, multimillion-dollar cases. They required deep research and a deft hand in managing political interests and boisterous parties.

Our prayers were answered, and Dad survived. His heart attack may have taught me about the fragility of life, but his recovery taught me volumes about our capacity to grow and change.

At six feet tall and over 200 pounds, Dad was a formidable man. He had big arms and strong hands. So, it was hard to witness the changes happening in him.

His recovery involved a severely modified diet. Cherished chocolate bars were replaced with radishes. No more sausages and burgers. At first, the dietary changes made him grumpy. But as he began to feel better, he adapted.

Dad's recovery included daily walking, and soon he was traversing the hills behind our home. He lost significant weight, and his thin physique looked foreign to me. But I could see he was healthier.

Most importantly, Dad's doctor enrolled him in a new behavior modification program for "Type A" personalities.

After when Dad returned to work, he continued to attend "Type A" meetings, and eventually chaired the meetings. He wrote weekly, handwritten letters of encouragement to the group's participants. They often contained the following, elegant preamble:

"The Fellowship, a select brotherhood of those who have endured, feared, striven, and lived, dedicated to absorbing from shared ex-

perience, a knowledge of our disability, the means to cope, and a heightened will to appreciate and merit our second chance."

The positive changes in my father were significant. He spent more time sitting on the patio with his cats, brushing them and scattering treats to their delighted purrs. He became more reflective, savored meals, and listened intently.

It was a complete transformation.

Dad's heart attack forced him into an emotional wintering. His months of recuperation were like a protective cocoon, providing the time and space needed to heal and emerge stronger.

Seasons when the leaves fall from us

Sooner or later in life, we will face unwanted challenges. Whether a health crisis or unexpected career change, we may suddenly find ourselves in a period or season of emotional wintering.

Author Katherine May explores all of this in her beautiful book *"Wintering: The Power of Rest and Retreat in Difficult Times."*

May's book explores her husband's illness, her son quitting school, and her own medical challenges. She learned how to endure difficult times and embrace the opportunities they offered.

"We have seasons when we flourish and seasons when the leaves fall from us, revealing our bare bones. Given time, they grow again. "-Katherine May, Wintering: The Power of Rest and Retreat in Difficult Times

Reading May's book called up all the memories of my father's heart attack and recovery, as well as my wife's journey last year with breast cancer.

The book even unearthed memories of my childhood, and the times I was home sick from school.

There are gaps in the mesh of the everyday world

As a boy, I was prone to respiratory illnesses like bronchitis.

I had to repeat the second grade because of a prolonged illness. It was my first emotional wintering. Yet despite the worry of missing school, being home sick was not entirely unpleasant.

I remember spending the days drawing, watching acrobatic squirrels in the oak trees outside my bedroom window, and sleeping comfortably for long stretches. My mother cared for me tenderly, bringing my favorite meals of soft-boiled eggs, toast, and apple juice.

No one wants to fall ill or face a life-changing circumstance, but the time we spend in these emotional winters can change us for the better. We can emerge with a deeper appreciation for our health or a refined view of what we want our future to look like.

Sometimes illness and adversity can teach us things about ourselves.

"There are gaps in the mesh of the everyday world, and sometimes they open up and you fall through them into somewhere else. Somewhere else runs at a different pace to the here and now, where everyone else carries on. Somewhere else is where ghosts live, concealed from view and only glimpsed by people in the real world. Somewhere else exists at a delay, so that you can't quite keep pace. Perhaps I was already teetering on the brink of somewhere else anyway; but now I fell through, as simply and discreetly as dust sifting between the floorboards. I was surprised to find that I felt at home there. Winter had begun."-Katherine May, Wintering: The Power of Rest and Retreat in Difficult Times."

Winter is not the death of the life cycle, but its crucible

The art of emotional wintering is about accepting these times in our lives when we will fall through the cracks. It's about taking advantage of rest and retreat to heal, grow, and discover new things about ourselves.

My father's heart attack was a wake-up call. Removed from the frenetic pace of work-life, his recuperation and emotional wintering provided the time and space to rest, reflect, heal, and change.

He emerged a better man. More patient. More attuned to the things that mattered most, like his health and family.

"Winter is not the death of the life cycle, but its crucible."-Katherine May, Wintering: The Power of Rest and Retreat in Difficult Times

I went through my own crucible in the second grade. All that time at home, recovering from illness, made me yearn for school again. When I finally returned, I brought with me a deeper appreciation and focus on my studies.

You will go through your own crucibles and times of emotional wintering. They're seldom wanted and often inconvenient.

Just remember that the art of emotional wintering involves acceptance and willingness to reflect. Time will slow down, and during this dreamlike season, you may feel adrift. But it will pass.

Be patient. Take each day as it comes. Focus on the long view.

When we greet the winter and let it in, we realize that healing and recovery take time. But they also instruct.

The sun will shine again, and we can emerge stronger, wiser, and filled with an emotional peace. It's a kind of peace that will carry us into spring, summer, and across the golden landscape of our future.

Chapter Fifty-Three

Why Your Second Mountain Is the Answer

You played by the rules. Kept your head down, went to school, and embarked on a promising career. While others got distracted, you embraced a strong work ethic.

Promotions followed. You and your spouse moved out of that tiny apartment and bought a house. Kids came along, and the rhythms of life changed, but you remained disciplined.

You stuck to a lean diet, exercised regularly, got up early, and made your bed every morning. There were amazing vacations, nice cars, and sound investments for your retirement.

According to the author David Brooks, you've made it to the top of your first mountain. The goals that you achieved are the ones American culture endorses: to reach financial success, make your mark, and live happily ever after.

But there's a problem. You feel all knotted up inside. Unsettled. As the dust jacket on David Brooks' book *"The Second Mountain: The Quest for a Moral Life"* states:

"But when they get to the top of that mountain, something happens. They look around and find the view...unsatisfying. They realize: This wasn't my mountain after all. There's another, bigger mountain out there that is actually my mountain."

The second mountain

According to Brooks' book, on the second mountain:

"Life moves from self-centered to other-centered. They want the things that are truly worth wanting, not the things other people tell them to want. They embrace a life of interdependence, not independence. They surrender to a life of commitment."

When we're still climbing that first mountain of success, we tend to cast a wary eye at commitments. We might be committed to our spouse and kids but avoid outside commitments. Namely, because they compete with our precious time.

When I was a police chief, I had a busy work schedule. I was hyper-focused on my career and tried to avoid seemingly unnecessary commitments. I joined the local Rotary club, not for philanthropic reasons, but to benefit my career.

I knew being in the Rotary club would benefit my reputation and provide important community connections. I wasn't alone. There were business people in my Rotary club who joined for similar, self-centric reasons.

But a funny thing started to happen. Our Rotary club often took on weekend community projects. We assisted elderly residents by installing safety rails in their homes. We volunteered at the City's annual electronic waste clean-up day.

I remember working those "e-waste" cleanups. Residents drove up to our drop off location. "Hey Chief, how are you doing," many would say, adding, "Thanks for being here and helping out!"

I was surprised at the sheer number of people I knew. I enjoyed the conversations, learning things about our city and its residents. It felt good to greet familiar faces and catch up on events. I started to see the community as something more than a piece of my professional career. I realized that the community was like an extension of my family.

The community was my people. My tribe. I felt a sort of kinship to them. Looking back, I realize this was a turning point, as I moved from self-centered to other-centered.

As a police chief, I had reached the pinnacle of my law enforcement career. I had a good income, benefits, and professional respect. I reached the top of my first mountain, but those Rotary experiences made me realize that I was dissatisfied with the view.

My second mountain was calling.

The vanity of ambition

According to David Brooks' book, four commitments define a life of meaning and purpose:

-Commitment to a spouse (and family)

-Commitment to a vocation

-Commitment to a philosophy or faith

-Commitment to a community

When we're on our first mountain, we may indeed love our spouse and family, but we are still victims of hyper individualism. The spouse and kids are part of the successful image in our heads. We are still stuck in the vanity of ambition.

There was a time in American culture when communities mattered more. Farmers helped one another out. City neighborhoods were tight knit, as families came together to watch each other's kids. People worked in one position or company their whole lives. Everyone went to the same bank. The same butcher.

It's not like that so much anymore. Society is more mobile, fractured, and consumed with digital life. We're more connected yet have more loneliness and existential angst.

David Brooks writes of those old American communities:

"That moral ecology had a lot of virtues. It emphasized humility, reticence, and self-effacement. The message was you're no better than anybody else, but nobody is better than you. It held that self-love-egotism, narcissism- is the root of much evil. If you talked

about yourself too much, people would call you conceited, and they would turn up your nose."

Of course, the old American culture had its failings. There was racism. Housewives were often trapped, unable to pursue careers. The point is, there was less of the hyper individualism we see today.

A second, timeless, larger self

Visit Instagram and you'll see endless, vainglorious posts of people flexing in the gym. "Look at me!" they seem to be exclaiming. When we're on the first mountain of our lives, we are self-centric. It takes time to move from self-centered to other-centered. But eventually, as we reach the top of our first mountain, we experience a stomach level sadness. We feel lost.

We begin to intuit that maybe, just maybe, it's not all about us. Perhaps life has a deeper meaning than six-pack abs and Facebook likes. Your heart begins to whisper to you. A longing for meaning surfaces in your soul, and as C. S. Lewis writes, we notice:

"The scent of a flower we have not found, the echo of a tune we have not heard, news from a country we have never yet visited."

And so, we descend into the valley. That confusing, no man's land between our first mountain and second mountain. As David Brooks notes, the *"shallow food"* of ambition won't satisfy this deeper hunger in us. We discover that money, titles, and vacations don't shape our moral purpose. We need something more meaningful.

This is when we start to look more closely at our vocations, which are different than our careers. Careers are all about marketing your talents and professional skills to make a good living. A vocation is less about your ego and more about a true calling. Perhaps it's an injustice you want to fight or the deepest expression of your creative self. It's a holy thing.

This recognition that you are meant for something deeper and more meaningful is best captured in the words of the poet Rilke, who said:

"The knowledge comes to me that I have space within me for a second, timeless, larger self."

Our transformation happens in the valley, as we begin to find our vocation. We also burrow deeper into the substrate of our souls, finding purpose in religious faith and/or a commitment to a philosophy. Life becomes about serving something greater than ourselves. We become acquainted with the joys of deep commitments and service to an ideal or others.

As David Brooks writes:

"Fulfillment and joy are on the far side of service."

We discover that commitments and sacrifices to a greater cause or purpose shape our moral foundation. As the theologian Tim Keller notes, real freedom *"is not so much the absence of restrictions as finding the right ones."*

A cause or purpose outside of ourselves

When I lived in California, I knew a young man named Elliot who created a successful martial arts school after he graduated from high school. My son achieved his black belt at Elliot's martial arts school.

I used to think that Elliot found his calling. That he was already on his second mountain. He was so passionate about the martial arts, and a gifted instructor. He married a beautiful young woman who was also a martial artist. The world was his oyster. But then, Elliot's marriage ended. Later, he decided to sell his martial arts school. I was surprised by all of this.

A few years went by, and I received a Facebook post from Elliot. He started a GoFundMe campaign to build a skatepark in Mexico for children in a small village. It was obvious from the post that Elliot was passionate about the project.

He knew the people in this small Mexican village and was committed to helping improve their lives. I made my donation with a smile. Elliot had found his calling. He was on his second mountain.

Our lives seem to go best when in service to others or a worthy ideal. A cause or purpose outside of ourselves. When we pursue an ideal, we don't mind the restrictions and hardships that accompany the journey.

When we're young, we crave freedom. We don't want to be tied down or restricted in any way. We are hyper-individualistic. As we move to our second mountain, things change. We understand that sometimes restrictions can lead to greater freedom.

For example, if you want to enjoy the freedom of playing concert level, classical piano, you need to embrace years of practice and study. Such an effort may feel restrictive but will lead to immense creative freedom.

Enrich your moral character

If you want to have a meaningful life, you need to find your second mountain. You need to move from self-centric living to other-centric living. This can be found in deepening your commitment to your spouse and family. Learning to listen much closer and making their growth and happiness more important than your own.

If you want to have a meaningful life, you need to find your vocation. Your true calling. The thing you love doing deep down in your soul, regardless of whether it makes money. In my case, I retired early from my police career because I could no longer ignore the siren song of my creative being. I knew that writing and creating art would feed my soul and inspire others.

Yes, we must make a living. Sometimes our true vocation is not something that earns an income. Thus, we learn to become pragmatic jugglers. We find a job or career to make money and craft our schedule to make time for our vocation. In this way, we continue to grow and start climbing our second mountain.

If you want to have a meaningful life, committing to a healthy philosophy or faith helps. It's about believing in and pursuing something greater than yourself. Whether it's a religion, ideal, or humanitarian purpose, such a commitment can enrich your moral character.

Some people join a political cause, which is fine, so long as the ideal is worthy. However, once politics becomes your ethnic and moral identity (David Brooks warns), it becomes impossible to compromise, because compromise becomes dishonor.

As David Brooks goes on to note:

"These days, partisanship for many people is not about which party has the better policies. It's a conflict between the saved and the damned. People often use partisan identity to fill the void left when their other attachments wither away- ethnic, neighborhood, religious, communal, and familial."

Lastly, if you want to have a meaningful life, rediscover the benefits of committing to a community. Perhaps it's the community in your small town. Serving on your city council, or in the local soup kitchen.

For a loner like me, I strive to serve my online community of readers and collectors of my artwork. I commit to producing the best writing and artwork I can, to educate, entertain, and hopefully enrich the lives of others.

My work involves a lot of reading, research, and artistic trial and error. It can sometimes be exhausting but is also deeply fulfilling. Especially when I hear from readers who tell me how much my work helped them, or collectors who say my artwork uplifts them.

The view is spectacular

There's nothing wrong with financial and career success. It's not a sin to work out and improve your appearance. A lot of us strive for such things on our first mountain. But when you start hearing those internal whispers from within your soul, listen.

When the view from atop the first mountain loses its luster, pay attention. Your second mountain is calling, and let me tell you, the view from the second mountain is spectacular.

Chapter Fifty-Four

Guess Who Has the Most Power in a Relationship?

We had been to their apartment twice in the last two months. This was the third time. As before, the neighbors called, no doubt tired of the loud arguments that echoed through the thin apartment walls.

She opened the door. Her hair was messy and eyes red from crying.

"Hi Lisa," I said, "I'm Officer John Weiss. We met last month."

"Oh, yeah. We're fine, just arguing. My husband, Steve, can be a jerk sometimes," she said.

"Okay, well, my partner and I just need to talk to you and your husband separately to make sure everyone is okay," I said.

I feel a bit invisible to him

My partner and I determined that no crime had occurred. Lisa was a stay-at-home mother. Steve was a mechanic who liked to hit the pub with his buddies after work. Their infant child, miraculously, slept through all the yelling.

Their arguments centered around Lisa feeling taken for granted. Steve made the money. Steve hung out with his buddies after work.

It was obvious, despite her frustrations, that Lisa loved Steve. "Sometimes he brings me flowers. He works hard, and he's a good Dad. It's just that sometimes I feel a bit invisible to him," she once told me.

My partner and I dealt with a lot of couples and situations like this. Some turned into domestic violence incidents, but many were the kind of common arguments that spouses have.

Money, sex, addictions, and children are often the issues that couples fight over. But beneath the surface, unmet expectations and diminished self-respect can be the real problems.

Too soon old, too late smart

The late Gordon Livingston, M.D. was a graduate of West Point and Johns Hopkins School of Medicine. Awarded the Bronze star for valor in Vietnam, he went on to become a psychiatrist and writer.

In thirteen months, Dr. Livingston lost one son to suicide and another to leukemia. He deeply understood the human condition and tragedies of life, and poured wisdom into his eloquent, succinct books.

One of my favorite books by Dr. Livingston is *"Too Soon Old, Too Late Smart: Thirty True Things You Need to Know Now."*

If this book had been published in the early 1990s, and I had read it as a rookie cop, I would have had some valuable advice for Lisa. Specifically, chapter five of Dr. Livingston's book, which contained the following title:

"Any relationship is under the control of the person who cares the least."

A sort of enlightened self-interest

It was clear to my partner and I that Steve had taken his wife Lisa for granted. He was the income winner. He had the freedom to socialize with his buddies after work. Lisa was home all day with their child. She made dinner for Steve when he came home.

Steve wasn't a bad guy. He was always polite and apologetic with us. But whether intentional or not, he seemed to care less about his marriage than Lisa.

It isn't supposed to be this way. We all dream of falling in love and entering a relationship built on mutual love, respect, and admiration.

Maybe the problem is in how we approach relationships? Instead of accepting our partners the way they are, perhaps we foist too many expectations on them?

Listen to Dr. Livingston as he describes how most people find a partner:

"The ways in which people come together and choose each other place a great emphasis on the potent combination of sexual attraction and a sort of enlightened self-interest that evaluates the other person on a series of qualities and achievements: education, earning potential, shared interests, trustworthiness, and philosophy of life. Each person's assessment of a prospective mate using these standards creates a certain set of expectations. It is the failure of these expectations over time that causes relationships to dissolve."

So, what do you do when expectations are not met? How do you right the ship if your partner cares less than you do about the relationship?

Good communication is important. You must broach difficult issues and feelings with your partner. Lisa did that in her relationship with Steve. She knew he held the power and she felt taken advantage of. Steve promised to change, but somehow things always slid back to the same old problems.

Higher quality alternatives

Psychologist Esther Ghijsen noted in the article *"Love Hurts"* for United Academics Magazine the following:

"Research shows that the more power someone has in a relationship, the less committed he is to it (Grauerholz, 1987)."

If you're the one without the power in a relationship, what should you do? Here's what Dr. Ghijsen advises:

"In order to gain back control, you need to acknowledge your fears, and then toss them aside. A new study shows that the one who's in power in a relationship also has 'higher quality alternatives' in life — which means his family, free time, friends, and other dating partners are of greater value to him. Here lies the key to solving your problem: start building those alternatives yourself. Go out with friends, start that new course or class, host a dinner party for your family — invest some time in people that are not your lover."

A lot of marriages risk the slow march towards alienation. Eventually, one ends up showing and/or expressing less respect and affection for the other.

According to Dr. Livingston, the person who cares less *"appears to be a bid to seize control of the relationship."* Dr. Livington goes on to note the following:

"That this effort has been successful can be seen when one spouse has a greater investment in reconciliation and is much more upset at the prospect of ending the marriage. When I point out to people that much of the distress they are feeling is not shared by their partner and that this is the source of their feeling 'out of control,' they are usually quick to recognize their predicament. While it takes two people to create a relationship, it takes only one to end it."

It's possible to reinvent yourself. You are not defined by who you are today or the status of your relationship. People can improve themselves, and their relationships.

Everything is within your power

Consider the story of Joseph Pilates. He was sickly as a child and studied various self-improvement systems. He examined Eastern practices like Zen Buddhism and admired the ancient Greek ideal of man perfected in body, mind, and spirit.

An article about Joseph Pilates in VeryWellFit.com noted:

"German-born Joseph Pilates was living in England and working as a circus performer and boxer when he was placed in forced

internment in England at the outbreak of World War I. While in the internment camp, he began to develop the floor exercises that evolved into what we now know as the Pilates mat work."

Joseph Pilates, against great hurdles, changed who he was. From a sickly child to a self-confident, physically fit man.

Even with meager resources, it's possible to change your life. That's precisely what Lisa did.

Several months went by after our last domestic disturbance call involving Lisa and Steve. I worried that maybe things fell apart and they divorced. Then one day while on duty, I bumped into Lisa at a coffee shop.

"Hi Lisa, how are you?" I asked.

"Officer Weiss, hello. I'm good. Real good," she said. There was a radiance about her, and she looked fit and happy. I noticed she was wearing exercise clothing.

"Been working out?" I said.

"Yeah. I found a Pilates class here in town awhile back. It's been great. I met these two girls there, and we became great friends. They have kids too, and we hang out a lot."

Lisa went on to tell me that the Pilates class saved her marriage. She got physically fit and gained new friends. Her self-esteem and self-confidence grew. And it didn't hurt that her fitness attracted the admiration and glances of other men.

"At first it drove Steve crazy. Every time he saw some guy looking at me, he got jealous. But then he noticed my new circle of girlfriends and the life I was creating for myself. Since then, Steve has been great. He's home right now with our daughter, so I have to run." Lisa smiled and thanked me for helping her out.

"Everything is within your power, and your power is within you." — *Janice Trachtman*

Just like Joseph Pilates, Lisa was in a difficult situation, but she marshaled the resources she had, and transformed herself into a strong, independent woman.

She invested in herself and changed the power dynamic in her relationship. As a result, her husband Steve saw her differently, and stopped taking her for granted.

This is how you avoid becoming a victim. You invest in yourself. You refuse to put your happiness at the mercy of another's attention or approval. You give love and respect but expect both in return.

There are no guarantees in life, and some relationships are unhealthy despite best efforts. But for many, taking an approach like Lisa's can rebalance the power in a relationship.

Invest in your fitness, find good friends, and show your significant other your independent, self-confident side. Doing so could change your relationship for the better.

Chapter Fifty-Five

How to Be Memorable in Social Settings

My father was not one for weekend parties and social gatherings. He was much happier at home, cutting weeds on the hillside or ensconced in his favorite reading chair with a good book.

Unfortunately for Dad, my mother was the opposite of him. She loved a good party. Whenever invited to a neighborhood get together or weekend BBQ, Mom always prodded my father into attending.

"I am not someone who likes cocktail parties or large dinner parties, but I have to attend them often. I much prefer very small dinners with close friends." -Tom Ford

One of our neighbors was a neurosurgeon. He and his wife lived in a huge, impressive, colonial-style home with a long, winding driveway. They threw lavish parties, often outside on their sprawling front lawn.

Occasionally, I would tag along to the parties with my parents. Partly in the hope of meeting girls my age, and partly to watch the spectacle of nicely dressed adults getting plastered. It never ceased to amaze me the things inebriated adults would confide in me.

"As a child, I always enjoyed — my parents used to have these little cocktail parties — and I always loved trying to get the adults to tell me things they weren't supposed to say. And in many ways, that's what my job is today; it's getting people to tell me things that they probably are otherwise not supposed to say." -Andrew Ross Sorkin

Politicians and diapers

My father was an administrative law judge, bibliophile, historian, and teetotaler. Standing six feet and a solid 220 lbs., he possessed a self-assured, commanding presence. Yet, he was reserved, preferring to observe more than engage.

It was fun watching my father at big parties. While some folks worked the room and struck up conversations, Dad preferred to stroll the periphery, having quiet conversations here and there.

Parties at the neurosurgeon's house invariably got louder. Once guests moved inside, conversations sometimes turned to politics. There were always a few opinionated folks who talked the loudest, challenging others and spoiling for a good debate.

Once, during a heated conversation, a man turned towards my father and said, "Judge, we haven't heard from you yet. What's your opinion on this?"

I don't remember the political issue, but I do remember my father's unorthodox response. Instead of taking a position, he said something like:

"Good people on both sides of this debate ought to sideline their partisan dogma and study the history behind it. The complexity of the past doesn't allow for one-sided conclusions."

From there, Dad led the group on a brief history lesson of the issue, and summed things up with a humorous quote from Mark Twain:

"Politicians and diapers must be changed often, and for the same reason."

The crowd laughed heartily, and even the most opinionated in the group was disarmed by Dad's impartial response and memorable quote. I sensed that few would remember the opinionated voices at the party, but many would remember the articulate judge and his funny Mark Twain quote.

Elegance is not about being noticed

We all want to make a good impression on others. For some, it's also important to make the right connections. To do this, there are things we can do to be memorable. The key is to be memorable in a positive way, not a negative way.

"Elegance is not about being noticed, it's about being remembered." -Giorgio Armani

For example, you could dress like a complete clown and get a lot of attention at a party. Or you could become raving drunk and make an utter fool of yourself. Both are memorable, but not in a good way.

What follows are five tips to make yourself more memorable (in a positive way) in social settings. The list is far from exhaustive but will give you a good start.

1. Uncommon answers

Parties and social gatherings often involve superficial chit chat. People meet or are introduced to one another, and the conversation begins with predictable questions and comments. Things like, "So, where are you from?" or "What do you do for a living?"

The answers to these conversation openers are typically unremarkable. One might respond with, "Me? Oh, I'm from Los Gatos, California," or "I'm a soldier." Such responses may be honest and true, but unremarkable.

Imagine, however, if you responded to such questions with more uncommon answers. For example, consider the following example between a woman named Jill and a man named Mark.

"So, Mark, where are you from?" asked Jill.

"I'm from a northern California town named after the screams of mountain lions prowling in the night. Early settlers used to call it 'La Rinconada de Los Gatos (Cat's Corner)' but today it's known as Los Gatos," Mark replied.

Jill smiled and said, "That's interesting. May I ask what you do for a living?"

"Perhaps you've heard the phrase 'We sleep soundly in our beds because rough men stand ready in the night to visit violence on those who would do us harm.' Some say the phrase is from George Orwell. Others attribute it to the film critic and essayist Richard Grenier. Anyway, I'm one of those rough men. I'm an Army ranger."

Think about more uncommon, interesting ways you can describe where you're from and what you do for a living. Doing so will make you memorable and open the door to more interesting and enjoyable conversations.

2. Dress for success

Looks and appearance aren't everything, but people do make judgments about you based on how you're dressed. You don't need expensive clothes and fancy brands to dress elegantly.

"Fashion is a tool...to compete in life outside the home. People like you better, without knowing why, because people always react well to a person they like the looks of." -Mary Quant

My father told me to err on the side of dressing well versus dressing casually. I noticed that people react to me differently when I attend parties in a sports coat and crisp button-down shirt versus a polo shirt and jeans.

Elegantly dressed people stand out and tend to be more memorable than casually dressed folks. Of course, there are exceptions. You probably wouldn't wear an evening gown to a pool party. The point here is that part of being memorable is dressing well and looking your best.

3. Music to their ears

No question smiling and making eye contact with others is a good way to connect and make a positive impression. However, if you want to be memorable, focus on remembering people's names. After all, it's the centerpiece of their identity.

The reason names are hard to remember is because they're arbitrary, just like telephone numbers and addresses. There's often not a lot of associations in your brain for random names. Even if you know someone else with the same name, you still tend to forget the new person's name.

If you meet someone new and they tell you their name, don't respond with, "Nice to meet you." Instead, add their name at the end: "Nice to meet you, Sarah." Make an effort to work the person's name into your conversation. Don't overdo it but try to use their name periodically while talking.

Mnemonics can help, too, such as rhymes or word associations. For example, if I met a guy with squinty eyes named "Clint," I might associate his name with the actor Clint Eastwood, who is famous for his menacing squint.

Remembering and using people's names is music to their ears. With a little effort, you can get better at remembering names, which helps you become more memorable. After all, a lot of people are bad at remembering names. Do the opposite, and you'll stand out in a good way.

4. Undivided attention

Remember when you were a kid craving the attention of your mother or father? You'll see kids in a playground yelling, "Mommy, look at me," or "Daddy, watch!" Kids want the undivided attention of their parents. When Mom or Dad is watching, kids feel important, loved, and valued.

The same is true when we grow up, except that we no longer wave our hands and say, "Look at me." Rather, we simply take note of who is paying attention to us and who isn't.

Ever been in a conversation with someone who keeps checking their phone or watch? Or maybe they're scanning the room behind you while you're talking. When people do this to us, we feel slighted. Or maybe we feel insecure and assume we're not interesting.

"Everyone is always in need of something that another person can give, be it undivided attention; a kind word or deep empathy. There is no better use of a life than to be attentive to such needs." -Jonathan Safran Foer

The reality is that we live in an attention economy, where our phones, tablets, and laptops all vie for our attention. Pop-ups and social media are designed to distract us down rabbit holes and sales funnels.

We have grown accustomed to distraction and crave instant gratification. As a result, our social skills suffer, along with our attention.

If you want to be memorable, get good at giving people your undivided attention. Keep your phone in your pocket. Listen closely to what others are saying. Repeat back parts of what they say and ask lots of questions.

People love to talk about themselves and having someone listen to them provides validation and appreciation.

5. To fill up and live

One of my dad's secret weapons was his love of books and reading. He had a large library, containing everything from the Harvard classics to history books, non-fiction works, and novels.

Most evenings, while my mother, sister, and I were watching television, Dad was in his leather chair reading.

Books expose us to other worlds, people, perspectives, and experiences. Unlike many blog posts and social media feeds, traditionally published books are better edited and more professionally written.

The reality is that taking a new book to market is expensive, and publishers look for the best work to invest their time and money in.

I used to be an information junkie, often watching cable news shows and parroting their talking points. I enjoyed diving into political debates with others. Over time, however, I began to see how pointless much of this was. I started to turn to books, to acquire deeper knowledge and understanding.

"She reads books as one would breathe air, to fill up and live."
-Annie Dillard

People have their political views and biases, and they're hard to change. Nothing is more boring than listening to two blowhards argue the same political dogma and jargon heard on the cable news shows.

This is why my father stood out at the party mentioned above. Because he didn't get in the gutter with partisan politics. He rose above it by sharing a historical perspective, followed by the wisdom of Mark Twain.

Being well-read arms you with unexpected bits of wisdom and knowledge, making you memorable and interesting in social settings.

For example, I was at a gathering once where a woman reflected on the difficulties of aging. I responded with a quote from Shakespeare's sonnet 19:

"Devouring Time, blunt thou the lion's paws."

Then I followed up with a quote from the choreographer Twyla Tharp:

"Age is not the enemy. Stagnation is the enemy. Complacency is the enemy. Stasis is the enemy."

Sharing wisdom and knowledge from good books elevates the conversation, prods people to think deeper, and makes you more memorable in social settings. Just be judicious in how much you share, so that you don't come off sounding like an intellectual show off or an annoying pedant.

A good first impression

According to Will Rogers, you don't get a second chance to make a good first impression. To that end, take advantage of the above five tips.

Come up with some uncommon answers about yourself, that will surprise and delight people. Dress elegantly and focus on remembering people's names. Give them your undivided attention and keep company with good books.

Do these things, and people will remember you. They'll tell others about how interesting you are. You'll make helpful connections, potentially expand your circle of friends, and become more memorable. All of which can enrich your life and put you in a better position to enrich the lives of others.

Chapter Fifty-Six

This Is What Happens When You Simplify Your Life

Sometimes competence and ambition work against us. We follow conventional wisdom and get a good education. We dive into a career, work hard, and ascend to higher levels of responsibility and leadership.

We reach the top echelons and move into corner offices. We have authority, power, and respect. The only problem is that we're unhappy and unfulfilled.

Just ask Linda Souza. She obtained a master's degree in global marketing, communications, and advertising. She spent many years at different startups. She liked the creativity of her work, but as she ascended into higher positions, things changed.

As Souza told The Huffington Post, "It wasn't that interesting," adding, "But it sort of felt like, this is what you do to continue to advance."

A sense of possibility

Souza became vice president of marketing for a Los Angeles-based tech startup. Unfortunately, the creative work she used to enjoy gave way to Monday morning meetings and forecasting dull budget models.

What do you do when your professional work no longer brings you fulfillment? For Linda Souza, the answer was simple: Become a circus performer.

According to an article in The Huffington Post, Souza "found a coupon for two introductory aerial classes on an online discount site and signed up on a whim, hoping to try something new after a breakup."

"There'll always be serendipity involved in discovery." -Jeff Bezos

Before long, Souza was hooked. She went on to become an instructor as an aerial performer. She convinced her boss to cut back her hours to three days a week, which allowed more time to pursue her new passion.

Souza acknowledged that she's lucky to have a flexible tech job allowing more time to teach aerial classes. The reduced income has meant no more big vacations, and less shopping, but she's happier.

As The Huffington Post article noted: *"Instead of more material things, Souza said, she has gained a sense of possibility, time to explore an unexpected passion, and the freedom to tap into her creativity and physical strength."*

Enormously overloaded property room

Edgar Alwin Payne was an American Western landscape painter and muralist. His book, Composition of Outdoor Painting, is somewhat of a bible for many dedicated landscape painters.

Payne writes in his book that landscapes are, "enormously overloaded property rooms." All that stuff out there, from rocks and trees to mountains, streams, and clouds, can be intimidating to paint. They can overwhelm an aspiring landscape painter.

"The art of art, the glory of expression and the sunshine of the light of letters, is simplicity." -Walt Whitman

The solution is to break things down. Landscape painters start by asking themselves what the painting is about. What is the main idea?

Then the painter tackles the big shapes, to create a pleasing design and composition. Doing this makes it much easier, later, to render fine details. However, the strongest paintings keep things simple. They focus on the main idea, and not all the extraneous detail.

A successful landscape painting requires the artist to do two things: ***Organize and simplify***

The principles of successful landscape painting are a good analogy for successful living. If you want to get more out of life, it helps to organize and simplify.

Our lives get more stressful when there are endless details and complications. We get bogged down with the minutia and forget the big picture. We get lost in that enormous property room of life and lose sight of the things that make us happiest.

A good landscape painter starts by asking what the painting will be about. What's the main idea? Similarly, we need to ask ourselves what our life is about? What is the main idea?

My life is about creativity. Namely, writing and creating artwork. I retired early from my law enforcement career, sacrificing a larger pension to pursue my main idea.

Even during the busy years of my police career and raising my son, I organized and simplified facets of my life to have more time for my writing and artwork.

Like a complicated landscape, there were many distractions, commitments, and obligations. By organizing and simplifying, I was able to craft a more successful life.

Everything in my life actually had a purpose

Sometimes, it's the unexpected upsets in life that can unexpectedly open the door to effective organizing and downsizing. Consider the story of Joshua Fields Millburn.

Millburn was making a six-figure salary at a demanding job but blowing his income on endless shopping. Then life got difficult. His mother died of cancer and his marriage fell apart.

Millburn happened to watch a Twitter video about minimalism, and it changed his life. Minimalism is all about identifying what is essential in your life and eliminating the rest. In short, less is more.

Millburn began unloading all the stuff he realized he didn't need. He spent eight months getting rid of everything until he had only 280 possessions left. He managed to pay off over $100,000 in debt, moved, and launched the successful website The Minimalists with his buddy Ryan Nicodemus.

Millburn was finally able to focus on two things that were important to him: his writing career, and physical fitness.

In an interview with The Huffington Post, Millburn said, "As I pared down my stuff, I started changing how I viewed things," adding, "Then everything in my life actually had a purpose or brought me joy."

"Too many people spend money they haven't earned, to buy things they don't want, to impress people they don't like." -Will Rogers

Like a successful landscape painter who focuses on the big idea instead of the details, Millburn organized and simplified his life. As a result, he is healthier and happier today.

How about you? Are you drowning in the endless details and minutia of life? Are you ready to organize and simplify your life? Here are several tips to help you organize and simplify that enormously overloaded property room of life.

How to simplify your life

The following 5 tips all flow from a minimalist philosophy that less is more.

Consume less

In this day and age of ubiquitous technology, choosing to consume less may seem counterintuitive. Many people are glued to their TVs, social media, text messages, and endless Amazon deliveries. They don't want to "miss out" on anything. But are they truly happy?

Take a close look at your budget and ask what you need. Think how much fitter you'd be if you used all that TV and social media time to exercise? Not to mention if you skipped more of those beer-busts and wine parties.

Imagine the reduced stress of a simpler wardrobe, instead of a stuffed closet. Ditto for that garage of yours that has become its own "enormously overloaded property room."

Learn to say no

People are happy to spend your time for you if you let them. I used to be shy about saying no to people, and as a result, I got walked all over. They would march into my office and distract me when I was busy. Others would flatter me and then ask for something that infringed on my time.

Eventually, out of frustration, I learned the power of saying no. I was gracious but became adept at turning people down. When they pressed, I would say, "Thanks for thinking of me, but I'll never reach my personal goals as a writer and artist if I take on more responsibilities."

"You have to decide what your highest priorities are and have the courage pleasantly, smilingly, and non-apologetically- to say "no" to other things. And the way to do that is by having a bigger yes burning inside." -Stephen Covey

I made time for important events, like weddings and funerals. And sometimes, I'd say yes to commitments for a big reason, like investing in a valued friendship. But for the less important, myriad requests that came my way, I got comfortable turning people down. So can you.

Stop living in the past

Who we used to be, and the things that happened to us in the past, don't get to define who we are today, or who we can become tomorrow.

Part of organizing and simplifying your life is learning to let go of self-limiting thoughts born out of past experiences. For some, professional help may be needed to deal with past issues of abuse or neglect. The key is to organize and simplify your mind so that the past no longer stands in the way of your dreams.

"When you hold onto a script that doesn't serve you, you leave no space to write a new one that does." -Jennifer Ho

It's helpful to write down in a journal the person you want to become. Next, identify the habits and routines necessary for that vision to come to fruition. From there, create a calendar to track your progress. Block in pockets of time to work on the things that matter most to you.

Let go of the past, envision the future you deserve, and anything is possible.

Downsize/relocate

Along the lines of consuming less, consider downsizing your life. Do you need to be chained to that big mortgage or BMW payments? What if you moved to a smaller house and traded in that status car for a more affordable, used vehicle?

Smaller homes cost less, require less stuff to furnish them, require less cleaning and maintenance.

A reliable Toyota will cost you a lot less than a Mercedes. When fewer things "own" us, we end up with more cash and time to pursue our passions. Relocation is another option. After I retired early from my police career, I moved from Northern California to Southern Nevada. I found a superior house for less money and lower property taxes. Even better, Nevada has no state income tax, thus saving me more of my hard-earned pension.

Moving also afforded me anonymity. Lots of people knew me in the small town where I served as chief of police. Coffee shop visits inevitably turned into unexpected encounters. I often found my quiet reading time interrupted to answer questions about the police department or town politics.

"If what you are doing is not moving you towards your goals, then it's moving you away from your goals." -Brian Tracy

As much as I liked the locals in town, I needed space to read, think, and write. Not to mention, retired police chiefs are often asked to sit on boards or get involved in city projects. After 26 years of community service, I was ready to embrace my creative life. Relocating to a different city gave me the freedom to start a new life of art and writing.

Abandon toxic relationships

According to Kelly Campbell, Ph.D., associate professor of psychology and human development at California State University, San Bernardino, "A toxic relationship is one that adversely impacts a person's health and well-being."

In an article at mydomaine.com, Dr. Campbell goes on to state:

"Because we spend so much of our time and energy on a romantic partner, these relationships are especially influential on our well-being. When they are going well, we are usually doing well. But when they are not going well, our health and happiness will likely be negatively affected."

If you feel like you're walking on eggshells in your relationship or putting in all the effort with little in return, these can be red flags. Other warning signs can be if your partner is overly controlling, or you feel your self-esteem stifled by your partner. As Dr. Campbell notes in the article:

"If you notice that your partner is jealous, competitive, and generally unhappy when you are doing well, then that's a huge red flag."

Toxic relationships can also exist in friendships. At some point, you must evaluate if the positives outweigh the negatives.

The next step is to address your concerns with your partner or friend. This is seldom easy, but positive change will never happen unless you identify the issues and work together to fix them.

Sometimes people can change, and a toxic relationship can evolve into a healthy one. If not, then it's time to move on. Ending toxic relationships is difficult, but you deserve to be happy.

Addressing toxic relationships is part of organizing and simplifying your life. Letting go of such relationships removes a huge weight and allows you to get on with your life.

It's never too late

Linda Souza simplified her life by cutting back on work hours and embracing her passion for aerial performance.

The late painter Edgar Alwin Payne taught artists to organize and simplify their landscape paintings. He likened the complexity of landscapes to an "enormously overloaded" property room. Much like the endless details and commitments in our lives can overwhelm us. The key is to organize and simplify.

Joshua Fields Millburn walked away from a six-figure job and countless possessions because his life was too complicated and unfulfilling. He organized and simplified. The changes allowed him to relocate and focus on his physical fitness and writing career.

I retired early from my law enforcement career, sacrificing a bigger pension because I wanted to write and create artwork fulltime.

I organized and simplified my life. I sold, donated, and trashed a bunch of stuff. I adopted a simpler wardrobe. I moved to a more affordable city with lower taxes. The result is that I'm happier and able to pursue my passions. This is what happens when you simplify your life.

How about you?

It's never too late to organize and simplify your life. Take advantage of the tips in this article. Learn more about the benefits of minimalism. Doing so might just change the whole trajectory of your life and move you closer to your dreams.

Chapter Fifty-Seven

How Trying to Be Happy Makes You Miserable

In 2014 I started blogging on my website JohnPWeiss.com. I knew very little about blogging but enjoyed writing poignant little stories and posting articles about the creative arts.

I seldom received comments on my blog posts, but the process of writing was enjoyable to me. It helped me address new ideas, refine my thinking, and explore my creativity.

Then social media ruined everything.

Get noticed in a noisy world

Facebook and Instagram led me to the websites of successful bloggers. They had legions of followers and seemed to be making a boatload of money off their books, courses, and products. They were online celebrities.

Suddenly, I wanted to be like those successful bloggers, which was strange. I built my website, JohnPWeiss.com, to showcase my fine art paintings. I planned to retire from my law enforcement career and become a full-time artist, not a blogger.

Then one day I discovered Michael Hyatt's book, *"Platform: Get Noticed In A Noisy World."* Hyatt is a successful blogger, and I read his book cover to cover.

I started to mimic Hyatt's style of blog posts. My content changed, too. I began writing more about personal development, and less about the creative arts.

I still wasn't happy

Later, I discovered another successful blogger, Jeff Goins. I flew down to Franklin, Tennessee, for Jeff's first "Tribe Writer" conference, and learned a great deal about blogging.

Next, I hired the former chief content writer for Copyblogger Media (now Rainmaker Digital), Demian Farnworth, to teach me copywriting. In short, I completely immersed myself in blogging.

Finally, I discovered the website Medium.com and began posting articles there. I even took a course (Medium Mastery) by Thomas Kuegler to improve my exposure on Medium.

My painting productivity suffered, but my blogging became more successful. With effort and consistency, my followers grew substantially. I wasn't a blogging superstar like Michael Hyatt or Jeff Goins, but I started to generate a good monthly income from my blogging.

Yet, I still wasn't happy.

I kept comparing my success to big-time bloggers. Even though I generated an enviable following, I wasn't happy. I paid too much attention to my stats. I was emulating other bloggers, instead of following my own path. It was sort of like playing a song I hated, over and over again.

Writing blog posts wasn't much fun anymore. It became a grind. The more I focused on finding happiness with my blogging, the more miserable I became.

"Unhappiness is not knowing what we want and then killing ourselves to get it." -Don Herold

Despite increasing success and income, I started to resent the whole blogging thing. More than once I considered quitting altogether and going back to a quiet life of painting and writing poignant little stories.

We try too hard to be happy

A research study found that one of the reasons we're not happy is because we try too hard to be happy.

The study's co-author, Brock Bastian, is a social psychologist at the University of Melbourne School of Psychological Sciences. In an email to Time.com, Bastian noted:

"Happiness is a good thing, but setting it up as something to be achieved tends to fail."

Mark Manson, the author of the best-selling book, *"The Subtle Art of Not Giving a F***,"* wrote:

"The desire for more positive experience is itself a negative experience. And, paradoxically, the acceptance of one's negative experience is itself a positive experience."

In other words, the more we pursue feeling happy, the less happy we become. Because it reinforces what we lack, whether money, looks, fame, etc.

The built-in metrics of social media (likes, claps, followers, etc.) lures us into comparing our stats with others, thus exacerbating our unhappiness. Instead of being pleased with our work, we fret about how well we're competing.

"Comparison is the thief of joy." -Theodore Roosevelt

The more I fixated on becoming a blogging success like Michael Hyatt and Jeff Goins, the more unhappy I became. When we focus on what we don't have, we fail to appreciate (and leverage) what we do have.

So, if we try too hard to be happy, what's the alternative?

What quickens your heart?

I finally sat down one day and asked myself an important question: Why was I trying to become a successful blogger like Michael Hyatt and Jeff Goins? I had a good retirement income from my police career and originally planned to become a landscape painter.

The other important question I asked myself was: To what end? Where did I hope to arrive at? What was the ultimate goal? Money? Fame? An inflated ego?

I came to realize that my obsessive-compulsive nature hijacked my goals. Before diving deep into blogging, the thing that made me happiest was creating art and writing from the heart. My greatest joy came from improving my craft, not social media likes and more newsletter subscribers.

So, I stopped emulating the bigtime bloggers and worrying about my stats. I began putting more time into my cartoon illustrations and crafting essays that I enjoyed writing. I pursued more authentic work.

I reduced my output of blog posts, to free up time for my fine art painting, and projects like books and courses I want to create. Fewer articles meant less income, but I'm enjoying the work more now. It feels meaningful and fulfilling. I never really wanted to be a big-time blogger, with all the attendant headaches that working on that scale requires.

Another question worth asking is this: **What quickens your heart?**

What activity, passion or pursuit gets you excited? What do you love doing more than anything else? What do you most look forward to? What brings you true fulfillment and joy?

Once you figure out what quickens your heart, the next step is to craft your life around it. This doesn't mean being reckless and giving up your day job or neglecting family responsibilities, but it does mean reprioritizing. Saying no to the unimportant things, so you can chase the thing(s) you love the most.

Something important and meaningful

Have you explored the underlying motivations for what you think will make you happy? Honest and close examination may uncover some uncomfortable realizations.

Maybe you're in law school because your older sister became a lawyer and that's what your family expects you to do. Except you hate it, and deep down, always wanted to become a marine biologist.

Perhaps your girlfriend pushed you into CrossFit because she's a fitness buff and disapproves of your diminutive beer gut. Except you aren't into hardcore fitness. Your passion is the craft brewery you started. You want to enjoy your passion and grow your business, not spend every day doing burpees and power-lifting.

Sometimes we think our happiness will come from meeting the expectations of others, but that's a recipe for disappointment. Why tie our joy to the approval of others? It only empowers them and steals our independence.

Best-selling author James Clear wrote a succinct, three-sentence summation of Mark Manson's book, *"The Subtle Art of Not Giving A F***":*

*"Finding something important and meaningful in your life is the most productive use of your time and energy. This is true because every life has problems associated with it and finding meaning in your life will help you sustain the effort needed to overcome the particular problems you face. Thus, we can say that the key to living a good life is not giving a f*** about more things, but rather, giving a f*** only about the things that align with your personal values."*

Stop focusing so much on happiness and instead ask yourself what's important and meaningful in your life.

For many people, it's their creative passion (painting, writing, photography, music, etc.). For others, it's helping people, raising great children, higher education, or caring for their family.

When we stop comparing ourselves to others, looking for approval, and chasing the next level of success, we can slow down and focus on what's important and meaningful. Happiness may come and go but pursuing what's important and meaningful will lead to a more fulfilling life.

Solving problems and achieving

All the truly valuable things in life don't come easy. Fitness, great kids, mastery of difficult skills, and helping others require effort, pain, sacrifice, discipline and more.

Pursuing such valuable things is both important and meaningful, but runs counter to the instant gratification world we live in. It's much easier to surf the couch, watch Netflix, or space out on social media. The problem is that these diversions won't get you where you want to go in life.

True happiness comes from solving problems and achieving. True happiness comes from taking action against laziness, indifference, addictions, denial, and negativity. True happiness comes from being honest with ourselves and living authentic lives.

"Happiness is when what you think, what you say, and what you do are in harmony." -Mahatma Gandhi

When we do hard things in the service of what's important and meaningful, our sense of accomplishment lasts longer than happiness.

Rest satisfied with what we have

The Roman Stoic philosopher Seneca argued that putting things off is the biggest waste of our lives. Deep down, most of us know that our happiness won't come from comparison, trying to please others, or pursuing things that fail to quicken our hearts. Yet we keep putting off the important and meaningful things in our lives.

"True happiness is to enjoy the present, without anxious dependence upon the future, not to amuse ourselves with either hopes or fears but to rest satisfied with what we have, which is sufficient, for he that is so wants nothing. The greatest blessings of mankind are within us and within our reach. A wise man is content with his lot, whatever it may be, without wishing for what he has not." -Seneca

Stop worrying about happiness. Get busy chasing your passion. Do the hard work. Make sacrifices. Solve problems and achieve. Embrace what's important and meaningful. Remember to have gratitude. Do these things, and you'll find that the whole happiness thing will take care of itself.

Chapter Fifty-Eight

How to Escape Your Family to Save Yourself

Imagine being born into a family of survivalists with extreme religious beliefs. Your bipolar father is convinced the end of days is approaching and prepares by stockpiling canned peaches, weapons, and fuel.

Your father distrusts traditional doctors and the medical establishment as wicked servants of the "socialist' government. Your family relies on your mother's herbalism and divine healing for all your medical needs.

You have no birth certificate and never attended school, as your father believes all you need is the Bible. Your older brother becomes sadistic and violent, often dragging you by the hair and forcing your face into the toilet to purge your wickedness.

Isolated from mainstream society, all you have are the beauty of the Idaho mountains and kindness of your grandmother. The only glimmer of hope is when another brother leaves the family to go to college. He returns periodically and tells you that there's a world out there, and it will look a lot different once your father is no longer whispering his view of it in your ear.

So, you teach yourself mathematics, science, and grammar. You take the ACT and miraculously get accepted into Brigham Young University. But there's a problem. Your father disapproves and says your place is back home, working with the family. In fact, he suggests that the devil has a hold of you, and if you don't return, you'll be lost to the family forever.

Hope lies in dreams

You love your family, despite their disfunction. Against their objections, you stay on in school and distinguish yourself academically. Despite economic hardship, a kindly professor helps you get a scholarship. You are encouraged to apply at Harvard for advanced studies, and then Cambridge University in England. Against all odds, you are accepted.

"Hope lies in dreams, in imagination, and in the courage of those who dare to make dreams into reality." -Jonas Salk

What would you do? The love and approval of your family weigh heavily on your mind and heart. All you have to do is walk away from your education and embrace your family's way of life.

Making the decision harder, your family is no longer poor. Your mother miraculously healed your father after a terrible accident, and her celebrity as a healer and herb specialist spread. The family created an online business for their herbs, tinctures, and oils, making them wealthy. It would be easy to go back and join them.

You miss your family and worry if you travel to England for your education, you may never be able to come home again. Your parents even travel to the university to see you and encourage you not to continue with your education. "Come home," they say. The guilt you feel leads to a mental breakdown, nearly costing you your education.

What would you do?

What it means to self-create

Everything described above, and more, happened to the author Tara Westover. Her bestselling book, *"Educated- A Memoir"* detailed all the hardships she endured.

Despite the disapproval of her parents, she studied psychology, politics, philosophy, and history at Brigham Young University. For the first time in her life, she learned about the Holocaust and the Civil Rights Movement.

Imagine how hard it must have been to defy her dictatorial father. Her whole life and perception of the world had been defined by her father's teachings. As Westover wrote in her book:

"Everything I had worked for, all my years of study, had been to purchase for myself this one privilege: to see and experience more truths than those given to me by my father, and to use those truths to construct my own mind. I had come to believe that the ability to evaluate many ideas, many histories, many points of view, was at the heart of what it means to self-create."

Westover studied at Harvard and Cambridge, where she earned a Ph.D. in history in 2014. The success of her memoir brought recognition and fame, but at a steep cost. She has been shunned by her family.

Westover experienced tremendous guilt for defying her father's wishes. Even though she knew the pursuit of education was a good thing, there was still guilt. She wrote in her memoir:

"But vindication has no power over guilt. No amount of anger or rage directed at others can subdue it, because guilt is never about them. Guilt is the fear of one's own wretchedness. It has nothing to do with other people."

In the end, Westover learned to focus on what she needed, instead of what her father demanded. She explained it this way:

"I shed my guilt when I accepted my decision on its own terms, without endlessly prosecuting old grievances, without weighing his sins against mine. Without thinking of my father at all. I learned to

accept my decision for my own sake, because of me, not because of him. Because I needed it, not because he deserved it."

Don't be trapped by dogma

Tara Westover is not the only person to have defied the unfair expectations of loved ones to become her own person. To become who she was meant to be. There are many people who found the courage to pursue their dreams, despite their parent's objections.

An article in MentalFloss.com notes that the singer Katy Perry was raised as an evangelical Christian. Her parents, both pastors, embraced a strict religious code of conduct. For example, things like co-ed dances were not allowed.

Despite Katy Perry's success, her mother has said, *"We strongly disagree with how she's been conducting herself."* Her mother added, *"...and she knows how disappointed we are."* Yet, despite this stinging disapproval, Katy Perry found the courage to follow her own dreams.

The actor and singer Kris Kristofferson graduated with a master's degree in literature in 1960, according to a Mentalfloss.com article. Kristofferson was a Rhodes Scholar who studied at Oxford. He served in the Army, and upon discharge, was offered to teach at West Point. However, against his parents' wishes, Kristofferson turned down the teaching offer and moved to Nashville to become a songwriter.

Kristofferson's family disapproved, feeling that he denied himself a solid future. They disowned him. Kristofferson dealt with the rejection of his parents by putting his pain into writing songs.

"Your time is limited, so don't waste it living someone else's life. Don't be trapped by dogma- which is living with the results of other people's thinking. Don't let the noise of others' opinions drown out your own inner voice. And most important, have the courage to follow your heart and intuition." -Steve Jobs

Making a person

The bottom line is that your family is not you. They may be a part of you. They may have shaped aspects of your personality and outlook on life. But you are your own individual. No one has the right to lay claim on your life. Who you are, or who you wish to become, is up to you.

Perhaps the most important thing you can do for yourself is to obtain a good education. The pursuit of knowledge enriches the mind and deepens your understanding of the world. As Tara Westover wrote:

"An education is not so much about making a living as making a person."

How much of ourselves do we owe to our loved ones? Where do healthy parental expectations for their children end and unfair demands begin? No doubt, when we are young, we must rely on our parents for guidance and support.

In youth, we often lack the education, experiences, and wisdom to decide big life decisions. If we're lucky, we have wise parents to guide us to adulthood. But sometimes, people aren't so lucky. Their parents may be misguided, mentally ill or mean-spirited. What are we to do then?

For Tara Westover, she turned to her grandmother, who encouraged her to get an education. Westover intuitively knew that her grandmother meant the best for her. Perhaps that's a good measure for dealing with the demands of loved ones. Ask yourself if their guidance benefits themselves or you.

"Education is the passport to the future, for tomorrow belongs to those who prepare for it today." -Malcolm X

Education is the key to personal growth. It need not come from traditional schools and universities. There are many forms of education, from books and videos to technical schools and life experiences.

Education was the key to Tara Westover escaping her family to save herself. Of course, along the way, you must be sure you're not buying into your own lies. Some young people defy well-meaning parents because they think they have all the answers when they don't. Again, education is the key to checking your own biases, false narratives, and self-lies.

"The man who lies to himself and listens to his own lie comes to such a pass that he cannot distinguish the truth within him." -Fyodor Dostoevsky

It's possible to save yourself and become the person you always wanted to be. Whether it's family, a loved one or friends who are holding you back, you have the power to direct your own future. So long as you don't lie to yourself with delusions of grandeur, and seek real and meaningful education, you can pursue and achieve your dreams.

Many of us are blessed to have parents and families that support us in life. Even when they disagree with our choices, they are still there for us. Sadly, some parents and families are not like this. They may be blinded by their own stringent beliefs. Perhaps they were victims of controlling or unsupportive parents themselves.

Try the best you can to find peace with your parents and loved ones, but if education and experience have shown you that they are wrong, you must chart your own course. You have a right to save yourself and pursue your dreams.

It may not be easy, but it's possible. Tara Westover did it. So did Katy Perry, Kris Kristofferson, and countless others. Pursue the gift of a good education, believe in yourself, and become the person you always dreamed of being.

Chapter Fifty-Nine

Do You Make This Mistake in Conversations?

Years ago, I suffered an exercise-related injury. My doctor referred me to a physical therapist. On my first appointment, the physical therapist welcomed me and introduced himself as Michael. He patiently asked questions about my injury, listened intently, and explained what we would work on.

For several weeks, Michael helped me recover from my injury. As much as I appreciated his professional help, what I enjoyed more was his conversational style. He was easy to talk to and a superb listener. He asked a lot of questions and was interested in my answers. There was no competition. I felt like it was important for him to learn more about me. When my physical rehabilitation ended, I missed the weekly conversations with Michael.

My doctor (when I lived in California) was another person whose conversations I always enjoyed. We occasionally met for lunch, and he always asked questions and showed interest in what I had to say. He listened well and was able to share his own stories and insights in a noncompetitive, flowing manner.

We tended to talk about ideas more than everyday stuff, and I came away enriched by our conversations.

The poor quality of conversations today

What I seem to notice, increasingly, is the poor quality of conversations today. Perhaps the ubiquity of social media, texting and digital communication has made us all impatient, distracted, rude conversationalists. We tend to talk at one another rather than with one another.

Just the other day, I was enjoying a latte in Starbucks, sketching in my journal. I couldn't help but overhear a conversation next to me between two women. I don't know their names, so we'll call them Carole and Linda. It went something like this:

Carole: *"So, how's your daughter Jennifer doing?"*

Linda: *"Oh, she's doing fine. We got her a tutor for math, 'cause she's been struggling a little bit. Oh, and she's trying out for the girls' basketball team, so we'll see."*

Carole: *"Our Joseph is still on the varsity football team. We went to his game last Friday night. It was terrific. Look, let me show you (pulling out her phone and scrolling through pictures of the game). See, here he is making a touchdown. Oh, and he's still eyeing Stanford University. It's more expensive than the state university, but George and I know it will open doors for him. Joseph might even get a football scholarship. We're working on that."*

Linda: *"Well that's great. Oh hey, did I mention that Bob and I are thinking about going to Hawaii this summer? We haven't had a vacation in a while, so we're pretty..."*

Carole (interrupting): *"Oh, George and I went to Hawaii last year! Remember, I showed you pictures. We rented this amazing guest house right on the beach. Now that George got a promotion at work, we're talking about going to Italy this summer. Don't get me wrong, Hawaii was fun, but there's just something about Europe that's exciting. We were going to do one of those tour groups but decided to explore on our own. Like we did when we went to Scotland last year. Did I ever tell you what happened when we visited Edinburgh?"*

It went on like that. Carole monopolized the conversation, often interrupting Linda to talk about herself and her family. Worse, Carole kept "one-upping" Linda. Whatever Linda had to say, Carole would counter with something better. The more I eavesdropped (I shouldn't have but they were loud) the more annoyed I became with Carole.

"There cannot be greater rudeness than to interrupt another in the current of his discourse."-John Locke

Competition disguised as conversation

How people converse tells you a lot about them. Egocentric people like everything to be about them, so they steer conversations back to their favorite topic: themselves. Shy, reserved people tend to listen more, but also fail to jump in and share. As a result, they get steamrolled in conversations.

Boisterous, overconfident people think they know everything and interrupt frequently to share their "brilliance." Insecure people sometimes play the "one-upmanship" game, needing to go one better than whatever your accomplishment or success might have been.

Then there is the substance of conversations. It's natural to begin conversations with standard pleasantries and superficial chit chat. The best conversations move past this, delving into a deeper back and forth. Perhaps sharing with one another about recent struggles or successes. Concerns and dreams. Each listening intently, not monopolizing the discussion, and contributing equally.

Or the discussion forays into the realm of ideas. Things learned from books or lessons derived from a meaningful movie. These types of conversations are far more enriching than superficial gossip.

"Great minds discuss ideas; average minds discuss events; small minds discuss people." -Eleanor Roosevelt

A lot of conversations become competitions disguised as conversations. Each person is not really listening. They're formulating and preparing their next thought and readying to interrupt. Neither is really learning anything from the other. It's an awkward dance of egos.

"There is a difference between listening and waiting for your turn to speak." -Simon Sinek

Even worse are the conversation hogs who hold you hostage with their long stories, recounting every mundane detail. Their stories frame themselves as heroes, brilliantly outsmarting everyone else and winning the day.

Or they devolve into a long rant, bitching and complaining about real or imagined slights. People who hold court over others might think they have a rapt audience, but they don't. Their audience can't wait for the pain to end.

I'm currently reading Tara Westover's memoir, *"Educated."* Microsoft founder Bill Gates interviewed Westover. On his website, GatesNotes.com, Gates describes Westover's book as follows:

"Tara was raised in a Mormon survivalist home in rural Idaho. Her dad had very non-mainstream views about the government. He believed doomsday was coming, and that the family should interact with the health and education systems as little as possible. As a result, she didn't step foot in a classroom until she was 17, and major medical crises went untreated (her mother suffered a brain injury in a car accident and never fully recovered)."

In his website video interview, Bill Gates talks with Tara Westover about her book. While this is more of an interview than a strict conversation, Gates displays all the earmarks of a wonderful conversationalist. He asks brief questions. He nods affirmatively and listens intently. Gates is a brilliant man, but he has no need to pontificate, lecture or tell long-winded stories. He is truly interested in what Tara Westover has to say.

Do more listening than talking

My wife took me to a beautiful winery once along the northern coast of California. We attended a special dinner and were seated with several other couples. The conversation was polite, as we all remarked on the beauty of our surroundings. But then a woman in the group made an overtly political comment, and in my youthful impetuousness, I couldn't let it go.

Soon the woman and I were engaged in a heated political discussion. The woman's date was older than her. A distinguished gentleman with white hair and an impeccable suit, he seemed bemused by our debate. He had listened quietly for quite some time. At some point, someone asked his opinion.

He leaned forward, and with a smile and twinkle in his eye, started to share an interesting story from history. It related to our political debate indirectly but took on its own form. The gentleman weaved a short story around it. About hope, loss, and how fruitless some of our battles are. It was brilliant. Elegant. Above the fray.

My wife missed it, having abandoned the table with another woman. My debate partner and I had been disarmed and shut down by this wise, articulate gentleman. I learned a lesson that night about humility.

"Most of the successful people I've known are the ones who do more listening than talking."-Bernard Baruch

Here's the bottom line. We all do it. We all get caught up in ourselves from time to time. We want to be the center of attention. Our egos get the best of us. But the problem is, doing so often makes us utter bores.

The mistake we make in conversations is making it all about us.

People love a great listener. There's a sense of validation when someone listens closely to what you have to say, nods affirmatively, and paraphrases back parts of what you said. When we discipline ourselves to stop steering the conversation back to ourselves, something amazing happens. People start to open to us. They begin to trust us more. They go home after the conversation and tell others what a brilliant conversationalist you are.

Tips for better conversations

What follows are some helpful guidelines to improve your conversations. Learn and employ these tips and watch what happens. You may find people seeking you out more for coffee, lunch or just to talk. People will start speaking highly of you, as someone who really listens and converses well.

Stop trying to be right

What is it with our need to be right all the time? It gets in the way of understanding others. Instead of trying to win a debate, how about trying to better understand where the other person is coming from?

Ask deeper questions, like, "Tell me why you believe that. I'd like to understand better." Even if you disagree, you might gain valuable insights. Everyone has their beliefs and stories. If you're always trying to slam them with your rehearsed talking points, then you're not really conversing. You're just feeding your ego.

There's an old saying that sums up the importance of listening:

"God gave us two ears and one mouth for a reason. So you listen twice as much as you talk."

If you're talking, then you're missing an opportunity to learn from others. Even people we dislike or disagree with may have wisdom to share. What kind of arrogance assures us that we have all the answers and everyone else is wrong? Learn to listen more.

Stop hogging the conversation

Perhaps you are a clever person and have tons of wisdom to impart. Maybe you possess a slew of personal stories about your successes and brilliant escapades. Guess what, most people aren't all that interested. They may feign interest, but chances are they aren't.

Yes, there are exceptions to this. If you are a paid speaker, people are probably there to learn from you. Or maybe you're a soldier home from deployment, and your family can't wait to hear about your tour of service. But for the rest of the time, at coffee or dinner with friends, don't inflict long, uninvited stories about yourself on others.

My Dad was a Type A personality, which means he was impatient and authoritative. It caused him to have a heart attack, and he received counseling on how to better manage his Type A impatience. He once told me the following advice:

"In the middle of a story you're telling friends at dinner, excuse yourself to use the restroom. When you come back and sit down, wait, and see if anyone asks you to resume your story. Don't be upset if they don't. Our every day, personal stories are not always fascinating to others."

Stop the one-upmanship

Some people just have to do you one better. Mention your promotion at work, and they'll have to tell you about theirs, and why it's more remarkable. Talk about how proud you are of your kid, and they'll mention something better about their kid. It's a twisted kind of insecurity. Like they have to compete with you.

We see this too with intellectual snobbery. The academic who has to correct others and proceed with a mini lecture on a particular topic. To most people, this kind of behavior looks like you're wearing a signboard that says, "I'm totally insecure."

Ask questions

The famous attorney Gerry Spence once wrote a book about winning arguments. It was an unconventional book, and different from the usual texts on logic and debate. In one part of the book, he talked about the uncommon knowledge found in others. The wisdom of truck drivers and janitors that cannot be found in books.

If we are to learn more about people and life, we should view each person as an exquisite interview opportunity. Like you, they have their own experiences and stories to tell. Why rehash your life story when you can learn from others? Learn to ask more questions.

"The size of our universe shrinks considerably when we place ourselves at the center. And the people who are most focused on themselves are the least satisfied in life." -Joshua Becker

Embrace active listening

If you really want to blow people away as a conversationalist, don't just listen attentively. Learn to paraphrase back what they said. Here's an example:

"So that's how come I'm so excited, Steve. I studied for months, took the sign language exam, and passed the first time with 100%! Now I can apply for that new job and if I get it, I'll get a raise!"

"Wow, congrats Beth. It's not easy to study sign language for months and ace the exam! When will you apply for that better paying job?"

In the above example, Steve clearly paid attention to Beth, and then paraphrased back the main parts of her story. This validates what she's saying and feeling. She will remember and appreciate Steve's interest a lot more than if he had turned the conversation into a story about his own work or job successes.

Give reciprocity

We all have times when we just must tell our story. Maybe something exciting happened at work, or we're still raving about a great movie we saw. Everyone has the need to share their experiences and stories. The trick is to learn to give and take. Learn the art of reciprocity. Don't make it all about you. When you finish your story, say, "Enough about me, what's new with you?"

Conversations are not competitions. They're a chance to connect, laugh, cry, and learn from others. Steer clear of mundane stories. Follow the tips outlined above, don't make it all about you, and soon everyone will be saying what a remarkable conversationalist you are. But the best part is that you'll start connecting on a deeper level, learn new things, and find greater joy in the conversations you have.

Chapter Sixty

How to Age With Elegance

Imagine being born in 1911 to a peasant Sikh family in Punjab, India. Your legs are so frail that you're unable to walk until the age of five. The village kids call you danda, or stick.

In time, you grow stronger. You become an avid amateur runner. Unable to attend school or read, you begin working alongside your father on the farm. Eventually you marry, start a family and farm of your own.

You teach your children how to farm and love your family dearly. But then tragedy strikes. Your wife dies in 1992 and your eldest daughter passes away due to complications from childbirth.

In 1994 your fifth son, Kuldip, dies in a construction accident. The depth of loss sends you into a deep depression and emotional turmoil. You move to England to live with your son, and spend your days at home, watching television.

Running breathes new life into you

One day, you see the London marathon. It rekindles an old passion for running when you were younger. So, at the young age of 89, you return to running.

You show up for training at Redbridge, Essex, wearing a three-piece suit. Fortunately, the coach works with you, gets you into appropriate attire, and soon you're in the 2000 London Marathon.

Running breathes new life into you. At the age of 93, you complete a marathon in 6 hours, 54 minutes. You beat the world best for anyone in the 90-plus age bracket.

In 2004, you're featured in an Adidas advertising campaign with celebrities like Muhammad Ali and David Beckham. You end up breaking records, and complete marathons at age 100 and 101.

Despite experiencing racism, you cast a charitable eye towards your fellow man. You become an advocate for health and wellness, encouraging people to eat healthily and treat others and all things with respect.

In 2012 you carry the Olympic torch. You refuse to accumulate personal wealth from sponsorships and donate the money to charity.

The first 20 miles are not difficult

Now that you've imagined such a remarkable life, meet the man behind the biography. His name is Fauja Singh, and he's 108 years old.

According to Wikipedia.org, Singh *"attributes his physical longevity to abstaining from smoking and alcohol and following a simple, vegetarian diet."*

This is what Singh has said about marathons:

"The first 20 miles are not difficult. As for last six miles, I run while talking to God."

Fauja Singh, despite a difficult childhood and great personal loss, exemplifies dignity, grace, persistence, and charity. He is a model for how to age with elegance, and in the process, inspire others to be the best they can be.

We can learn a lot from Fauja Singh. About the power of not giving up. About the importance of finding something you enjoy throwing yourself into. Not to mention, the merits of exercise and a healthy diet.

Equally important is Fauja Singh's charitable giving. Since his basic needs are met, he donates his sponsorship monies to charity. This not only helps others, but no doubt fills his own heart with a sense of purpose and joy.

Aging is not for the faint of heart

I remember when my father used to stand up from his reading chair. He'd place his beefy hands on his knees, lean forward and grunt. Then he'd turn to me and say, "Don't get old, Johnny."

"What's the alternative," I used to think to myself. "Dying young?"

Watching my parents age, with all their physical indignities and ailments, was instructive. I studied the way my father, despite a bad heart and aching body, found solace in his books and outdoor yard work.

My mother, despite being marooned in her lift chair due to advanced Parkinson's disease, found joy in reading, news programs, conversations, and favorite desserts.

My mother also took the time to listen to her young caretakers who shared their love lives and family troubles. Mom rendered wise advice and kind encouragements, interspersed with a few jokes and a wonderful sense of humor.

Mom refused to give up and dress sloppily. She took pleasure in coordinating her outfits and jewelry. Not because she was trying to impress anyone, but because she had self-respect. "It feels good to look presentable," she told me.

The interior of the soul

There's plenty of advice on how to age well. Stuff like eating right, exercise, plenty of sleep, managing stress and drinking lots of water. All important things to focus on.

Of course, some folks struggle with their aging appearance, enlisting the help of dyes, Botox, hair transplants, beauty treatments and plastic surgery. In some cases, it helps, in others it makes things worse.

Society today focuses incessantly on youth and exterior beauty, at the expense of intellectual growth and interior beauty.

"There is one spectacle grander than the sea, that is the sky; there is one spectacle grander than the sky, that is the interior of the soul."
— *Victor Hugo*

The problem with this shallow celebration of youth and beauty is that we miss the more important thing: Developing our minds and character.

Thus, many become ill-equipped for the indignities of aging. They rush to gyms or cosmetic surgeons to somehow put the genie of youth back in the bottle. But the genie is gone.

Pleasure is a shadow

There's nothing wrong with focusing on good health, and we all have a little vanity. We want to look our best, at any age. But what about your interior life? What about your mind? How are you equipping yourself for the road ahead?

The thing that helped my father and mother with the rigors of aging is that they never stopped developing their minds. Books were my father's best friends, and their lessons and stories provided perspective and answers for him about this grand journey of life.

My mother read regularly. Jousting with new ideas kept her mind engaged, nimble and growing. Not to mention, a curious and well-read mind makes for an interesting person.

"Pleasure is a shadow, wealth is vanity, and power a pageant; but knowledge is ecstatic in enjoyment, perennial in frame, unlimited in space and indefinite in duration." — *DeWitt Clinton*

The knowledge of yourself

Loving our families and friends, personal development, travel, new experiences, never ending education of our minds, helping others, and pursuit of our creative passions all create memories and an emotional armor that we can call upon in old age.

Long after our looks fade, these things become our closest allies as we march slowly toward the void. To allow vanity and narcissism to feed your ego is to deny yourself a deeper, more fulfilling, and meaningful existence.

"The knowledge of yourself will preserve you from vanity." — Miguel de Cervantes

I know it's not easy. The bloom of youth, when our bodies are beautiful and strong, is a hard thing to relinquish.

I can only imagine how devastating it is for glamorous movie stars, whose careers and personas rely heavily on their appearance. Then, over the years, they witness on screen their slow, public disintegration.

The poet Dylan Thomas seems to recommend that we fight back against Father Time, when he wrote:

"Do not go gentle into that good night,
Old age should burn and rave at close of day;
Rage, rage against the dying of the light."

My sense is that we should do all we can to avoid the "dying of the light." We should eat right, exercise, and get plenty of sleep. Not so much for vanity's sake, but to sustain us for the road ahead.

More importantly, we should continue to develop our minds and character. It's no coincidence that the people we admire most tend to have an interior beauty and deep character.

Learn to gently let go of your youth when the time comes. Dress in a flattering way that reflects your personal aesthetic, but don't become a cartoon of your younger self. Age with style and elegance.

Read broadly to keep feeding your mind. Cherish your family, friends, and passions. Help others.

In these ways you will shine now and in the twilight of your life. Your light will eclipse the dandies, fops, and egos, who have yet to discover their true centers and deeper meaning of life.

This is how you age with elegance and refuse to "go gentle into that good night."

Chapter Sixty-One

This Is Why You Need to Say Yes

It's been many years, but I remember the phone call like it was yesterday. I was in my office at the Scotts Valley Police Department. It had been a busy day and I was looking forward to heading home for dinner.

"Hey John, it's Bob. I have a silly little favor to ask you. It's a silly little thing, really."

This was not a typical phone call from Bob. Usually, when the district attorney calls a police chief, he either praises your agency about a case or suggests how things could've been handled better.

"Hi Bob, what's up?" I asked.

"John, the county treasurer bowed out. He can't do it this year. You're one of the most artistic guys I know. It'll be something you can cross off your bucket list," Bob said.

He was buttering me up, and I knew it.

"What exactly do you want me to cross off my bucket list, Bob?" I asked warily.

"It's a silly little thing, really," he said, which now had me worried.

He continued, "They need a public figure to perform in the holiday Nutcracker production. It's really a lot of fun. Do you think you could do it with me?"

...

I remembered the newspaper coverage of the previous year's performance — Bob and the county treasurer in ridiculous outfits with makeup. I envisioned some of our department's SWAT team members reacting with, "Hey, did you see the chief doing ballet in leotards with the district attorney?" I would never live it down.

I searched for excuses.

"What kind of commitment is this, Bob?"

He replied, "John, it's nothing. Piece of cake. Just a few practice sessions at the ballet center."

I didn't want to do it. I had other commitments. I searched for an out.

Bob chimed in: "People enjoy it, John. You're the most artistic guy I know. It's a silly little thing … something to cross off your bucket list."

Defeated (you can't argue with an attorney), I gave in. "Fine, Bob, fine. I'll do it."

...

Two months of weekend practices later, it's finally opening night. I'm in a dressing room looking like some turn-of-the-century clown with ruffles and makeup. Speaking of makeup, I'm applying a touch of rouge to Bob's cheeks, per his request.

You can't make this stuff up! Bob was beaming.

"See John, I told you this would be great," he said.

The curtains went up and out we shuffled to a full audience, bright lights, and the music of "The Nutcracker." Of course, the professional ballet dancers were magnificent, but Bob and I held our own as novice extras.

After the performance, it was champagne and laughs back in the dressing room. We took funny pictures, congratulated one another, and ventured off to find our wives.

A few years later, Bob passed away after a valiant fight with cancer. Ever the classy guy and competent leader, he planned his own memorial and left the stage with grace and dignity.

Little did I know how thankful I would be that Bob talked me into "The Nutcracker." He shared a side of himself I had not been privileged to see in our professional associations.

We spend a lot of time pursuing our careers. Chasing the prize of money, recognition, benefits, etc. It's easy to say no to unexpected opportunities. After all, we're all busy. Who has time?

Some things are worth making time for.

...

When people reach out to you with an invitation to step out of your comfort zone, think hard before you decline. It could turn out to be something amazing. I'm so thankful Bob called me, and we did "The Nutcracker" together.

Bob may have thought our Nutcracker experience was just a "silly little thing," but actually, it was a time with him I'll never forget. A wonderful experience to "check off my bucket list." And for that, I am most grateful.

Years ago, my good friend John visited me with an adventurous vacation proposal.

"White water rafting!" John said, with a gleam in his eye. "I looked into it, and we can get a group of guys for a weekend trip. It'll be awesome. The water table is insane right now. We're talking category four and five rapids!"

I had zero interest in white water rafting.

"Don't people die on those category five rapids?" I asked.

"Don't be such a wimp," John said. "Live a little."

"That's the point, I want to keep living!" I told John. But it was to no avail. John was already on the phone to our buddy Bruce, who didn't hesitate to say yes. Soon, John had his group of guys, and there was no way for me to wiggle out of it.

We drove up north to river country and met up with our guides. There was a long bus ride down a treacherous road with sharp cliffs on one side.

"What have I gotten myself into," I thought.

...

At water's edge, we packed our gear into the rafts, slipped on our dry suits and helmets, and shoved off.

The initial ride down the river was scenic and peaceful, but it wasn't long before we encountered rough water. As we navigated boulders and more dramatic waterfall drops, our crazy guide asked if we wanted to tackle some serious water.

"No, no we don't. We want to hit shore and picnic somewhere," I thought to myself.

"Hell yeah, let's do some category five action," John shouted to our guide. To my horror, our buddy Bruce high-fived him in agreement.

There are moments in life you never forget because you survived them. Such was the case for the second half of our river adventure.

Our crazy guide, egged on by John and Bruce, soon had us charging category five rapids, full of ear-deafening, crashing waters and enormous boulders.

At one fork in the river, we went over an angry juncture of rocks and cascading water, into a swirling vortex below. Our raft partially capsized, ejecting everyone (including the guide) except me.

Stunned that I somehow remained in the raft, I noticed our guide clinging to the end of one of the oars, grasping to climb back into the raft.

"That was epic!" the guide yelled as he crawled back into the raft.

"We're all going to die," I thought to myself.

...

Eventually, everyone found their way back into the raft and the adventure continued. That night we camped along the river shore underneath bright stars and surrounded by singing crickets.

There were laughter and beer and tall stories. John and I lay our sleeping bags on a small ridge. In the morning, John's sleeping bag was invaded by ants. I laughed hard as he jumped out of his bag, cursing. Miraculously the ants ignored my sleeping bag.

By the end of the trip, we were all exhausted but triumphant. We had conquered the angry rapids and emerged mostly unscathed.

We had stories to share with family and friends back home. Most importantly, we invested in one another. Deepened our friendships and created lasting memories.

Little did I know that several years later, lost in the fog of depression following a bitter divorce, John would take his life. I was devastated the day I received the news and still suffer from his loss.

"I collect memories. I look for opportunities to try new things, go to new places, and meet new people all the time." — Marcel Wanders

Memories are the only things that lessen the pain. Particularly that crazy white water rafting trip. Thank God I went on that trip and resisted the urge to bow out.

...

If we let work, responsibilities, and commitments take over our lives, we'll deny ourselves experiences that lead to rich memories and fuller lives. Like my experience with Bob at the Nutcracker or tackling white water rapids with my friend John.

I often write about the importance of deep work and saying no to distractions, unnecessary obligations, and commitments. But for every rule, there's often a flip side.

"Some talk to you in their free time, and some free their time to talk to you." — hplyrikz.com

Sometimes, we need to set aside our work and say yes to family and friends. Sometimes, we need to do silly things or row for our lives down category five rapids.

This is why you need to say yes more. Because quality memories matter. Because no one lives forever. Because life is meant to be lived.

I miss Bob and John, but I give thanks every day that I joined them on our adventures. The memories make me smile and feel like a part of my friends live on, in my heart.

They are memories that keep on giving.

Chapter Sixty-Two

What Life Should Be About

"Dad, I don't want to," I said to my father. "The boys will make fun of me. Can't we let someone else take her?"

"What if you were her, Johnny? Wouldn't you want someone to help you? To take you home?" Dad smiled at me, but I still felt resistant. The emotions of youth can blur your conscience.

The little girl's name was Melinda and car trouble prevented her mother from picking her up after school. As other parents arrived, the school's principal asked if someone could help. My father, ever the kind soul, volunteered.

The principal provided Dad with Melinda's home address, which wasn't far from our home. Dad introduced himself to Melinda and said we would give her a ride home.

As some of my friends snickered and laughed in the distance, Dad opened the door to our car and Melinda slid into the front passenger seat with a smile.

I crawled into the backseat and shot an angry stare at my friends. As we drove away, I imagined the teasing I'd receive the next day at school.

Melinda was a pleasant, intellectually disabled girl who showed up at the private school I attended one chilly fall day.

When she first strolled into our fifth-grade class, we knew she was different. She had a light complexion, mouse-brown hair, kind eyes, and a slight lisp when she spoke. It took her a moment to form thoughts and words.

She seemed awkward in her school uniform and cardigan sweater. And since children are cruel, it didn't take long before little spit wads were flung her way in class. Other times, snickers and mean jokes were directed at her.

"Children are very cruel, yes. Of course. Children are extraordinarily cruel little creatures."- Dennis Potter

Young, immature and wanting to fit in, I joked about Melinda just like my friends did. Funny that I had forgotten what it was like to be the new kid at school. The feelings of trepidation and aloneness.

It wasn't long ago that I bounced around from public to private school. How quickly I forgot my own awkwardness in wearing the private school uniform. Not to mention the fear of not making any friends or fitting in. I failed to imagine how an intellectual disability would only amplify all those feelings.

We drove Melinda home and Dad engaged her in polite conversation. In her own staccato way, she chatted freely about her favorite things, TV shows, and pets. She liked some of the same television shows I did.

When we arrived at her house, Dad looked at me in the backseat. "Johnny, be a gentleman and walk Melinda to her front door, please."

I was mortified. It was bad enough that I had to be seen taking her home, but now I had to walk to her house with her!

Begrudgingly, I got out of the car, opened the door for Melinda, and walked to her front door. Halfway up the walkway, she turned to me with a sweet smile, looked into my eyes and said, "Thank you, J-J-Johnny, for being so nice to me."

I don't think I'll ever forget that moment. How it stripped away my selfish pride and made me see her sweetness. Her humanity. Maybe even her pain and vulnerability.

When I got back into the car, Dad patted me on the leg and said, "I know you didn't want to take her home, Johnny, but it was the right thing to do. Thank you for walking her to the door."

"It's okay," I told my dad, "I guess she's alright."

The next day at school my friends didn't waste much time. "How's your girlfriend, John?" one of the boys asked with a grin.

"She's not my girlfriend," I said, "We just helped her out."

The teasing continued for a few days but eventually leveled off. As for me, something had changed inside. Suddenly, some of my friends didn't seem all that cool anymore. In a way, they were kind of ugly. Always making fun of the weaker or awkward kids.

Over time, I started to distance myself from some of those friends. Melinda, perhaps sensing the shift in me, began talking to me more. I found her to be consistently pleasant with never a negative thing to say about anyone.

It made me wonder about who really possessed the intellectual disability.

Fast forward many years. I'm a young man in a theater watching a Tom Hanks movie. It's about an intellectually disabled man. It chronicles the bullying he received in his boyhood, his deep love of a girl, and his remarkable path to manhood.

Forrest Gump was a movie about love, but it offered so many more life lessons.

Here are the top three lessons that I took away from the movie.

Authenticity

Forrest Gump was unapologetically who he was. No pretension. No posturing. No ego. He loved to mow his own grass. Even when he became successful, he still mowed his own lawn.

How many of us do the things we do for the approval or attention of others? Are we living in the gym to build an amazing body for ourselves or for the admiration of others? Do we get someone else to mow the lawn because it's beneath us?

Do we buy expensive cars for ourselves or our image? There's nothing wrong with fitness and success, but it should reflect our authentic selves, not a need to impress others.

Nonjudgmental

Maybe those who have suffered the cruelties of others better understand the gifts of kindness and being nonjudgmental.

Forrest Gump was pure and nonjudgmental. Even when his childhood love, Jenny, came back home to see him, there was no judgment. Just Forrest's acceptance, gratitude, and love.

Forrest Gump managed to see the good in everyone that few of us would find. He may have had a disability, but he understood what love was.

If only the rest of us could see the world the way Forrest Gump does.

Honesty

Forrest Gump was always honest, whether people liked it or not. What you saw is what you got. No deception. No doublespeak. What a rare thing today.

Yes, we all tell little white lies from time to time. Usually, benevolent lies to avoid hurt feelings in others. "No honey, your bottom doesn't look too big in that spandex outfit."

Imagine if we could be more honest. If we could find a way, to tell the truth gently. Perhaps, in the long run, we'd avoid more misunderstandings and hurt feelings. Maybe we'd get closer to the things that really matter?

Funny, after all these years, I'm still thinking about Melinda and those early school days. I barely remember the names of the boys I hung out with back then, but I still remember Melinda.

Grace in others has a way of doing that. It stays with you through the years. My father's kindness was another kind of grace.

I've tried to shape my own behavior and life after people like my father and Melinda. Sometimes I have fallen short, as we all do, but their memory serves as a reliable guidepost.

One of my favorite poems is the *Desiderata* (Latin: "Things Desired") by Max Ehrmann.

The poem reminds us to strive for high ideals. To treat others kindly, accept others for who they are, and be gentle with ourselves. Pretty much everything Forrest Gump did.

Beyond the lessons of Forrest Gump, the Desiderata captures what life should be about. It's worth reading:

Go placidly amid the noise and the haste, and remember what peace there may be in silence. As far as possible, without surrender, be on good terms with all persons.

Speak your truth quietly and clearly; and listen to others, even to the dull and the ignorant; they too have their story.

Avoid loud and aggressive persons; they are vexatious to the spirit.

If you compare yourself with others, you may become vain or bitter, for always there will be greater and lesser persons than yourself.

Enjoy your achievements as well as your plans. Keep interested in your own career, however humble; it is a real possession in the changing fortunes of time.

Exercise caution in your business affairs, for the world is full of trickery. But let this not blind you to what virtue there is; many persons strive for high ideals, and everywhere life is full of heroism.

Be yourself. Especially do not feign affection. Neither be cynical about love; for in the face of all aridity and disenchantment, it is as perennial as the grass.

Take kindly the counsel of the years, gracefully surrendering the things of youth.

Nurture strength of spirit to shield you in sudden misfortune. But do not distress yourself with dark imaginings. Many fears are born of fatigue and loneliness.

Beyond a wholesome discipline, be gentle with yourself. You are a child of the universe no less than the trees and the stars; you have a right to be here.

And whether or not it is clear to you, no doubt the universe is unfolding as it should. Therefore be at peace with God, whatever you conceive Him to be. And whatever your labors and aspirations, in the noisy confusion of life, keep peace in your soul. With all its sham, drudgery and broken dreams, it is still a beautiful world. Be cheerful. Strive to be happy.

What about you? Who have you shaped your life after? Who has inspired you to be a better person? It's never too late to craft a better you.

Perhaps the lessons of Forrest Gump, or the wisdom of the *Desiderata*, will help you discover what life is about.

Because, as the poem so eloquently states: *"With all its sham, drudgery and broken dreams, it is still a beautiful world."*

May you experience such beauty in your life.

Chapter Sixty-Three

Are You Aware of the Nasty Habit Killing Your Dreams?

We all have this little voice inside our heads, chattering away behind the scenes. Stuff like, "You're too fat. You're not good enough. You'll never get promoted. You don't have what it takes. No one will like it. Why do I try? Who cares?"

It's a sadistic, negative little voice.

Other times, a dose of optimism courses through our being and the little voice becomes a cheerleader. It prattles on with encouragements like, "You're the best. You can do this. You are beautiful. You are special. You're a superstar."

Sounds nice. Encouraging. Maybe even helpful for the moment. Except the voice is unreliable. Sometimes it forewarns us. Other times it leads us astray.

The voice seems to vacillate between self-limiting thoughts and egocentric blandishments. Either way, that little voice can't be trusted.

We all lie to ourselves. Some of us do a decent job of honest, self-evaluation, but we often have our blind spots and misperceptions. And that's a problem because it distracts us from living a more joyful life.

Hide your true self

Best-selling author Joshua Becker is a self-described "minimalist." His popular website, BecomingMinimalist.com, is all about choosing a simpler life. Less stuff and more living.

Becker's blog post *"9 Easy Ways to Become Unsatisfied With Life"* outlines behavior that leads to unhappiness. Things like focusing on ourselves, worshiping money, blaming others, etc.

One negative behavior on Becker's list is *"Hide your true self."* Why do we find it so hard to be, or become our authentic selves? By failing to grow into our true selves, we are shortchanged from truly living. We feel this nagging sense of incompleteness.

Another important point Becker makes has to do with egocentrism or focusing always on ourselves. As Becker notes:

"The size of our universe shrinks considerably when we place ourselves at the center. And the people who are most focused on themselves are the least satisfied in life."

Some of us can look beyond ourselves and seek inspiration from others. We often find heroes to look up to. People we'd like to be like. Such individuals can inspire us to become more or to improve who we are. But we should never forget our own uniqueness. That's the thing that sets us apart from everybody else, despite what our internal dialogue might be saying.

Out of the shadows

The little voice in our head is always comparing, complaining, worrying. It tells us to copy the person we admire. Try to be like that person. Which is fine up to a point. There's nothing wrong with emulating positive traits in others. But we can never be someone else. Nor should we want to be a cheap imitation.

"Authenticity can't be replicated or faked. You're either real or you're not." -Bibi Bourelly

Other voices can chip away at our authenticity. Sometimes parents refuse to accept all or part of who their children are. Maybe a father frowns on a son's desire to be an artist. Or a mother refuses to accept her daughter's sexuality.

It takes bravery to step out of the shadows of other people's expectations and be who you really are. Yet, if we are to live a joyful life, we must stop lying to ourselves and take what our internal voice says with a grain of salt.

How do you know if you're lying to yourself? Basically, it just doesn't feel right. It gnaws at you. Like the guy who refuses to address his alcoholism. He denies his addiction. Tells himself he can stick to just a few glasses of wine. But the cravings persist. Deep down, he knows. He's lying to himself.

Or the woman who swears that her abusive husband will change. He seemed apologetic after the last time he struck her. Maybe this time will be different? But of course, she knows the truth.

Voice of doubt

The little voice inside our head, fueled by fear and insecurity, likes to lie to us. It masks its lies in false charm and is slow to reveal the truth.

It's like a charitable friend who says you look fabulous in that new outfit. But if you probe long enough and ask for the truth, the friend will eventually admit that yes, maybe you do need to lose a few pounds.

So, what is the nasty habit that's killing your dreams? ***Unreliable self-talk.***

It's something we all do. Even the most self-confident people have moments when the voice of doubt starts its nasty work. Questioning. Doubting. Reliving past failures and cajoling our insecurities.

Or the little voice does the opposite and caters to our ego. It tells you how great you are. How talented and brilliant your work is.

Don't fall for it.

If you want to achieve your dreams, you must put unreliable self-talk in its place. Here's how:

Fact check

Sure, you might be convinced that the manuscript you spent two years slaving over will be a publishing sensation. But before you start popping champagne corks in premature celebration, ship your tome off to a few editors.

Do some fact checking, to see if your work truly measures up. Compare it to the work of others. Also, if impartial editors shred your baby, don't despair. Better to find out early and learn from the experience. Better to keep growing than listen to that lying voice in your head.

The same approach holds for negative self-talk. If you got passed over for a promotion, don't assume it's because you suck. It's possible a more qualified candidate was selected. Try to find out what the winning candidate possesses that you don't. Then work to develop those skills.

Seek unbiased feedback

Your Mom loves your paintings. So do your friends and family. They don't want to hurt your feelings, so they lie to you. They do it with benevolent hearts, but nevertheless, false praise won't get you where you want to go.

Be wary as well for the opposite side of family/friends' praise, which is unfair criticism. Sometimes maladjusted people make themselves feel better by tearing down other people.

"Between flattery and admiration there often flows a river of contempt."- Minna Antrim

Don't rely on your jealous sister for feedback. Or that buddy who's always competing with you needlessly. Find outsiders who don't know you to get unbiased, straightforward feedback about you or your work.

Accept change

The voice in your head is always running, and it hates change. Status quo is much easier than upsets, changing course and having to learn new things. Learning to accept change rather than fighting it will help calm that internal dialogue.

My transition from police work to creative work was a big change.

Toward the end of my law enforcement career, I knew I was ready for a change. I yearned to throw myself into my creative life, but fear made me hesitant about retiring early. The voice in my head said to hold off, but my heart said otherwise. So, I accepted that change was inevitable, and I retired early. It was the right move for me.

Manage your attention

Don't be held hostage by your internal conversations because they're frequently fueled by insecurity, fear, jealousy, conceit, or false bravado. Also, they can distract from paying attention to more important things.

Get your attention off your internal conversations by educating yourself. Seek the council of wise people whom you respect. Tell them your story. Your circumstances. Ask them if you should be feeling insecure or invincible.

When we put our energy into productive problem solving instead of negative self-talk, we correct course more quickly or confirm that we are on course.

As former FBI agent LaRay Quy wrote in TheLadders.com:

"Energy follows attention — wherever your attention is focused, your energy will follow. If your inner critic is beating you up about a failure, your failing will be the one thing you focus on."

Let go of perfectionism

People don't succeed because they're perfect, they succeed because they work around their imperfections. Your unreliable self-talk is like quicksand. It focuses endlessly on your faults, and you get stuck there. You're no longer able to see your strengths, or how to navigate around your flaws.

I was never strong in math and science. As a police chief, I had a multi-million-dollar budget to manage, and complicated computer and communications systems to purchase and maintain.

To combat my shortcomings, I had my systems administrator draw rudimentary maps on my grease board. She simplified our computer and communications systems to help me understand the concepts.

This enabled me to have a working understanding of our systems and needs. But most importantly, I employed experts in these systems that I could rely on to help me make good decisions. Doing so also freed me to focus on other things I was more talented with.

Beauty and humility

No one is perfect at everything. Find support for the areas you are not talented in so that you can put more energy into the areas you're great at. Doing so will mute that negative self-talk and allow you to be more successful.

"There is beauty and humility in imperfection." -Guillermo del Toro

None of us get to escape our internal dialogue. Sometimes, the voice within can helpfully guide us through difficult situations. Unfortunately, that same voice can appeal to our insecurities and shortcomings.

Follow the steps outlined above and learn to manage your unreliable self-talk. Doing so will bring you more success and happiness, and that'll be something worth talking about!

Chapter Sixty-Four

You Need These People in Your Life - But You Ignore Them

The flight was turbulent, and I was fairly new to air travel. With each bump and strain of the jet engines, my heart lurched, and I felt a sense of dread.

I was flying to a convention of editorial cartoonists in Minnesota. Excited as I was to hang out with other cartoonists, the rough flight put me in a state of high anxiety.

There was a calm looking fellow across from me, who could tell I was a white-knuckle flier.

"Don't fly much?" he asked with a smile.

"No, this is my third flight, ever. I don't like heights, and I hate turbulence!" I gripped the armrests on my seat tightly.

"If you like, I might be able to help a little," he said. "Give me your right hand."

Happy for any distraction, I complied.

"I'm a massage therapist and specialize in pulling out negative energy," he said as he began kneading his thumbs into the palm of my hand. "Just try to relax, breathe, and feel the stress work out."

Being a pragmatic guy, I was skeptical of anyone claiming mystical abilities, but I went along with it anyway.

The guy started to work on my fingers. As he reached each fingertip, he let go and then shook his hand, as if releasing the negative energy "pulled out" from each finger.

It was strangely relaxing. He finished and then asked for my other hand, repeating the same process.

"People store so much stress inside themselves, and they don't know how to get rid of it," he said. "You have to learn how to breathe better, clear your mind, calm yourself and let the stress work itself out."

"I think a lot of the stress will disappear when we land," I said with a smile.

"No, you've got other stress in your hands. I can feel it. You need to work on that, too."

When he said that, I thought about some of the relationships and work-related challenges I was working on. Still not sold on the mystical stuff, I was amazed how much he helped me calm down. And he was right about the other stress in my life.

After he finished the hand massage, we talked for a bit about travel and our work. Before I knew it, we were preparing to land, and I thanked him for helping me out.

Put on our happy face

In this age of digital distractions, we tend to disappear into our smartphone screens rather than talk to strangers.

Walk into any coffee shop and look around you. Most people waiting in line are busy scrolling on their phones. Some customers may be engaged in conversation, but many are glued to their laptops and tablets.

People tend to avoid having conversations with strangers, whether in a coffee shop or commuting on public transportation.

Many fear that they'll say something dumb or worry that the other person will talk their ear off. In reality, there are many benefits in striking up a conversation with a stranger.

When we talk with loved ones and friends, we often use a sort of shorthand. Our conversations can be more superficial.

Talking with a stranger is different. We tend to behave our best. As an article in the New York Times notes:

"The great thing about strangers is that we tend to put on our happy face when we meet them, reserving our crankier side for the people we know and love. When one of us, Liz, was in graduate school, she noticed that her boyfriend, Benjamin, felt free to act grumpy around her. But if he was forced to interact with a stranger or acquaintance, he would perk right up. Then his own pleasant behavior would often erase his bad mood..."

Talking with strangers can change our perspectives. Meeting people who are not like us is a great way to broaden our views, and shatter some of our biases. And best of all, it enhances our mood.

The ethics of strangers

As the world seems to feel more and more insular and hostile, I've found increasing hope and pleasure in talking to strangers. I've discovered that people really aren't that different from one another.

"Our very lives depend on the ethics of strangers, and most of us are always strangers to other people." -Bill Moyers

When I visit the grocery store, I always make a point to chat with the cashier. Even the smallest of conversations seem to make both myself, and the cashier, feel a little better.

"Looks like you guys are pretty busy today," I'll offer.

"Yeah, it gets like this before the weekend," the cashier replies.

"Bet it makes the shift go by faster, though."

"Yeah, it really does," the cashier says with a smile.

"Well thanks very much, I'll catch you next time," I'll say.

What I find is that, on subsequent visits, the cashier and I will remember one another, and often jump right into a new conversation. There's a sense of familiarity and friendliness, which improves both our moods.

My wife once told me about something she called "Greyhound therapy." When I looked at her quizzically, she explained:

"You know, when you're on a bus and you strike up a conversation with a total stranger. And before long you find yourself sharing feelings and thoughts that you maybe never even shared with your closest friends."

The beauty of strangers is that they don't know us. We're free from all pretensions and can engage in a more honest, direct conversation. Sometimes it's just easier to talk with a stranger, who is not invested in a relationship with you. Also, the feedback you get is likely to be more honest.

"...sometimes one feels freer speaking to a stranger than to people one knows. Why is that?"

"Probably because a stranger sees us the way we are, not as he wishes to think we are."

— *Carlos Ruiz Zafón, The Shadow of the Wind*

When we express simple pleasantries with strangers like "hello" or "how are you" we are not really asking for an answer. The purpose of the salutation is to acknowledge their presence and humanity. It builds goodwill and a sense of peace and community.

Beautiful interruptions

We are brought up to be careful, even fearful around strangers. While it is true that we cannot know the intentions of every stranger, most people we meet are not out to harm us.

The trick is to read the behavior of others more than the categories in our heads. We use categories to simplify how we perceive the world. A guy in a uniform is a "cop." The stooped over, wrinkled fellow with a cane is an "old man."

The problem with these categories is that they can become a pathway to bias. Without talking to these strangers, we don't know what they are really like. And we might just miss out on their wisdom, charm, or unique personality.

The "cop" on the corner might be into jazz music as much as you are. That "old man" with the cane might have some advice for you on how to deal with loneliness or losing your spouse.

Author Kio Stark gave a helpful TedTalk about why you should talk to strangers. As she notes:

"When you talk to strangers, you're making beautiful interruptions into the expected narrative of your daily life — and theirs."

A whole new world

When my son was young, he was riding his bike home from school. Somehow, he lost control of his bike and flew over the handlebars.

As he lay on the sidewalk, a few strangers came running to his aid. They helped him up, asked if he was okay, and checked to see if his bike was damaged. Luckily, only my son's pride was hurt.

I remember, when he told me about the incident, the sense of pride I felt in my community and the good-hearted people who came to help my son.

As a police officer, I often came to the aid of accident victims. I could always see it in their eyes, even when they were too scared or injured to speak. The look of gratitude. The relief that someone cared. The renewed sense of hope, that perfect strangers look out for one another.

We need strangers in our lives more than we think, but we tend to ignore them. Fear of crime, embarrassment or the unknown keeps us avoiding eye contact. We reach for the distractions of our phone screens.

What if we tried a little harder to interact with strangers? What if we struck up a few more friendly conversations? At the market, coffee shop or bus stop?

Doing so just might open a whole new world. Every human being you meet is a walking historian of their lives and experiences. You never know what you might learn, or how your own story might inspire them.

Research indicates that interacting with strangers can uplift your mood and improve your day. So, the next time you're at the market or in a line at Starbucks, strike up a conversation with someone you don't know. You might be pleasantly surprised by how good it will make you feel.

Chapter Sixty-Five

How to Escape a Life of Mediocrity

Maybe you are nervous, uncertain, and afraid. Perhaps you're weighing the risks and rewards. Maybe you're not. But you know you want a change. A different outcome.

Something inside you persists, pushes, and cajoles until you can't ignore it anymore. And so, throwing caution to the wind, you leap. Like a young eagle who leaves the nest for the first time, you leap.

You instinctively know that the comfort of the nest isn't enough. When the fear of staying is greater than the fear of leaving, you leap.

Charging that cliff

Think back on the accomplishments and breakthroughs in your life. Some may have been due to good fortune and luck. But the most satisfying and meaningful growth often comes from the leap. From the aftermath of charging that cliff and throwing oneself into the abyss.

Diving into the abyss is scary. At first, it may feel like you're falling. But then, at some point you experience what the young eagle leaving the nest feels. Exhilaration. Freedom. The thrill of entering a whole new world. New possibilities and dreams.

"Living with fear stops us taking risks, and if you don't go out on the branch, you're never going to get the best fruit." — Sarah Parish

Country music artist Tim McGraw wouldn't go on stage without a drink. He needed a little "liquid courage" to perform. But it didn't end there.

He'd get trashed and drunk call his wife. He'd slur. Then, to hide his inebriation, he'd text her. Except everything was misspelled, and she knew.

Finally, after one last bender and hangover, he flew into Florida to start a new concert tour. And he decided to quit. He took the leap.

It certainly could not have been easy. The superstar lifestyle is not conducive to sobriety. But he took the leap anyway, and never looked back. Today, he is in the best shape of his life and more successful than ever.

My fear of flying

For me, venturing outside the nest and leaping meant getting on a plane. I had a fear of flying and heights. The fear prevented me from taking trips I should have taken.

Then an opportunity came to study landscape painting with renowned artist Scott L. Christensen. My wife shot down all my excuses about expenses, time away from work and upcoming obligations. She knew they were sad facades, masking the real issue. My fear of flying.

Defeated, I packed my art gear, stepped on that big plane, and threw caution to the wind. I hated every bump and flashing "fasten seatbelt" sign.

But then we landed in Idaho, and I felt it. Exhilaration. The joy of conquering my fear. That turning point led to more painting trips to study with Christensen and significant, personal growth as an artist.

What's holding you back?

What's holding you back? Your weight? An addiction? An un-healthy relationship? Depression? Uncertainty and fear? All these challenges have real solutions, if you're ready to leave the nest once and for all. If you're ready to take the leap and soar.

Yes, sometimes the flight is bumpy. Sometimes it's the wrong leap and we fall. Some falls take longer to recover from than others. But playing it safe and never leaping is its own kind of hell.

An article in Rhapsodystrategies.com noted the following:

"We are inspired by people who go beyond the norm and push the boundaries of possibility. Mediocrity, on the other hand, does not inspire. Nor does it lead to greatness. Success, however, you define it, will elude you unless you are willing to push the limits you have placed on yourself and that others have placed on you."

What a tragedy to not live boldly and pursue one's passions. If you want to soar, you must leap.

Nobody knows the magic bullet

Start by weighing the pros and cons. Figure out what the best case and worst-case scenarios are. What can you do to limit the consequences of the risk?

There's nothing wrong with doing your homework. But at some point, you need to act. You need to listen to you heart. You need to take the leap.

"Don't listen to anybody. Nobody knows the magic bullet. If they did, they'd sell it and make a fortune. Follow your gut. Follow your instincts. Every once in a while, take a chance." — Michael Cudlitz

It's easier to take risks and throw caution to the wind when we're young. When we don't have a family depending on us. But this doesn't mean we can't take risks later in life. We just need to be smart about it.

They took the leap

I've known people who made major career changes. People who were unhappy in their work but had a family to provide for. So, they didn't dive out of the nest carelessly.

They took their time. They planned and prepared. They minimized the risks through proper planning and patience. But then, they took the leap.

For some, the leap meant less money but more happiness. For others, the leap changed their lives for the better. For some, they stumbled, and had to regroup. But at least they tried and learned from the effort.

"Character cannot be developed in ease and quiet. Only through experience of trial and suffering can the soul be strengthened, ambition inspired, and success achieved." — Helen Keller

If you feel stuck right now, don't give up. Don't live a life of mediocrity. Meaningful change may require research, planning and patience. Be smart about it, but don't settle for your unhappiness.

You'll know when the timing is right. When you're ready to leave the nest. When that day comes, draw a deep breath. Exhale.

Then, take the leap. Feel what it's like to soar. To finally fly, to the better future that awaits you.

Chapter Sixty-Six

How the Power of Simplicity Can Improve Your Life

Nobody in the police department, including me, looked forward to the annual inspection.

It was a two-day event. The first day involved an early morning review of the troops. The police chief, along with a guest inspector, scrutinized every member of the police department.

A Lieutenant, holding a clipboard to record our scores, shadowed the Chief and guest inspector as they studied our uniforms, equipment, polished boots, and overall presentation.

City council members, other government officials, family, and friends were all invited to watch the early morning troop inspection. Afterward, there were speeches from the Mayor, Police Chief, and guest inspector.

Following the troop inspection, the Chief and guest inspector reviewed all our patrol cars, police motorcycles, ATVs, and related equipment. Next came an indoor and outdoor facility inspection, that lasted the rest of that day and the day after.

Every division of the department was examined. Files were checked. The integrity of the evidence room and armory were reviewed. A white glove was used to find dust on surfaces.

Each year, police staff spent weeks preparing for the two-day inspection. Naturally, there were complaints and gripes. It was a lot of work.

But it taught us some valuable lessons.

Hack away at the inessentials

If you ever spent a day or two cleaning out your closet, then you might understand how we felt after the annual police department inspection was over.

Anticipating and doing the hard work of cleaning, organizing, and downsizing is never fun. But the sense of accomplishment, and the feeling of being unburdened, is wonderful.

The annual inspection wasn't just about showing pride in our police department and profession. It was also about decluttering, refining our systems, and identifying ways to work smarter.

Every inspection uncovered waste, as well as ideas for how to simplify and improve our work.

Later in my career, when I became police chief, I continued the annual inspections. I recognized how important they were in helping us to simplify, declutter, and perform more efficiently.

There were many divisions within the police department, such as communications, administration, investigations, services, and operations. The annual inspection helped us identify the main goals and objectives of these divisions, as well as what was unnecessary and inessential.

"It is not a daily increase, but a daily decrease. Hack away at the inessentials. — Bruce Lee

Eliminating the inessential in my work life carried over into my personal life. I reevaluated how I was spending my time.

This led to saying no to commitments that complicated my life. I also began decluttering my home and art studio, so that fewer things got in the way of my priorities.

I sold a bunch of paint boxes I didn't need, donated art books that no longer interested me, and quit a few hobbies (like golf) that were preventing me from focusing on my passion for writing and artwork.

By simplifying my life as much as possible, I felt freer and unburdened.

Imagine what would happen if you did the same.

Simplicity is the ultimate sophistication

Our lives seem more complicated than ever.

In these busy days of social media, information overload, and fear of missing out, it's easy to keep adding stuff and complexity to our lives. But it often leads to overload, unhappiness, and burnout.

For example, I have Instagram and Facebook accounts. I started them, begrudgingly, to increase exposure for my creative work.

A website isn't enough these days. Even with decent SEO, nobody seems to directly visit websites anymore. So, one must leverage social media, where the audiences are.

But good Lord, what a pain in the rear. You must post constantly, respond to comments, and reciprocate by following others. All of this takes time away from developing one's artwork or creative craft.

I'm currently in the process of working on a new book, a collection of my best essays over the last two years.

I plan to self-publish on Amazon's KDP, but first I must learn all the formatting rules. And then I have to demystify the Canva app to create my book cover, which also must comply with specific KDP format rules. Ugh!

"Simplicity is the ultimate sophistication." — Clare Boothe Luce

Yes, there are YouTube videos to help me, but they're time-consuming.

To simplify, I'll probably contract out the book formatting work to a digital wizard on Fiverr. While it's important to keep up with new technology, it's also smart to delegate difficult tasks. That way you can save precious time and focus on what you're good at.

Try to find the simplest way to do things.

Keep your eye on a specific goal, and don't let the complexities of technology slow you down. Farm out difficult tasks or have someone more knowledgeable help you.

Simplify, simplify

When I first got into photography, a photographer friend of mine tried to convince me to purchase a Leica Q2 camera. He told me that I'd love its simplicity, fixed lens, and an uncomplicated menu.

The Leica Q2 makes it easy to shoot great pictures, and not waste your time experimenting with different lenses.

Unfortunately, the Leica Q2 is over $5K, and I had a string of unexpected expenses (house plumbing issues, my son's truck repair, a big veterinarian bill, etc.).

I bought a more affordable Sony A6600 camera, and a couple of prime lenses.

The Sony A6600 is a compact, beautiful camera, but its menus are deep and complicated. Unlike the Leica Q2, it's not as easy to quickly adjust exposure, ISO, etc. I must dive into the menus to do that.

"Our life is frittered away by detail. Simplify, simplify." — Henry David Thoreau, Walden and Other Writings

The Sony A6600 wasn't simple. Yes, I'm learning the camera, and it will get easier. But once again, I've found that complicated technology isn't fun.

I don't need endless features in a camera. I just want to take some decent pictures.

This is why smartphone cameras are so popular. You just point, shoot, and immediately share your photos with friends or upload them to social media.

Yes, today's expensive mirrorless cameras take "technically" better photos than smartphones. But you must divine the complicated camera menu, figure out how to transfer the photos to your phone or computer, and sometimes do post-processing with apps like Lightroom.

Also, most cameras are bigger and less convenient to carry than a smartphone. If future iPhones can improve bokeh and dynamic range, I might just say goodbye to my Sony.

The more I simplify the tools I use for creative work, the happier I seem to be.

A simple and unassuming manner of life

I used to work in color, but not so much these days.

My painting palette has shrunk down to the primaries, and white paint. Even then, I find myself painting more monochromatic pieces.

The same with my cartoons.

I like the contrast, simplicity, and elegance of black and white cartoons. Maybe because, as a boy, I fell in love with elaborately drawn political cartoons in newspapers, which were always in black and white.

I prefer shooting black and white photos, without the distraction of color. There's just something elegant and timeless about the simplicity of monochromatic images.

Simplicity frees you.

I'll take the simplicity and elegance of books, journals, and fountain pens any day over the complexity of Sony camera menus, social media algorithms, and Amazon KDP formatting hieroglyphics.

My wardrobe consists of solid colors and interchangeable pieces. When traveling, I bring quick-drying clothes that I can wash in a hotel sink. It reduces what I pack.

"Possessions, outward success, publicity, luxury — to me these have always been contemptible. I believe that a simple and unas-

suming manner of life is best for everyone, best for both the body and the mind." — *Albert Einstein*

I delete apps I don't need on my iPhone and try to do the same on my computer. I stripped away sidebars and other unnecessary distractions on my website.

Less is often more.

In every aspect of my life, I try to simplify and remove the inessential. What remains are the important things. Namely, my health, family, and creative work.

How about you? What complexities and unnecessary distractions are hindering you? What digital timewasters, overcommitments, and energy-draining clutter are keeping you from your best life?

Start simplifying, and the world might be your oyster.

Chapter Sixty-Seven

Never Get Out of Bed Before Noon

There is a proliferation of early bird aficionados writing self-improvement articles about their morning routines.

They want us to join them in the dark morning hours to meditate, drink Kombucha, write in journals, guzzle gallons of water, run half-marathons, and take ice-cold showers.

No thanks.

I much prefer to stay in a nice, warm bed for as long as possible. So does my cat, and he's the most stress-free little dude I know.

"I love sleep. My life has the tendency to fall apart when I'm awake, you know?" — Ernest Hemingway

I did the early morning thing for many years in my law enforcement career. As a police chief, I was often the first one at the office, to take advantage of the quiet.

I'd catch up on emails, phone messages, and in-basket tasks. Then I would attend the morning patrol briefings, catch the on-coming and off-going patrol officers, and visit for a bit.

I was very efficient during the workweek thanks to my early morning routine. I think I even felt a tad smug about it. Like I had one up on other people.

But every weekend I slept in whenever possible, and it was magnificent.

The second mouse gets the cheese

My natural circadian rhythm mirrors the swing shifts I used to work as a rookie cop on patrol.

Those shifts started at 3 PM and ended at 11 PM. After work, I'd come home and jump in the hot tub with my roommate (he was a cop working swing shift too).

We'd hit the sack around 1 AM and snooze until 9 or 10 AM. Best sleep ever. Then we'd get up for some exercise, laundry, errands, and go back to work at 3 PM.

"The early bird gets the worm, but the second mouse gets the cheese." — Stephen Wright

Unfortunately, those halcyon days didn't last. When I joined the police administration as a young Lieutenant, my schedule became Mondays through Fridays, 7 AM to 5 PM.

But this was a lie because to get anything done, I had to rise at the crack of dawn, before interruptions and unexpected crises ate up my day.

So, I understand the wisdom behind the early bird gurus. Starting early can help you get ahead.

But here's the thing about wisdom, sometimes it contradicts other wisdom. For example, the inimitable, late poet and novelist Charles Bukowski famously said, *"Never get out of bed before noon."*

I liked him the moment I read that quote.

Sleep is the best meditation

Yes, Bukowski was an alcoholic who lived a debauched lifestyle. He would have been canceled in a minute today. I won't defend his failings, but I like a lot of his writing and wisdom.

This brings me back to his advice about sleeping in. Advice that was likely born out of many hangovers. Or maybe he truly believed that sleep trumps pre-dawn initiative and exhausting morning routines.

"Sleep is the best meditation." — *Dalai Lama*

The point is nobody has a lock on what's the best way to live your life. The early morning crowd may get the worm, and I may get the cheese.

In other words, take all these self-help gurus with a grain of salt. Including me.

I get my best work done at night, and then the cat and I get up when the sun has warmed the house and the thought of fresh coffee lures me out of my slumber cocoon. I guess we're kind of like Charles Bukowski, except neither of us drinks alcoholic beverages.

If you function better at night, then stay up late and sleep in. If you're killing it with those early morning routines, more power to you.

The point is everyone is different.

Don't let the early morning gurus, or the Charles Bukowski night owls, tell you what's best for you.

Listen to your body, and you decide.

As for me, I won't be checking my emails or messages until after lunch.

Chapter Sixty-Eight

The Exciting Whisper Moving Through the Aisles of Your Spirit

It's funny the things that stay with you in life.

The hallway outside my parent's bedroom contained a framed essay titled, "Keep Alive the Dream in the Heart," by the late author and theologian Howard Thurman. I don't know where my father acquired the essay, but it clearly meant something to him.

I wish I had asked him about it, but I never did.

Things hung on walls either inspire us daily or become invisible. Fortunately for me, I often stopped to read the essay on the wall and ponder its meaning. I never forgot it.

The essay opens with the following:

"As long as a man has a dream in his heart, he cannot lose the significance of living. It is a part of the pretensions of modern life to traffic in what is generally called 'realism.' There is much insistence upon being practical, down to earth. Such things as dreams are won't

to be regarded as romantic or as a badge of immaturity, or as escape hatches for the human spirit."

The world is full of people whose dreams were crushed by others preaching pragmatism over romanticism. Luckily for me, my father was a curious blend of both pragmatism and romanticism.

The quiet persistence in the heart

My boyhood dreams swirled with thoughts of becoming a professional tennis player like my idol, Jimmy Connors. I also fancied the idea of becoming a rock star, playing the keyboard, and singing like Dennis DeYoung in the band Styx.

My father was big on education and often counseled me to find a reliable, conservative career path. Something with a good salary, benefits, and pension.

And yet, Dad paid for a coach to help me with my tennis. As a result, I made the high school varsity tennis team.

"The dream is the quiet persistence in the heart that enables a man to ride out the storms of his churning experiences. It is the exciting whisper moving through the aisles of his spirit answering the monotony of limitless days of dull routine."-Howard Thurman, Keep Alive the Dream in the Heart

Dad also bought a baby grand piano and paid for years of piano lessons. During my adolescence, I joined my first rock band and needed a portable keyboard/synthesizer and amplifier. Dad bought them for me.

I think my father knew that Wimbledon was a long shot for me, as well as performing in coliseums filled with screaming fans. But Dad didn't want me to lose "the significance of living."

He wanted his boy to have dreams.

The dream in the heart is the outlet

During my tennis years, my mother dutifully drove me around to tournaments and practice sessions. I won a few trophies and fashioned my entire style and technique after Jimmy Connors.

Puberty hastened my rock band aspirations, where I thought playing keyboards and singing would impress the girls. My high school and college rock band experiences did attract a few admirers, but by then my dreams were evolving.

"The dream in the heart is the outlet. It is one with the living water welling up from the very springs of Being, nourishing and sustaining all of life. Where there is no dream, the life becomes a swamp, a dreary dead place and, deep within, a man's heart begins to rot."-Howard Thurman, Keep Alive the Dream in the Heart

I realized that being a professional musician, with its endless travel and uncertain livelihood, was no longer my dream. I decided to pursue a career in law enforcement, where there was adventure and the chance to help people.

My father no doubt breathed a sigh of relief.

Life is a broken-winged bird

The thing is, during my early years, I needed those dreams. They brought me life experiences, joy, and growth. They moved me forward.

But then the dreams changed.

"Hold fast to dreams,
For if dreams die
Life is a broken-winged bird,
That cannot fly."
-Langston Hughes

During my law enforcement years, I started rediscovering my love of cartooning. I moonlighted as an editorial cartoonist for the county newspaper. And I began painting landscapes in oils.

Most recently creative writing and monochromatic photography have captured my interest. The past dreams build a sort of foundation and allow me to creatively grow.

As long as I feel excitement within my heart, I know the dream is moving me forward.

Your crucial link with the eternal

A few years ago, I bought Howard Thurman's book *"Meditations of the Heart."* Mostly because it contained the essay, *"Keep Alive the Dream in the Heart,"* which makes me think of my father.

The first section of the book contains the following:

"There is in every person an inward sea, and in that sea there is an island and on that island there is an altar and standing guard before that altar is the 'angel with the flaming sword.' Nothing can get by that angel to be placed upon that altar unless it has the mark of your inner authority. Nothing passes 'the angel with the flaming sword' to be placed upon your altar unless it be a part of 'the fluid area of your consent.' This is your crucial link with the Eternal."

Don't let anyone trample on your dreams. Your altar, where the visions and hopes for the future are held.

Hold close to your dreams, those exciting whispers moving through the aisles of your spirit. Because they are where we find the significance of living.

Also by John P. Weiss

*An Artful Life: Inspirational Stories and Essays
for the Artist in Everyone*

*The Cartoon Art of John P. Weiss: A Collection of John P. Weiss's
Cartoon Illustrations from His Blog
Posts and Articles*

About the Author

John P. Weiss is a writer, artist, photographer, and former chief of police with twenty-six years of law enforcement experience. He holds a master's degree in criminal justice administration, and his work appears in The Guardian, Thrive Global, Good Men Project, Becoming Minimalist, NBC News, and elsewhere online. He lives with his family in Nevada. Visit John at JohnPWeiss.com.

Made in the USA
Las Vegas, NV
25 February 2023